HISTORICAL TRAILS
OF
EASTERN PENNSYLVANIA

HISTORICAL TRAILS OF EASTERN PENNSYLVANIA

Anthony D. Fredericks

THE COUNTRYMAN PRESS
WOODSTOCK, VERMONT

Interior photographs by the author unless otherwise specified
Frontispiece photo: The ironmaster's mansion at Cornwell Iron Furnace in Lebanon County, built in 1773
Book design by Susan Livingston
Composition by Chelsea Cloeter

Published by The Countryman Press,
P.O. Box 748, Woodstock, VT 05091

Distributed by W. W. Norton & Company, Inc.,
500 Fifth Avenue, New York, NY 10110

Printed in the United States of America

10 9 8 7 6 5 4 3 2 1

Historical Trails of Eastern Pennsylvania
978-1-58157-183-7

TO KIM SUTTON—

Definitely for the laughter, certainly for the friendship

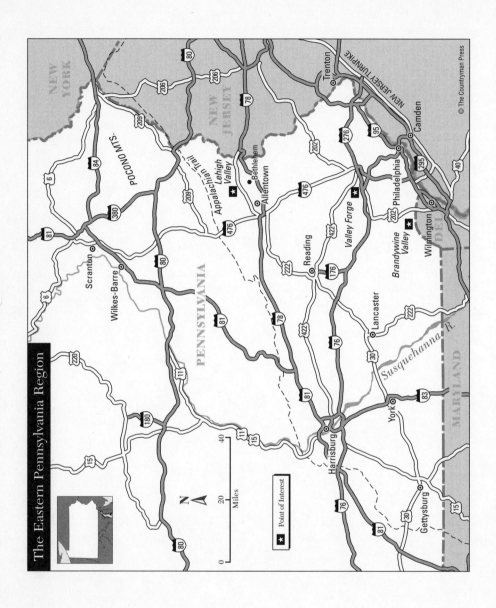

The Eastern Pennsylvania Region

Point of Interest

© The Countryman Press

CONTENTS

Let freedom ring!

Introduction

*"Travel is like a tonic for me… I need it
to recharge my batteries."* —Norman Rockwell

Many people who visit Pennsylvania are aware that the country's historical roots are firmly planted in the cobbled streets and colonial architecture of Philadelphia. They know of Constitution Hall and Independence Hall and the Liberty Bell. These sites traditionally get tens of thousands of visitors every year. They are the photos that adorn the covers of history books and are featured in every travel magazine since the invention of the interstate highway system. But the history of this region is much more than that found in the City of Brotherly Love. It's the hex barns just outside the rural town of Kutztown, it's a row of mansions built by lumber barons in the city of Williamsport, it's an aging ferry battling the currents on the Susquehanna River, it's a monument to a fallen Civil War soldier in the remote town of Greencastle, and it's a stone house in Kennett Square that once sheltered a family of former slaves working their way north. In so many ways, the history of the United States is the history of Pennsylvania.

The earliest travelers in eastern Pennsylvania were the Lenni Lenape Indians who traversed the countryside over a well-planned sequence of footpaths that skirted mountains, traversed forests, and crossed numerous streams. That many of those Native American paths served as the prototypes for the state's modern-day highways is a testament to their need to get from point A to point B in the most efficient way possible. In fact, most of the travel of early Native Americans was by land, rather than by water. Eventually these very functional footpaths evolved into bridle paths, then wagon roads, then the asphalt four-lanes that dominant the modern Pennsylvania landscape.

It is many of those same paths that I want to share in this book. I invite you to come along with me on long-ago byways and historical throughways that will bring the past alive and offer a you-are-there perspective. I'd like to show you some incredible sights and people who made this part of the country so rich in heritage and history. I'd like to take you over endless rural roads, through delightful small towns and villages, past architectural wonders, and around revolutionary battlefields that highlight impressive historical treasures and visual riches. This is what eastern Pennsylvania is all about—a feast for both the spirit and the eyes. Its past awaits your discovery.

> **F**AST FACT: The Allegheny Path, particularly the section between Philadelphia and Harrisburg, was a popular footpath for both Native Americans and early Europeans during colonial times. Part of today's Pennsylvania Turnpike (I-76) follows that same route.

ABOUT THIS GUIDE

Those visiting Pennsylvania for the first time will quickly discover that the state is awash in history, culture, and dramatic vistas. This is a state with something for everyone—from vibrant urban centers pulsing with art and color and noise to vast open spaces where the only

Pennsylvania's unique (and classic) historical marker

The Susquehanna River is part of Pennsylvania's history.

sign of civilization may be a discarded candy wrapper on the side of the road. In so many ways, Pennsylvania is a state rich with possibilities and ripe for exploration—a state founded on a diverse and varied historical past.

The chapters in this book are loosely grouped around select historical places and events. Each chapter presents an itinerary for a road trip or walking tour designed to last several hours, an entire day, a weekend, or several days. Some tours offer traditional tourist destinations, as well as some lesser-known historical sites throughout the region. From time to time, I had to manipulate some historical chronology for the sake of consistency. Nevertheless, it is the history that predominates—a history of famous (and infamous) individuals, a history of cultural and economic events, and a history of war, insurrection and general malfeasance. You'll visit places where revolutions were started, fortunes made, journeys initiated, cultures established, battles fought, and issues argued.

We'll begin our travels in the historic centerpiece of the state—Philadelphia—where we'll walk along cobbled streets and tour fabled buildings just as those founding fathers did. From here, we will follow revolutionary roads and the route of the Underground Railroad; pass log cabins, hex barns, and Victorian mansions; cross covered bridges; and take a journey down the incredible Susquehanna River. We will end with one of the most pivotal battles in American history—the Battle of Gettysburg. The book concludes on a more peaceful note with a walking tour through historic Gettysburg—with some places you have to see to believe, including a 200-year-old tavern that brings all that history alive.

> **F**AST FACT: With a total of 46,055 square miles, Pennsylvania is the 33rd largest state in the United States.

In so many ways this was a most incredible book to write. I had the opportunity to revisit some of my favorite haunts, as well as discover several new places and sites throughout eastern Pennsylvania. I walked in the footsteps of some of my historical heroes and saw this state through their eyes and experiences. I was able to investigate places I had only heard about, but never seen. And the fact that I could crisscross the region and drink in the beautiful scenery through multiple ventures added a nice flourish to the inspiring places and people I met along the way.

I hope you will see this book as a way to separate yourself from the "hurry-up" world we live in and a way to re-connect with a simpler way of living—a way of distinctive architecture, patient transportation, trustful politicians, rich history, dynamic individuals, and wide open spaces. Eastern Pennsylvania is, as you will discover, a part of the county unlike any other—a region that excites, inspires and teaches. It's a history book you'll want to turn to time and time again.

HELPFUL HINTS

- Pennsylvania's nickname is the Keystone State because it was the middle colony of the original 13 colonies. Residents, however, often lovingly refer to it as "the Pothole State." A unique combination of geography and climatology produces a constant freeze and thaw cycle during the winter months that often does some serious damage to roads and highways. Lots of potholes can only mean one thing, especially in the summer—lots of road repairs. Select almost any road in the state and it is likely that there will be some form of construction work taking place at the height of the summer tourist season. Allow time for delays and bring along a healthy dose of patience.

- Since this book is focused exclusively on historical sites, you will not find many recommendations for restaurants, hotels, or other diversions. I'll make occasional suggestions for certain restaurants and places of lodging, but they must satisfy two strict prerequisites: first, they must have some historical value—that is, something that is 100 to 200 years old and at which a fairly important event took place. Second, it must be a place that I have personally visited. If I haven't spent some time or money in an establishment, then it is not included in these pages. If you decide to dine or room at a place suggested in this book, please know that I have done so too.

> **F**AST FACT: If Pennsylvania were an independent country, its economy would rank as the 18th largest in the world.

- Just to discombobulate first-time visitors to our state, the Pennsylvania Department of Transportation sometimes assigns confusing and irrational directional names to certain roads. For example, you will be heading due west on Route 1, even though the official state designation is "Route 1 South." It's always best to use a road map, rather than to rely solely on a car compass or GPS.

- Pennsylvania has a habit of ratcheting up the speed limit on long stretches of highway (say, to 55 miles per hour) and then just as quickly slowing things down considerably on your approach to a village or burg in the middle of nowhere. The slower speed limit is often posted on a sign hidden behind a large tree, inside a leafy hedge or amid the directional arrows for 16 converging roads. Please be aware that there are many small towns on almost every road in Pennsylvania—that means that there will be many "hurry up and slow down" areas throughout the state as well.

"I'LL HAVE THE COMBO, PLEASE."

The drives and tours profiled throughout this book provide you with up-close-and-personal experiences with Pennsylvania history. However, you might want to take advantage of the opportunity to combine two or more tours together for a unique travel experience. Here are a few suggestions:

The War Tour—Begin your journey with Civil War Trails (Chapter 14) and continue the trip into Gettysburg. Then add on the the Battle of Gettysburg tour (Chapter 15) and conclude with the In Historic Gettysburg tour (Chapter 16).

Old Order Pennsylvania—Start with the Pennsylvania Dutch tour (Chapter 8) and then add on An Amish Journey tour (Chapter 12) as well as the Around Lancaster County tour (Chapter 11).

Some Famous People—Start with the In Historic Philadelphia tour (Chapter 1) and continue over to the Revolutionary War Trails tour (Chapter 2) and finish with the Somebody Slept Here tour (Chapter 4).

Whatever you decide, don't try to complete any of the possible combo packages in one day-long, marathon drive. The history of Pennsylvania took a while…so should you.

- Pennsylvania goes out of its way to provide visitors with tons of travel information and data about every corner of the state. Contact them directly (Pennsylvania Tourism Office, Department of Community and Economic Development, Commonwealth Keystone Building, 400 North St., Fourth Floor, Harrisburg PA 17120-0225; 1-800-VISIT-PA), or visit their website (www.visitPA.com) for up-to-date maps, guides, and travel suggestions. Also check out their great quarterly travel magazine, *Pennsylvania Pursuits*.

Sharp-eyed readers will note that I have omitted some (normally important) information from all these tours. I have not provided any data regarding the hours of operation for museums or other historic sites, nor have I provided information on the fees or admission charges at those places. This is intentional.

Many sites change their rates on an irregular basis (in response to foot traffic as well as operating costs), often without notice. On many occasions, I re-visited selected sites to gather additional information and discovered that a $5 entrance fee three months ago had blossomed into a $7 fee. This also held true for the hours of operation. Many museums and other public venues are subject to the whims of the economy, funding sources, and even state government. Less revenue also often results in a reduction or modification of hours.

To avoid any confusion or disappointment, I provide you with the most current contact information (at the time of this writing) so you can verify the days and prices that are most compatible with your schedule or travel plans.

Now let's get on the road!

Independence Hall in Philadelphia

1 In Historic Philadelphia

Estimated length: 2–3 miles

Estimated time: 1 day (walking)

Combine this tour with: Chapters 3 and 4

Getting there: If you are staying in a hotel in Philadelphia, use public transportation or a taxi, and head over to the Independence Visitor Center. If you are driving into Philadelphia from somewhere outside the city, drive to the parking garage at the Visitor Center (on Sixth Street) and leave your car.

Highlights: This is a walking tour you will long remember. You'll have an opportunity to see exactly where a lot of history took place—making those old photographs in your high school history textbook seem pale by comparison. Be prepared to add to your photo album (and mental album)—this is a journey that will dazzle and amaze.

Ask most Americans to name the most historic city in the country and you will get little argument that Philadelphia answers that query. The city is known as the birthplace of freedom and of the new country, as well as the seat of democracy, for good reason.

It was here that our forefathers, in powdered wigs and buckled shoes, walked the cobblestone streets of the City of Brotherly Love and argued about rights, demanded justice, and shouted for freedom from the tyranny of English rule. This was the place where liberty and individual rights were first championed. This was the place where constitutional leaders made their case for "life, liberty and the pursuit of happiness" and where common folk fought for what they believed in with an unmatched fervor and sense of patriotism seldom seen in European capitals.

Colonial architecture in Elfreth's Alley

It has been said that history has an imperfect memory—that facts and events and personalities are sometimes compromised or sometimes bent in order to fit into neat historical packages. Individuals are shaven of their foibles, buildings are given a new coat of paint to make them shine, and events are viewed through a new set of lenses that, while not distorting the truth, bend it just a little. It would be quite easy to look back more than 200 years and reinvent or reframe the events that took place in Philadelphia. But the truth is, the Philadelphia events and individuals stand on their own merits. They don't need new dressing and they don't need a twist here and there to make them more palatable to legions of schoolchildren (or adults reading travel books).

I suppose that if Philadelphia is the birthplace of freedom and liberty for this country, then it is because great people rose up in difficult times to make it so. Walk these streets and you can almost hear the passionate voice of James Madison crying for the new constitution, hear the faint echoes of Benjamin Franklin whispering down cobblestone streets, and pick up the scratchings of Thomas Jefferson as he pens another draft of the Declaration of Independence. This is history alive; this is a city that celebrates its own history and past events with as much fervor as a diehard Phillies fan at Citizens Bank Park. The faces may have changed over the years, but the events have been locked into our collective consciousness as historical gems to celebrate, honor, and fervently remember.

NOTE: The following sites are presented in an order, while not chronologically correct, that will allow you to take a counterclockwise circuit of important historical sites in the historic district. This walking tour is planned so you will have maximum opportunities to visit all the sites within a full one-day visit.

1. Independence Visitor Center (1 N. Independence Mall West at Sixth and Market Streets)—This should be your first stop on any tour. You can load up all sorts of information and check in with friendly park rangers, who will steer you in the right direction and offer plenty of insight. This is also where you can obtain your free timed tour tickets for Independence Hall. These are first-come, first-served tickets and on busy summer days can be gone by noon, so be sure to get there early in the morning. Also, please note that restrooms are few and far between on this tour, so plan accordingly.

2. Independence Hall (Chestnut Street between Fifth and Sixth streets)—You'll have to walk past the Liberty Bell to get here (we'll return shortly), but this is a must-see on any trip into Philadelphia. Each member of your party will need a timed (free) ticket from the Independence Visitor Center to enter. You'll get a brief history lesson about the early years of this country, some of the influential individuals, and why this building is so important.

This may well be the most famous building in the country. It has been said that this is where the United States was born. As you will learn in the brief introduction by a park ranger, delegates from each of the 13 original colonies met in the Pennsylvania Assembly Room to adopt the Declaration of Independence, approve the Articles of Confederation, and herald the federal Constitution.

The building was constructed between 1732 and 1756 and designated as the new state house for Pennsylvania. Its design has been attributed to Alexander Hamilton, a well-known lawyer and speaker of the Pennsylvania Assembly.

This is also where the Second Continental Congress met (except for a brief period when the British occupied Philadelphia) and where George Washington was appointed commander-in-chief of the Continental Army. Most notably, it is where our independence from England was proclaimed by brave representatives from the 13 colonies.

As you enter the main part of the building, you will be led into the large room on the right. This is the Pennsylvania Supreme Court, where English law was upheld and where the fate of many prisoners was determined. You'll be able to see the witness box just as it was more than two centuries ago. You'll also note Pennsylvania's coat of arms above the judge's bench (After the reading of the Declaration of Independence on July 8, 1776, the original coat of arms—that of King George III—was ripped from the wall and burned).

You will next be led into the Pennsylvania Assembly Room, which is arranged

> **F**AST FACT: On the president's desk in the Pennsylvania Assembly Room is a silver ink stand designed by Philip Syng in 1752. This is the actual ink stand into which the delegates dipped their pens and signed both the Declaration of Independence and the U.S. Constitution.

in much the same manner as it was in the late 1770s. One original piece of furniture is the "rising sun" chair used by George Washington as he presided over the Constitutional Convention.

This is also the same hall in which delegates met to determine the fate of the new constitution. After considerable arguments made, positions affirmed, and platforms debated, the new constitution was drafted. It began with the immortal words, "We, the people of the United States, in order to form a more perfect union...." After all the haggling and all the arguing our new nation had a document that would govern its destiny and ensure rights for its citizens. Perhaps just as significant is the fact that that Constitution has served as a template for the constitutions of many other countries—a testament to the wisdom and foresightedness of its originators. That very document was signed right in this room.

3. Congress Hall (Chestnut Street between Fifth and Sixth Streets)—This building, immediately adjacent to Independence Hall, was originally constructed between 1787 and 1789. It was designated as the Philadelphia County Court House, but its role in American history far outstripped its original intent. Between 1770 and 1800, this was where the U.S. Congress met when Philadelphia was the capital of the United States. The House of Representatives met on the first floor of the building while the Senate met on the second floor. Since that time, we have come to call the Senate the "upper chamber" and the House of Representatives the "lower chamber." George Washington was sworn in for his second term as president in this building, and John Adams was sworn in as the second president of the United States.

Unfortunately, this building fell into disrepair and was abandoned in 1895. However, its historical value was eventually recognized and it was repaired and rebuilt to its present form—an accurate reconstruction of its former days. Walk through and you will see many of its original furnishings and hear the constant echoes of heroes and dignitaries long gone.

4. Old City Hall (Chestnut Street between Fifth and Sixth Streets) — This building also was significant when Philadelphia served as the nation's capital. It was here that the U.S. Supreme Court met from 1791 to 1800. Then the Supreme Court was moved to Washington, D.C., where it has been ever since. Noted Supreme Court justices who walked these hallowed halls include Chief Justice John Jay, Chief Justice Oliver Ellsworth, and Associate Justice John Marshall, who eventually became chief justice when the court convened in its permanent location.

5. Declaration House (Seventh and Market Streets) — Also known as the Graff House, this was where Thomas Jefferson resided when he was drafting the Declaration of Independence. Needing a quiet location away from the hubbub of activities taking place in Center City, Jefferson rented two rooms from Jacob Graff Jr. The 33-year-old delegate from Virginia, along with delegates Benjamin Franklin, John Adams, Robert R. Livingston, and Roger Sherman were charged with the task of crafting this signature document by the Continental Congress.

The original house was constructed in 1775 and has undergone many transformations over the years. It was even razed in the early 1880s and replaced with a bank building.

The current building is an accurate reconstruction of the original house. As you enter the first floor you will see

> **F**AST FACT: At one time during the Depression, the Tom Thumb Luncheonette occupied the corner of Seventh and Market.

several exhibits as well as a brief film on the drafting process. On the second floor is a bedroom and parlor, including restorations of the furniture Jefferson would have used during his stay. Please note that visiting hours are limited (12 to 2 PM each day).

6. Liberty Bell (Sixth Street between Market and Chestnut Streets (across from the visitor center) — One of the most iconic of all American symbols, the bell was originally commissioned from the London firm of Lester and Pack in 1752. It was cast with the quote "Proclaim LIBERTY throughout all the land unto all the inhabitants thereof," which comes from *Leviticus 25:10*. When it was first rung in Philadelphia, it immediately developed a crack. The bell was subsequently recast in 1753 using metal from the original bell.

The bell was little used until the 1830s when it was adopted by several abo-

> **F**AST FACT: With your back to Independence Hall, look closely at the bell and you'll note that "Pennsylvania" is spelled incorrectly. In fact, in the original Constitution, the spelling of the state is also missing an "n."

litionist societies who dubbed it "the Liberty Bell." Then sometime around 1846 a thin crack began to appear—affecting the sound of the bell. Shortly thereafter the crack was repaired and the bell was used to celebrate George Washington's birthday. During that ringing, the bell once again developed a crack. It has not been rung since.

In the latter part of the 19th century, the Liberty Bell toured the United States, attracting large crowds. Unfortunately, additional cracking (and some less-than-honest souvenir hunters) resulted in the loss of small pieces of the bell. In 1915 the bell was retired from its travels and permanently displayed in Philadelphia.

The bell is constructed of copper, tin, lead, zinc, arsenic, gold, and silver. It weighs approximately 2,000 pounds and hangs from what many believe is its original wooden yoke.

Our forefathers were (apparently) not good spellers.

The Second Bank of the United States

7. Second Bank of the United States (420 Chestnut Street)—Completed in 1824, this Greek Revival building was designed by William Strickland, who was also responsible for creating a number of Philadelphia's public buildings. Walk inside and you'll be dazzled by an impressive collection—not of money—but of nearly 185 paintings of colonial and federal leaders. Many of the portraits were done by artist Charles Willson Peale and later obtained by the city of Philadelphia after his death. Included in the portraits are George Washington, Benjamin Franklin, Thomas Jefferson, James Madison, John Paul Jones, and John Adams. Stepping into the gallery is like stepping into an oversized American history textbook.

FAST FACT: The Liberty Bell is owned by the city of Philadelphia, not by the U.S. government. After World War II, the city allowed the National Park Service to take custody of the bell, although Philadelphia still retains ownership.

Carpenters' Hall served as a hospital and arsenal during the Revolutionary war.

8. Carpenter's Hall (320 Chestnut Street)—This building was constructed between 1770 and 1773 by the Carpenter's Company—a coalition of carpenters formed in 1724 as a building trades group. In September 1774 the First Continental Congress met here to draw up a Declaration of Rights and Grievances and an appeal to King George III. After the little tea party some colonists had in Boston Harbor in December 1773, the British Parliament had come down hard on the colony of Massachusetts. Soon after, delegates convened in this hall and voiced some pretty inflammatory comments about England and the monarchy. It was here that Patrick Henry declared with rage, "Government is dissolved. Where are now your landmarks, your boundaries of colonies?" With those words and a few other sentences from equally irritated delegates, the American Revolution was off and running.

When first constructed, the building was nothing more than a simple meeting hall with crude fireplaces and plain wooden floors. What you will see today are the improvements made by the still-functioning Carpenter's Company—tile and marble floors, sturdy furniture, gilt and polish. Stand in the center of the first floor and imagine the inflammatory dialogue that ricocheted off the walls here more than two centuries ago.

9. The First Bank of the United States (Third Street between Chestnut and Walnut Streets)—This Federal-style structure is the oldest bank building in the United States (long before drive-up windows were invented). Built between 1795 and 1797, this was the government's financial headquarters until 1811, when its charter expired. This was an impressive building in its day—take a look at the American eagle on the tympanum of the pediment and the stately Corinthian capitals and you can see why this building inspired trust and solidity in the early

The Carpenters Company left its mark on the floor many years ago.

The First Bank of the United States garnered architectural acclaim when it was completed in 1797.

years of the new country. Unfortunately, the building is usually closed to the public, so you may not have the opportunity to walk its hallowed halls.

10. City Tavern (138 S. Second Street between Walnut and Chestnut Streets)— If you plan your journey appropriately, you can stop by this landmark tavern for a midday meal. The current building is an accurate reconstruction of the three-story hostelry that was constructed here in 1773. In colonial days, the tavern provided lodging and meeting places in which the social, business, and political activities of Philadelphia were conducted. The First Continental Congress held many informal meetings here and the Constitutional Convention convened its closing banquet here (George Washington was in attendance).

This is a restaurant that spares nothing to bring the flavor of colonial times directly to your table. The waitstaff is dressed in period costumes, the water goblets are made of pewter, and the entire atmosphere is absolutely colonial. You might want to start your colonial repast with one of my favorite beverages—the Thomas Jefferson 1774 Tavern Ale—a beer made using one of Jefferson's original recipes.

The menu at City Tavern is eclectic, dynamic, and mighty good. Head chef Walter Staib has penned several cookbooks and has been featured on a 13-episode series on PBS. Menu selections include roast duckling, venison medallions, and colonial turkey pot pie. By the time your meal is over, your taste buds will be singing "Yankee Doodle Dandy."

11. Franklin Court (between Third and Fourth Streets and Chestnut and Market Streets)—This historical site is distinguished by the fact that it is truly "a shell of its former self." What you will see here is not Benjamin Franklin's house, but rather an outline of it. Designed by architect Robert Venturi, this edifice is a simple outline of steel frames cast in the general outline of the house in which Franklin passed away in 1790. Erected in 1976, this frame is an approximation of Franklin's original house—a structure about which little is known, but much is speculated. This much we do know—his house was primarily constructed of brick in 1763 and it was the only home he ever owned. It was known that he built an addition to the house in 1786.

The underground museum beneath Franklin Court houses many Franklin artifacts, including his personal desk, a Franklin stove, and several of his inventions. There are also architectural excavations (including privy wells) and a film on Franklin's life.

Just a few short steps away is Franklin's house print shop (320 Market Street). Inside you'll see several of the printing presses and other publishing tools of the day—just like the ones Franklin would have used. You can also purchase posters and other memorabilia with quotes from Franklin's famous *Poor Richard's Almanac*.

12. B. Free Franklin Post Office and Museum (316 Market Street)—This is the only colonial-themed post office operated and maintained by the U.S. Postal Service. It has been in operation since it first opened in 1775 and you can still get letters canceled with the postmark "B. Free Franklin," which was what the na-

FAST FACT: This is the only active post office in the United States that does not fly the American flag. That's because there was not yet one in 1775 when Benjamin Franklin was appointed Postmaster General.

The Ben Franklin post office

tion's first postmaster used many decades ago. On the second floor is a small museum on postal history.

13. Christ Church (Second Street above Market)—This church is often referred to as "The Nation's Church" and has been an active Episcopalian church since 1695. A veritable *Who's Who* of historical figures worshiped in this church including Benjamin Franklin, George Washington, Betsy Ross, Absolom Jones, Benjamin Rush, and Robert Morris. This is also the church where the American Episcopal Church was founded. The steeple, financed through a lottery organized by Benjamin Franklin, was the tallest structure in the colonies for 75 years.

When you enter the church you'll notice several gravestones down the main aisle. Current tradition says that walking on a grave inside a church is a way of honoring the individual below. You'll definitely want to seek out Pew 58—the one in which George Washington sat. Other "famous" pews include Benjamin Franklin's (70), Betsy Ross's (12) and the Penn family's (60). Afterward, walk outside to the graveyard and find the graves of two of the signers of the

FAST FACT: The baptismal font dates from the 1300s (donated by All Hallows Church, London) and was the one in which William Penn was baptized.

Declaration of Independence—Robert Morris and James Wilson. Pierce Butler, a signer of the U.S. Constitution, is also buried here.

14. Elfreth's Alley (off Second Street between Arch and Race Streets)—If you want to step into a time portal you can't go wrong with this delightful slice of authentic Philadelphia real estate. This narrow alleyway is colonial Philadelphia at its finest. It has been continuously occupied since 1713, and the enclave of 33 colonial and Federal-style homes leaves nothing to the imagination. In the past, the homes were occupied by merchants, shipbuilders, carpenters, printers, cabinetmakers, silversmiths, and blacksmiths. Named for blacksmith Jeremiah Elfreth, this bricked street allows no cars and should be strolled slowly to take in all the architecture and history. You might want to stop in to No. 126, the Mantua Maker's Museum House, or No. 124, the Windsor Chairmaker's House. Please note that all these residences are private homes. Knocking on doors or peeking in windows is strongly discouraged.

Elfreth's Alley in Philadelphia: a Philadelphia neighborhood since 1713

15. Betsy Ross House (239 Arch Street)—This is a historical structure filled with several "maybe's." Maybe Betsy Ross lived in this house, maybe she created the first flag of the United States, and maybe she had a conversation with George Washington. The story of Betsy Ross has filled countless children's books and textbooks with an interesting mixture of supposition, legend, and fact. Here is what we do know for certain—the house at this location was originally built in about 1740. Although it has not been absolutely confirmed that Mrs. Ross lived in this specific location, we do know that she was a well-known seamstress and upholsterer. Her talents for making pennants and ensigns for the navy were highly regarded by many in colonial Philadelphia.

What we don't know for sure was whether Betsy Ross created the first flag. The story about her flag-making comes primarily through hearsay and the memories of her grandson, who passed along the original story in 1870. Unfortunately, the facts of the initial flag cannot be confirmed. What you will find in this house is Betsy's reading glasses and furniture that represents the period in which she lived. You'll also be able to visit her grave, which is in the courtyard immediately in front of the house. Here Betsy is buried along with her third husband, John Claypoole. Also located in the courtyard is the Betsy Ross Hot Dog Stand, where you can obtain a snack that is definitely not colonial in nature.

The grave of Betsy Ross (and her third husband)

Christ Church Burial Ground is the final resting place for five signers of the Declaration of Independence.

16. Christ Church Burial Ground (Fifth and Arch Streets)—Not only are five signers of the Declaration of Independence buried in this urban cemetery, so are a host of other notable individuals. In all, more than 4,000 people are interred in this two-acre plot including military heroes, medical pioneers, 10 mayors of Philadelphia, and various families of the colonial and Revolutionary era. Perhaps the most famous grave here is that of Benjamin Franklin. His gravesite is at the edge of the cemetery and can be seen from the adjacent sidewalk through an iron fence. It may be the most visited grave in the city—a fact you can confirm by the sheer number of pennies that have been tossed on it for good luck.

The earliest grave is that of Robert Wallace, who passed away in 1723; the most recent graves are from the late 1900s. Take a walk through this historic place and you will see some of the movers and shakers of early Philadelphia and the early years of the United States. Keep in mind that this is an active burial ground. Be careful where you walk and refrain from taking any grave rubbings.

17. National Constitution Center (Fifth and Arch Streets)—What better way to end your journey through American history than at the first and only museum

Signers Hall at the National Constitution Center allows you to mingle with your revolutionary heros.

dedicated to the history of the U.S. Constitution? A tour through this architecturally imposing building will reveal numerous exhibits filled with interactive displays and artifacts that demonstrate the importance of the U.S. Constitution and its impact on our daily lives. Be sure to take in "Freedom Rising"—a 17-minute multimedia journey through the story of the Constitution from its inception to today. Dramatic images, a circular screen, and a live actor will fill you with pride, patriotism, and awe at the power of three words: "We the People."

Upstairs you'll walk through several interactive displays, including the Presidential Oath of Office. Here you can take the actual presidential oath and have the occasion validated with a photo of you being administered that oath by a member of the Supreme Court with a crowd and several former presidents in the background.

Another highlight is Signers' Hall with its life-size statues of the signers of the U.S. Constitution, including Benjamin Franklin and George Washington. Be

---

FAST FACT: The U.S. Constitution is the shortest constitution (4,167 words, without signatures) used by any representative government in the world today. India has the world's longest—at approximately 117,000 words.

---

sure to have your photo taken with your favorite constitutional hero. After your visit, it's just a short walk back to Independence Visitor Center.

The tour above has been designed so that a family can easily walk it, spend time at the selected sites, take a break or two for refreshments, and complete the entire journey in a single day. Completing the entire tour will mean beginning early in the morning (starting no later than 8:45 AM at the Independence Visitor Center is recommended) and visiting all 17 stops by late afternoon.

For those who would like a shorter tour, here is a tour that will provide an equally amazing view of American history:

1. Independence Visitor Center

2. Independence Hall

3. Congress Hall

4. Old City Hall

6. The Liberty Bell Center

8. Carpenter's Hall

11. Franklin Court

12. B. Free Franklin Post Office and Museum

CONTACTS

Independence Visitor Center, 1 North Independence Mall, Philadelphia, PA 19106; (800) 537-7676; www.independencevisitorcenter.com.

DINING

The City Tavern Restaurant, 138 South Second St., Philadelphia, PA 19106; (215) 413-1443; www.citytavern.com.

Washington's headquarters at Valley Forge

2 Revolutionary War Trails

Estimated length: 70 miles

Estimated time: 2 days

Combine this tour with: Chapter 4

Getting there: Start at Washington Crossing Historic Park on the Delaware River. Afterward, you'll have to get on some of the arterial routes around the Philadelphia area in order to make it over to Valley Forge (considerably less history on these routes). After leaving Valley Forge, you'll take a quick jaunt down to Brandywine Battlefield. The drive is not chronological, but the history is eye-popping nonetheless.

Highlights: War and revolution are the themes here. Interestingly, our nation's first president figures prominently in all three of these sites. At one he was victorious, the other defeated; the third was a draw. You'll be able to imagine what southeastern Pennsylvania may have looked like over 200 years ago and see how it has evolved in more than two centuries of urban growth and development.

Shortly after the French and Indian war in 1763, the English won a series of victories over French forces that effectively nullified the French influence in the new colonies. Believing that the colonies were now their legal and just possessions, the English Parliament enacted a series of taxes on the colonists in order to raise money and let the colonies know who was in charge. One of the most pernicious was the Stamp Act of 1765—the first direct tax levied on the colonies by Parliament. This tax stipulated that all official documents (including newspapers, almanacs and even playing cards) were required to have stamps. This angered the colonists simply because they felt that taxes were imposed indiscriminately and without sufficient authority (there was no way to argue for or against them because the colonies did not have any official representatives in Parliament).

Believing England to be unfair, the colonists said the laws were both illegitimate and a violation of their rights as former Englishmen. Thus, in 1772 several enclaves of colonists began to draft Committees of Correspondence—semi-political units that would establish their own Provincial Congresses in each of the individual colonies. The geographical distance between the mother country and the new colonies helped to fan the fires of insurrection. Fired up by their new swagger and confidence, the colonies essentially rejected the power of Parliament and replaced it with their own governing bodies. They capped this continental divorce by expelling all the royal officials and politicians.

This did not sit very well with the folks in London. To top it off, the colonists established the First Continental Congress as their "official" ruling body (rather than acknowledging any overseas governing entity). The British, normally reserved, blew the proverbial political gasket. In short order, they sent combat troops, did away with many of the local governments, and imposed direct rule on the colonies by Parliament.

The colonies quickly assembled militia (albeit lightly armed and barely trained) in response to the British presence. Fighting erupted in 1775 after King George declared the colonies "in rebellion" and the members of Congress to be traitors. The ragtag army was commanded by George Washington and it was he, and the newly formed Second Continental Congress, who managed the war that would fill untold chapters of history books about the new country's quest for independence—the American Revolutionary War, the American War of Independence, or simply the Revolutionary War.

FAST FACT: The Revolutionary War was one of the longest military engagements in American history. It lasted from April 19, 1775, to September 3, 1783 (8 years, 4 months, 2 weeks, and 1 day).

The Revolutionary War was a war of attrition and survival. Constant conflicts and fierce battles such as the battles of Lexington and Concord, the capture of Fort Ticonderoga and New York City, the battles of Saratoga and Brandywine, the capture of Philadelphia, and the final engagement at Yorktown, Virginia, were testament to the ebb and flow of a war that engaged combatants from six different countries and saw its share of victories and defeats.

While the conflicts raged up and down the colonies—on both land and water—this tour will take us to three of the most significant sites in eastern Pennsylvania…sites that have been immortalized in story, song, and legend for countless generations.

To prevent overlap as you visit these sites, we are going to mix up our chronology just a little. We're going to start with one of the most iconic of all wartime scenes—Washington's grand river crossing, then leapfrog over another event to get to Valley Forge and the encampment of 1777, then come back in time to one of the most embarrassing defeats in Washington's service as General of the Continental Army—the Battle at Brandywine. Are you still with me?

Now let's cross the Delaware.

It was the winter of 1776 and General Washington and his ragged army had experienced a seemingly endless string of defeats. Failure seemed to be the watchword of the day and the morale of the troops was at an all-time low. In addition to a corps of dispirited troops, Washington had to contend with frequent desertions and the expiring enlistments of troops. On December 7 and 8, Washington was forced to exit New Jersey for the relative safety of Pennsylvania. Winter was fast closing in and a lack of adequate clothing and food was having a significant impact on troop morale.

Washington needed a victory…and fast.

During these times, it was accepted practice for armies to go into winter quarters to regroup, re-supply, and strategize for the start of the spring campaigns. In fact, the British commander, Cornwallis, was preparing to spend the winter season visiting his wife in London, believing his troops would be able to survive the winter. Most of the British troops returned to New York for the season. They left behind a contingent of Hessian soldiers, free agents paid for their military service, to garrison small outposts in and around Trenton, New Jersey.

Washington, ever the tactician, decided to spring a surprise on the Hessian troops and attack them when they least expected it. Not only was this a bold military maneuver, it was also a potential psychological lift for the beleaguered Continental Army. The original plan was for the Continentals to divide into three divisions and cross the river on the evening of December 25. Various types of boats were to be used—most notably large, heavy Durham boats.

FAST FACT: In the famous painting by Emmanuel Leutze—*Washington Crossing the Delaware*—the river in the painting is not modeled after the Delaware River, but rather the Rhine River in Germany where this masterpiece was originally painted.

Washington assembled his division near McConkey's Ferry in preparation for the crossing. By 4 PM, 2,400 troops, 18 cannons, and approximately 50 to 75 horses began their crossing of the semi-frozen river. The river was thick with ice and the crossing took considerably longer than anticipated. On top of that, weather conditions quickly deteriorated as a blinding snowstorm and sharp sleet descended on the region.

The weather prevented the supporting divisions from crossing the Delaware at their stations further to the south. Nevertheless, the boats under Washington's command were able to successfully make the journey.

Ultimately, the crossing took far longer than planned. Washington's troops began their 9-mile march toward Trenton at 4 AM and when they arrived at about 6 PM, they had lost the cover of darkness necessary for a surprise attack. However, in an artful two-pronged attack the Continental Army successfully and decisively defeated the Hessians.

The morale of the troops escalated and there was a new energy for Washington's command and his role as an effective leader. This single engagement gave new life to the American Revolution when it was needed the most.

In 1917 **Washington Crossing Historic Park** was established to perpetuate and preserve this site. Thousands of visitors come each year (there is no admission charge, but there is a fee for guided tours) to view the grounds, the historic buildings, and see an annual reenactment every year on Christmas Day. Visitors can witness re-enactors in Continental military dress cross the river in replica Durham boats.

At the visitors center at Washington Crossing Historic Park, I was greeted by two of the most entertaining guides ever—Tom Maddock and Bill Traubel. Both retired, these two gentlemen truly embody the heart and soul of great guides. They provided answers to my questions, supplied me with more documents and information that I ever expected, and brought a lot of sunshine into a day filled with many stops and many visits along the history highway.

How modern travelers get across the Delaware River

The park is divided into two separate sections—about 3.5 miles from each other. The southern section—known as McConkey's Ferry section has seven buildings for visitors to see; while the northern section—known as Thompson-Neely—has two buildings, a graveyard, a wildflower preserve, and a 125-foot tower. Visitors can view all the buildings on a self-guided tour or they can take an information-packed one-hour tour.

The first place I visited was the **McConkey's Ferry Inn**, an 18th-century inn owned by Samuel McConkey, who also operated a ferry business across the Delaware River (a steel bridge now spans the river near the famous crossing). According to tradition, the inn is where Washington and his aides ate dinner prior

McConkey's Ferry Inn at Washington Crossing

to the crossing on Christmas Day. A few additions have been made to the building over the intervening years. The inn was the only building here during the time of the crossing. Other buildings, constructed as part of the small town of Taylorsville (now known as Washington Crossing) during the early 1800s, are clustered around the site.

These buildings include the **Mahlon K. Taylor House** built in 1817 as the primary residence of the wealthy Taylor family. There's the **Taylorsville Store,** which was owned by Mahlon Taylor starting in 1828 and also served as the post office. Directly across the street is the **Frye House**, built from 1828 to 1830. It is thought that this house was constructed for a local blacksmith. Adjacent to the house is a reconstructed blacksmith house used for periodic demonstrations.

Down the pathway from the Frye House is the **Durham Boat House**. This 20th-century building houses all the Durham boat replicas used in the reenactment of the crossing every Christmas. Nearby is the **Hibbs House**, a restored 19th-century home that was also part of Taylorsville. This particular building may have been let out as a tenant house for various craftspeople.

After my visit here, I drove up to the Thompson-Neely section of the park. The first building I visited was the **Thompson-Neely House**, an 18th-century gem located along Pidcock Creek. During the winter of 1776-1777, this home was used to care for convalescing and wounded soldiers as well as troops who had come down with a variety of diseases and illnesses. If you take a guided tour, note the four sections of the home additions and modifications made by numerous generations of inhabitants. Nearby is the **Thompson-Neely Grist Mill**, a restored water-driven mill built in the 1830s.

One of my favorite spots in the park is the **gravesites** of Revolutionary War soldiers (many unknown) down near the river. These are soldiers who passed away during the winter of 1776-1777 and the setting is ideal. Heavily wooded and tranquil, it is a great location for a family hike along the Delaware River.

Not to be missed is the short drive to **Bowman's Hill Tower** just up Lurgan Road. This imposing 125-foot structure, built to commemorate the American Revolution, provides visitors with a commanding view of the Delaware River and en-

The Durham Boat House

FAST FACT: One legend is that Bowman's Hill was named for Dr. John Bowman, ship's surgeon to the pirate Captain Kidd. The legend goes one step further in claiming that pirate treasure is buried on the hill.

virons. You'll also be able to admire the ever-changing landscape of Bucks County and New Jersey in addition to getting a sense of the terrain over which Washington and his men journeyed that fateful night.

After exiting the tower, get into your car and head back south on PA 32. Take the ramp onto I-95 and then the exit for US 1 South. Take the exit for the Pennsylvania Turnpike (I-276) and head west. Take exit 326 to merge onto I-76 east toward Valley Forge. Take exit 327 for North Gulph Road and then North Outer Line Drive. Turn into Valley Forge National Historical Park. The drive will take you a little over one hour to complete and you'll see absolutely nothing historical—just endless ribbons of asphalt, strip malls, and fast-food restaurants.

Cannons guard the battlefield at Valley Forge National Historical Park.

A visit to **Valley Forge National Historical Park** will make all your high school history lessons seem pale by comparison. Here, you will journey along the same routes as your patriot forefathers—you will step back into history to experience a time and a place etched into the American consciousness—a period of time that has often been clouded by legend as generations of history writers have sought to portray this place as one of abject misery or insufferable conditions. In many respects, it may have been a critical determinant of the war's success—not because of any military engagement, but rather because of military preparation.

Let's take a brief look backward. On August 25, 1777, the British commander-in-chief, Sir William Howe, and nearly 17,000 troops landed at the head of the Chesapeake Bay. Their intent was to march northward and capture Philadelphia. Opposing them was General George Washington and his army of 12,000 soldiers. The two armies met at Brandywine on September 11 and the Continental Army was soundly thrashed. It was then that the Continental Congress exited Philadelphia and headed north for safer territory. On September 26, Howe marched into Philadelphia unopposed and set up camp. On October 4, General Washington unsuccessfully attacked the British in nearby Germantown, but was forced to retreat.

After fending off a British attack at White Marsh, Washington and his army marched into Valley Forge on December 19, 1777. This position, 20 miles from Philadelphia, was ideal. It was close enough for Washington to keep tabs on the British occupation of Philadelphia, yet sufficiently distant from the city to prevent any surprise attack. It also prevented any northern advancement of British troops. The 10,000 troops of the Continental Army immediately set about the task of constructing approximately 2,000 huts laid out along planned military roads. They also built miles of trenches, several earthen redoubts (forts), as well as a bridge over the nearby Schuylkill River.

While history textbooks are fond of portraying the troops as "downtrodden and miserable," they were anything but. While there was a shortage of provisions early in the encampment and supplies of clothing and other essential living items were often lacking, the troops were able to effectively meet the elements and survive quite well. It wasn't the weather or lack of food that

> **F**AST FACT: Most of the men who died at Valley Forge succumbed to diseases (not cold) during the spring months of March, April, and May 1778.

A replicated hut that anchored the outer line of defense

decimated the ranks, but rather the scourges of influenza, typhoid, typhus, and dysentery. Approximately 2,000 troops lost their lives during the six-month encampment.

Although we'll begin our tour at the **Visitor Center**, there are a few things you might want to consider beforehand. While the tour is most often done by car (be sure to get the informative brochure and one-page cell phone tour guide at the visitor center), it is possible to see the extent of Valley Forge via a trolley tour with a professional guide. These tours are fee-based and operate seasonally.

There are other ways to view Valley Forge too. For example, if you come during the spring or summer months, you'll note armies of joggers and cyclists touring the various stops around the park. The park has a separate brochure that lists 11 walking trails and six biking trails throughout the acreage. That same brochure also lists seven horse trails. The following description, however, assumes you will be using a motorized vehicle.

Begin your visit by stopping in the informative **Visitor Center (#1)**. Here you will discover helpful park rangers, lots of books and pamphlets, and a small snack area. There's a film to watch and the staff will keep you updated about seasonal events, programs, and activities.

The next stop is the **Muhlenberg Brigade (#2)**—note that most of the roads are one-way. Here is a collection of reconstructed huts where General Peter Muhlenberg's brigade was housed. These troops helped to anchor the outer line of defense. As you walk around the huts, be sure to peek inside. Note the sparse living conditions (eight bunks crowded against the walls), the rudimentary fireplace, and the complete lack of sanitation. Imagine spending an entire winter surviving the elements in these structures.

The next stop is the **National Memorial Arch (#3)**. This imposing structure was originally constructed in 1917 in order to commemorate the "patience and fidelity" of the troops who wintered here in 1777-1778. Exit your car and walk around and you can get a sense of its enormity. Look to the southeast and you'll see the direction from which Washington's troops arrived at the encampment.

The following stop is the very impressive **Wayne Statue (#4)**. This memorial is in an area where troops under the command of General Anthony Wayne camped. Although Wayne actually had a home a few miles from Valley Forge, he preferred to take up residence closer to the encampment, so he moved in with his cousin, Mrs. Joseph Walker, and her husband.

Close quarters inside a soldier's hut

FAST FACT: During the Revolutionary War, there were more troops in the Continental Army from Pennsylvania than from any other state.

The next stop on the tour is the must-see **Washington's Headquarters (#5)**. Here is where the general set up his field operations—in the Isaac Potts House. The house today is decorated in the same way it would have looked during the winter of 1776-1777. The landscape around the house is striking and you'll quickly appreciate why Washington selected this specific location. Be sure to ask the rangers about some of the home's furnishings. Inquire about tours at nearby Valley Forge Station.

Next you'll travel down South Inner Line Drive; make a 180-degree turn to the left and come back up East Inner Line Drive. Between these two roads lies an area of the park known as the inner line defenses. Today they are virtually impossible to see, but they were critical to the defense operations of Washington's army. Back in 1777, this area left the Americans very vulnerable to attacks from the south.

At the next stop you'll be able to see **Redoubt 3 (#6),** built to secure this critical area. These earthworks appear to be giant molehills, but they are the result of some complex engineering. A deep ditch was excavated in front to slow an attacking enemy. The dirt was heaped into *gabions*—baskets of interwoven branches. Bundles of branches called *fascines* were piled outside and inside the wall to protect the defenders. Then the entire work was usually covered with sod to absorb cannon fire. At this particular redoubt the inside walls were faced with stakes. This redoubt is a partial reconstruction of the original redoubt on the original site. The British never attacked the camp, so none of the redoubts were ever tested.

Next on the tour is **Artillery Park (#7)**. This was a training ground where troops under the command of Brigadier General Henry Knox trained and drilled. Along the edge of these training grounds are a few replica cannons, which were always ready to be sent to other areas of the encampment if they were needed. They offer great photo opportunities.

Next is a **statue of General von Steuben (#8)**. Baron Friedrich Wilhelm Augustus von Steuben was the proverbial "breath of fresh air" for the beleaguered troops when he arrived in February 1778. He was a former Prussian army officer and was uniquely skilled at turning ragtag troops into disciplined soldiers. In short order, he developed an intense hands-on training regimen that turned the disorganized troops into a sharp and efficient fighting machine. It was said that the Baron created a "relish for the trade of soldiering." He taught by example with in-your-face instruction and repetitive drills. His methods worked and the troops were hammered into a well-disciplined fighting force.

Next on the tour is the **Washington Memorial Chapel (#9)**. The chapel is on private land (it receives no funds from the Park Service) and was built as a tribute to George Washington and the American Patriots of the Revolution in 1903-1904. Be sure to pick up an informative brochure about the chapel and its distinctive interior at the visitor center.

In many history books, the encampment at Valley Force is portrayed as a winter of enormous suffering and great hardships. Certainly those conditions existed, but the real story lies not with the weather or the surroundings, but with the men who spent those months in this now scenic place. This is where morale was lifted, where troop readiness was hardened, and where spirits were raised in a brutal and savage conflict. Drive these grounds or

Baron Friedrich Wilhelm Augustus von Steuben

FAST FACT: The lectern to the right front of the chapel is the only memorial at Valley Forge to a British soldier. It honors General Edward Braddock.

walk its trails and you will sense specters of the past in every reconstructed hut or partially eroded redoubt. This is truly the story of tenacity, perseverance, and resolve in the face of great odds and of the formation of a fighting unit's spirit and drive.

After your tour of Valley Forge, you'll be getting into your car and driving backward through history to an earlier time and an earlier event in the Revolutionary War. Depart the park and get on PA 23 east. Merge onto US 422 east. Follow the signs for US 202 south. Stay on US 202 for approximately 23.3 miles until you get to US 1. Make a right turn and drive for an additional 1.8 miles and **Brandywine Battlefield State Park** will be on your right.

One of the major goals of the British campaign during the Revolutionary War was to take over Philadelphia. The city's status within the colonies was of such importance that its capture would bring both a territorial and psychological victory to the English army that would transcend any military victories.

British troops under the command of General Howe began their march toward the city on September 9, 1777. Washington and his aides firmly believed that they had the superior forces and military tactics sufficient to protect the city and prevent its capture. Washington decided to muscle his troops in the area of Chadds Ford, Pennsylvania, in order to stop the British advance. Chadds Ford was significant since it offered a safe and easy passage across the Brandywine River on the road from Head of Elk, Maryland (now Elkton). where the British troops landed, to Philadelphia.

Troops were placed at the southernmost possible crossing of the river (Pyle's Ford) and the northernmost crossing (Wistar's Ford). In doing so, Washington hoped to squeeze the British troops and force a fight at the more easily defended Chadds Ford. By securing these specific locations Washington was sure he could successfully defend a significant portion of the river.

But the British had other plans. A portion of their army was to march from Kennett Square to Chadds Ford, just as Washington suspected they would. However, the majority of the army would then march north of Wistar's Ford and cross the river at a location (one apparently unknown to Washington) and subsequently march south to surprise the Continentals. It seems as though the British had a better knowledge of the local geography—a knowledge that gave them the upper hand in the battle to follow.

On the morning of the battle—September 11, 1777—a heavy blanket of fog

Washington's Headquarters at Brandywine

covered the area. This provided the British troops with an excellent cover for their surprise attack. When the fog burned off, the British troops were well-positioned for the ensuing fight. Washington believed that the entire British army was approaching toward Chadds Ford and organized his troops accordingly. However, when the bulk of the opposition appeared on the American right flank it became apparent to Washington that he had been outmaneuvered. In the ensuing confusion, it was evident that the Americans would not be able to defend their position. Although they fought valiantly, the odds and the forces were against them.

By nightfall the battle was essentially over. The Americans retreated to Chester, and General Howe's troops camped in the fields surrounding Benjamin Ring's house and Gideon Gilpin's farm.

Over the course of the next several days, Howe's army advanced on Philadelphia. Washington's troops offered little resistance. The two armies maneuvered back and forth with no significant military engagements taking place. Philadelphia was firmly in the sights of the British. Congress quickly abandoned Philadelphia and high-tailed it for Lancaster and then York. On September 26, 1777, the city fell into the hands of the opposition. The loss was a significant low-point for the patriots.

It may seem odd to some that we celebrate a significant defeat in the war for independence. That the defeat was due to a basic unfamiliarity with the landscape, rather than the inexperience of the troops, may make this place slightly more revered. It does, however, stand as a significant skirmish and a testament to military tactics and wartime preparation.

Upon entering the park, drive up the short road to the right and stop at the **Visitor Center**. Here, you'll be able to see an interpretive exhibit and an audio-visual presentation of the Brandywine Battlefield. There's also a gift shop with the usual array of books and information that will help you understand this place in greater detail. This is where you can also sign up for tours of the two houses on the property

After you leave the visitor center parking lot, make a right turn on the park road and head over to the **Gideon Gilpin House**. Pull into the parking area and stroll over the meadow to the house where Gideon Gilpin, a Quaker farmer, and his family lived at the time of the battle. As a pacifist, Gilpin did not participate in the battle, but he suffered greatly nonetheless—marauding soldiers plundered and sacked his home. His farm was left in ruins. Unable to sustain the farm, Gilpin converted his home into a successful tavern, which operated on the site from 1778 to 1789. As you tour the house you'll note that it has been furnished in a style reminiscent of 1777.

Return to the park road and head back toward the visitor center. Drive past it and up the first road on your right. In short order you'll make a slight left into a parking lot and see the **Benjamin Ring House** below. This home was Washington's headquarters during the conflict. The location of the house was pivotal to Washington due to its proximity to Chadds Ford, where Washington expected the entire British army to cross. It was here on September 10 that Washington and his generals planned their defense of the area. Your tour of the house will reveal a structure that has been extensively reconstructed after years of abandon-

The Gideon Gilpin House

ment and a fire in the 1930s to look like it did in September 1777. The furniture is of a simple colonial style and the decorations are intentionally sparse.

After leaving the house, exit the park and turn right onto US 1 W. Travel for about .7 mile and turn right onto Creek Road. Shortly up the road on your right (at the Chadds Ford Historical Society Barn) is a small gravel lot. Pull in and look for the 1725 home. It was here that soldiers were stationed in front of and just north of the house. The house and the springhouse have been restored and are open seasonally.

Depart the gravel lot and continue up Creek Road. As you pass Brinton's Bridge, Wylie, and Meetinghouse Roads on your right, know that this was the area heavily manned by Washington's army. These were the fords across the Brandywine that Washington believed the British would use. Throughout the morning of the battle, contradictory reports were delivered by couriers riding down the road you are now on. Those reports, intensified by confusion over location and names of fords, resulted in the American commanders believing that the entire British army faced them at Chadds Ford. It wasn't until 2 in the afternoon, when the "dust rising in the backcountry" proved to be the bulk of the British forces descending on the somewhat confused Americans.

Make a right turn on West Street Road (also known as PA 926). It was this road that the Americans used to gain higher ground on the advancing British troops. Continue your journey to Birmingham Road and make a right turn. On the corner just across from you is **Samuel Jones Farm**. This was where the Americans congregated as they were being driven back from the road by the British. Continue your drive down Birmingham Road and shortly on your left will be **Lafayette Cemetery**. Turn left into the cemetery and park your car where the road divides. From here you can look back at the terrain the British crossed to attack the patriot line.

Continue down Birmingham Road until you get to the **Birmingham Friends Meeting** on the right. Park your car and walk beyond the mounting block into the old walled cemetery. This is where the Americans held off the British against very heavy odds. To the right is a low granite block marking the resting place of dead from both sides, buried in one common grave. Return to Birmingham Road and make a right turn. As you continue down Birmingham Road, you'll see **Birmingham Hill**, a county park. This was where the main American line formed and the location of intense hand-to-hand combat between the two armies.

At the corner of Birmingham and Wylie Roads, there is a Civil War cannon. This is another area in which intense fighting occurred. When Washington heard about the skirmishes in this area, he quickly concluded that the bulk of the British army was attacking from the rear, rather than from across the Brandywine. He realized his tactical mistake and quickly ordered a sizeable detachment of men to help supplement the troops fighting here.

As you continue down Birmingham Road, there is a significant area on the right. Then known as the **Bennett Farm** it is today obscured by some modern development. Nevertheless, this is where many casualties were brought, including General Lafayette, who had been wounded in his left leg as he rallied the troops nearby. Continue to the intersection of Birmingham and Brinton's Bridge Roads.

This was originally known as Dilworth Crossing and it is here that the last engagement of the day was fought just before nightfall. There are also some 18th-century buildings in the general area including a blacksmith's shop and house, the old Dilworth Inn, and a country store where wounded soldiers were treated.

> **F**AST FACT: General Howe believed that as a result of the actions at Brandywine, the Americans could be defeated; but it would be very difficult to conquer them.

Turn right onto Brinton's Bridge Road and continue until you come back to Creek Road. Make a left turn and you'll return to US 1 at Chadds Ford.

After the battle, the Americans retreated to Chester, 12 miles to the southeast. The British, exhausted and disoriented in a strange territory, spent five days recuperating and tending to their injured. Although Brandywine was a less-than-successful encounter for the Americans, it was a crucial test of their fortitude.

CONTACTS

Washington Crossing Historic Park, Box 103, Washington Crossing, PA 18977; Phone: 215-493-4076; www.ushistory.org/washingtoncrossing/index.htm.

Valley Forge National Historic Park, Upper Merion Township, PA; Phone: (610) 783-1099; www.nps.gov/vafo/index.htm.

Brandywine Battlefield, Baltimore Pike at Ring Road, P.O. Box 202, Chadds Ford, PA 19317; Phone: (610) 459-3342; www.ushistory.org/brandywine.

The Johnson House in Germantown was an important station on the Underground Railroad

3 The Underground Railroad

Estimated length: 66 miles

Estimated time: 1–2 days

Combine this tour with: Chapters 1 and 11

Getting there: You'll begin your trip in Philadelphia—one of the primary gathering places for slaves escaping to the north. You'll journey over to Fairmount Park and then up to Germantown to view two distinctive homes along the "railroad." Then, it's off to Kennett Square and finally to Christiana in Lancaster County—additional stations along this tortuous highway to freedom.

Highlights: This ride will open your eyes to the passion and promise of the Underground Railroad—specifically as it took place in Pennsylvania—one of the leading abolitionist states. You'll see where the "freedom seekers" hid, the houses that provided them sanctuary and meet the people who risked lives and fortunes to ensure their safety.

The Underground Railroad was not a railroad and had very little to do with rail travel at all. It was quite simply a multilayered web of clandestine routes, friendly "conductors," and small bands of loosely organized citizens used by escaping slaves to move northward into free states and Canada while avoiding those who would have them returned to their owners.

What made the Underground Railroad all the more remarkable was the fact that no one knew all the facts about the entire system. No single person knew all the routes, all the stops, or all the details about this clandestine movement. Each person or each organization knew just enough about their own part of the operation, but nothing about other elements in the network. The local knowledge

FOLLOW THE DRINKING GOURD

One of the popular folk songs of the day was "Follow the Drinking Gourd"— a ditty passed from slave to slave and plantation to plantation during the 1800s. Hidden within the lyrics to this song were specific directions for following the Underground Railroad.

Follow the drinking gourd!
Follow the drinking gourd.
For the old man is a-waiting for to carry you to freedom
If you follow the drinking gourd.
When the sun comes back, and the first quail calls,
Follow the drinking gourd.
For the old man is a-waiting for to carry you to freedom
If you follow the drinking gourd.
(Repeat chorus)
The riverbank makes a very good road,
The dead trees will show you the way.
Left foot, peg foot, traveling on,
Follow the drinking gourd.
(Repeat chorus)
The river ends between two hills,
Follow the drinking gourd.

might consist of nothing more than the hiding place of a stash of food, the location of a hidden passage into a cellar, the route to a hospitable church with clothing and needed supplies, or a few miles of trails through a wooded area far from the main thoroughfare. By keeping the knowledge local and specific, the chance for outsiders to infiltrate a community and learn about the entire operation was minimized considerably.

The Underground Railroad had several special terms. First, there were the conductors, or individuals who helped slaves move from one place to another. These conductors usually operated out of a station—a house or barn or something less formal such as a lean-to in the woods or crawl space in an attic. The conductors might provide transportation via a wagon, boat, or barge, or they might be able to guide slaves along an obscure forest trail. In order to avoid detection,

There's another river on the other side,
Follow the drinking gourd.
(Repeat chorus)
When the great big river meets the little river,
Follow the drinking gourd.
For the old man is a-waiting for to carry you to freedom
If you follow the drinking gourd.

The "drinking gourd" is a coded term for the Big Dipper. The two stars at the end of the Big Dipper constellation point to the North Star or Polaris— which is always above the North Pole. For slaves, north meant only one thing—freedom—and that's why Polaris was so critical in their escape plans.

"When the sun comes back, and the first quail calls" is code for spring— a time of the year when weather conditions were more favorable for travel and when passage might be significantly less hazardous.

The river that "ends between two hills" was the Tombigbee River located in both Alabama and Mississippi. The second river ("There's another river on the other side") was the Tennessee River, which flows southeast from Tennessee into Alabama. The "great big river" was the Ohio River, where conductors would be waiting to help fugitive slaves cross over into northern states.

most of the movement along the railroad took place at night. The distance covered might be a few miles or up to 20 miles if weather and other conditions were favorable. Most of the stations were spots where individuals or families could rest, eat, and hide with a relative degree of security.

Slaves traveling along the railroad typically moved in small groups. While most of the travel was by foot, some of the slave routes consisted of passage on river boats or wagons. The routes themselves were frequently indirect and bypassed large population centers. It was not unusual for slaves to never see another person on the danger-filled journey north, other than the various conductors along the way.

Since accurate records were not maintained along the Underground Railroad, it is difficult to know for sure how many slaves were helped in their quest

> **F**AST FACT: Pennsylvania was pivotal to the success of the Underground Railroad. Every one of the 67 counties in the state had at least one Underground Railroad station.

for freedom. Estimates indicate that perhaps as many as 100,000 slaves were assisted in the journey from the south up to northern states or Canada. It may well be argued that the railroad was but a small dent in the overall practice of slavery, but the fact that it worked at all must have had a psychological impact on plantation owners that far exceeded the numbers who eventually discovered a newfound freedom.

The first stop on this tour will be one of the most symbolic structures on the Underground Railroad system—**Mother Bethel African Methodist Episcopal Church**, which traces its roots to the Free African Society, which was founded in 1787. Originally, the Free African Society was a typical mutual aid society. The members made regular contributions to the treasury, and the funds were used to help members in times of illness or other personal calamity. The society began laying the foundation for civil rights activities and institutions.

Differences over denominational styles spurred Reverend Richard Allen, Reverend Absolom Jones, and businessman James Forten to leave the Methodist Episcopal Church and establish the African Episcopal Church of St. Thomas. By July 1794 a blacksmith's shop was dragged to the recently purchased site by a team of horses. The structure was renovated and converted into a fully functional church.

In 1816 Richard Allen called together black Methodists from throughout the region to create a new Methodist conference. This was the birth of the African Methodist Episcopal Church. Allen served as its first bishop. Allen was a fierce champion of the anti-slavery movement, and he became a spokesman for his people on both local and national issues. The church rose to become a beacon of hope for many African Americans. It was also a forum for many of the nation's great orators and a significant stop along the Underground Railroad.

The present building is the fourth church to stand on this spot—having been erected in 1889. On my journey through this historic structure, my guide, Sharon, shared with passion the stories and tales of the people that have passed through this building and the fervor they brought to the anti-slavery movement.

If you are interested in anything to do with the Underground Railroad, then

Mother Bethel African Methodist Episcopal Church

this is the building to begin your journey. Although the present building was erected in the late 1800s, the spirits of its founders and the messages they shared with countless congregations still linger here.

On your own tour, be sure to ask for an explanation of the exquisite stained glass windows that adorn the sanctuary walls. Every aspect of the Bible and the

The sanctuary of Mother Bethel Church

faith has been lovingly crafted in these murals. On the day of my visit, the sun was at its zenith and the colors flared out over the entire church—brightening each alcove and tinting every corner. The pews in which Sharon and I sat are all original to the building.

After our visit in the main sanctuary, Sharon took me into the small museum in the basement. Here are the graves of Richard Allen, Sarah Allen (his wife), and Morris Brown—the second consecrated bishop of the A.M.E Church. Also on display are memorabilia and artifacts of the church's early years. Included is a ballot box designed specifically for non-readers, a haunting collection of fugitive slave notices (along with the physical scars that helped to identify individual slaves and the tortures they regularly endured), anti-slavery posters, and church alters and accoutrements.

By the time my tour was over, I had been well-steeped in not only the history of this building, but the history of the people who have called it home for more than two centuries. That this

> **F**AST FACT: Mother Bethel Church stands on the oldest piece of land (since 1791) continuously owned by African Americans in the United States.

building was critical in pushing the abolitionist cause and in harboring those who tried to escape from the wrath of slavery is clearly evident in the hope and vision of its mission and of its ancestry.

After departing Mother Bethel Church, work your way up to the Vine Street Expressway (I-676) and drive west. Merge onto the Schuylkill Expressway (I-76) headed west. Take exit 341 for Montgomery Drive. Make a left at the end of the exit ramp and go under the expressway. Turn right onto Belmont Mansion Drive and in about one minute you'll arrive at the **Belmont Mansion** in Fairmount Park.

The Belmont estate was initially settled in 1683 by Jan Boelsen, a Dutch land speculator, and his tenant farmers. William Peters, an upper-class Englishman and Loyalist, bought the farm at Belmont Cottage in 1742, in order to create a country estate for his American family. William Peters worked as an agent of the Penn family in the governance of their properties.

Belmont Mansion is a good example of Palladian architecture. Notice the central hall, which takes up over half of the first floor, flanked by small side chambers and one or two small winding staircases on the sides. The Underground Railroad Museum is housed in the central hall of this house.

The museum is small and limited to a few artifacts and a handful of standing displays about the role of the Underground Railroad during the time that the Peters family lived in this dwelling. In 1800, Judge Peters was responsible for determining the fate of 134 Africans, who were illegally enslaved and shipped on American vessels in violation of the 1794 Slave Trade Law. Peters turned the Africans over to the stewardship of the Pennsylvania Abolitionist Society, thereby enabling the Africans to become free persons.

One of the most interesting posters in the museum is "The Door of No Return." It shows a photograph taken through a deteriorating concrete doorway looking out over an empty sea. The text reads:

Belmont Mansion overlooks Philadelphia.

"The Door of No Return" is the last place on African soil where native Africans viewed their homeland before being transported to the New World as slaves. An estimated 20 million Africans passed through the port of Goree Island in the mid-1500s and the mid-1800s. Goree Island was a slave-holding warehouse—a veritable center for the trade of men, women, and children. Millions of West Africans were taken away against their will.

One of the noteworthy features about the mansion (unfortunately, not available for viewing) was an underground passageway running from Belmont toward the river as well as an additional underground passageway to a bathhouse near the river. Archaeological research has also uncovered a tunnel in the basement of the mansion.

Your visit here will be short, but keep in mind that this house, with its impressive view of Philadelphia, was but one of many along the Underground Railroad that helped freedom seekers find a better life.

FAST FACT: In 1688, the first protest against slavery was signed in Germantown, Pennsylvania (at a house about one mile south of the Johnson House).

Depart the mansion and return to Montgomery Drive. Get back onto I-76 and continue west. Merge onto the Roosevelt Expressway (US 1). After about 1 mile, take the Roberts Avenue exit and head toward Germantown Avenue. Continue on Germantown Avenue until you get to its intersection with West Washington Lane. On the left will be the **Johnson House**.

No journey along the Underground Railroad would be complete without a visit to historic Germantown and the Johnson House. My personable tour leader was a master of narration—effectively detailing the specifics of the house while wrapping them up in personal stories, dynamic dialogue, and amazing commentary that sustains interest and brilliantly brings the past alive. This is a tour for anyone with even the slightest interest in the Underground Railroad—both kids and adults will discover much in this engaging stroll through rooms rich in historic echoes.

Constructed in 1768, the Johnson House is one of Germantown's oldest existing homes. The stone in the front is native to the area and, if you look closely, you'll notice the Dutch doors are also original to the house. The home was built by John Johnson as a wedding present for his son and his bride. John Johnson Jr.

FAST FACT: William Still, "the father of the Underground Railroad," assisted as many as 60 slaves a month from his Philadelphia home. He interviewed each person, recording a brief biography as well as the destination of each person. Years later, he published a book—*The Underground Railroad* (now out of print)—which provides one of the best and most carefully documented records of the passage of slaves through Pennsylvania.

operated a tannery business from his home and may have done some farming on the side.

As Quakers, the Johnsons ardently believed in non-violence. While the Battle of Germantown raged outside the front door in October 1777, the family quietly slipped into the cellar and waited for the fighting to end. Even when soldiers tramped through the house looking for food, the Johnsons refused to get involved. Their concealment in the basement may have been fortuitous: My tour guide was keen to point out the very visible scars from a single musket ball that had penetrated three doors (an outside door and two inside meeting room doors) and smashed into an interior windowsill.

When Samuel Johnson married in 1805, he moved into the house with his bride, Jennet Rowland Johnson. Ardent abolitionists, Samuel and Jennet opened their home as a station on the Underground Railroad providing sanctuary, food, clothing, and transportation to African freedom seekers. As we stood in one of the home's front rooms—the meeting room—my guide told me of the many prominent abolitionists who came to speak within these walls: Lucretia Mott, William Still, and (reportedly) Harriet Tubman. It was in this very room that plans were made and directions were installed to assist freedom seekers in their movement north.

The other front room originally served as an office for the Johnson's tanning business. On display are artifacts and relics of the house unearthed by students during an archaeological dig in the spring of 2005. It is here that my guide tells me one of the many stories associated with the house—part of the home's oral tradition. From this house, some slaves were (reportedly) placed into wooden coffins. The lids were nailed shut and several individual coffins were transported by hearse six miles to the next station.

Our journey through the house took me through another room and out into the back yard. My guide pointed out the small third-floor attic window in the back of the house—the window in which a whale-oil lamp may have burned. The light probably alerted slaves escaping across the nearby Wissahickon Creek of the location of a friendly house. As freedom seekers approached the house and knocked on the door they were instructed to share a pass-code; in this instance, it was "A friend of a friend sent me." The Johnsons then knew that the people before them, even in the middle of the night, were freedom seekers and needed a place to rest.

My guide then showed me the interior door in the kitchen that leads to an attic space. The stairs were well worn and scuffed from many years of use and sufficiently deteriorated that it was not possible to go up and view the attic space. Nevertheless, my guide related the story how on one very dark night the local sheriff came pounding on the front door with a search warrant in his hand. Jennet Johnson quickly shepherded a group of frightened runaway slaves up through a trap door in the attic and out onto the roof of the house. Scrambling below, Jennet opened the front door to the impatient sheriff. The sheriff came stomping into the house, madly searching everywhere for possible fugitives. He eventually arrived in the attic space above the kitchen, certain there were slaves hidden within. Little did he suspect that less than six inches above him,

A stairway to freedom in the kitchen of the Johnson House

hearts beating madly, was a corps of former slaves gripping the shingles with all their might. The sheriff eventually departed and the freedom seekers were escorted back into the house.

The upper rooms of the house contain Jennet's bedroom and a parlor. The parlor walls are festooned with multiple portraits of prominent abolitionists of the day—among them Harriet Tubman at age 90. I also saw heavy set of chains typical of those used to shackle slaves.

On the third floor are the four bedrooms used by the Johnson children (the diminutive Jennet bore 12 children). I could almost feel the hustle and bustle of daily family life in this house…and the presence of so many souls who inhabited these rooms, if only for a day or two, as they traveled along a faint trail of freedom.

By the time my tour was complete, my guide had provided me with a first-rate

The Kennett Underground Railroad Center

account of the passion and persistence of a single family devoted to a cause that continues to reverberate hundreds of years later. It was more than a journey through the rooms of a 250-year-old house; it was a passage through the stories and anecdotes of a family bent on righting a wrong, as well as a historic tour about a group of believers who unflinchingly pursued the concept of "liberty and justice for all."

After departing the Johnson House, direct your vehicle to US 1 south. From here, it's about 26.2 miles to the picturesque town of Chadds Ford. Continue another 4 miles and make a right turn at the traffic signal (PA 52 north). Drive north for about 2.2 miles and then make a slight left at the Y onto South Wawaset Road (PA 52 bends to the right). Drive straight ahead on South Wawaset Road for about

.1 mile and you'll note a colonial stone house on the left (there will be a bright yellow pedestrian sign on the right side of the road). Turn left into the driveway and park your car. You're now at the **Kennett Underground Railroad Center**—a local organization devoted to preserving "one of the greatest and most revered events in our country's history."

This house was the former home of Eusebius Barnard, a prominent Chester County Quaker and ardent abolitionist. His strident views against slavery resulted in his "retirement" (read: expulsion) from the Kennett Friends Meeting. He was instrumental, however, in the founding of the Progressive Friends Meeting—a group that took a considerably more hard-line approach to the issue of slavery. Barnard was also known for his progressive views on women's rights and temperance.

Barnard's home was also a significant stop on the Underground Railroad. Barnard was a well-known conductor and hid many slaves in his home on their way to freedom. My tour guide was Mary Dugan, a Quaker who expertly and passionately presided over the organization for many years. While Kennett Square is frequently touted as "the Mushroom Capital of the World" (dozens of mushroom farms and mushroom processors dot the area), Mary believes a more appropriate appellation should be "Hub of the Underground Railroad." Many former Underground Railroad safe houses are still in the area and although they are for the most part in private hands, her group has listed a map of several Kennett Square houses on the museum's website. Narrated tours are also available at various times throughout the summer.

One of the elements of the Barnard House is a replica of a hiding place in a shed behind the main structure. In another room mannequins are bedded down in front of the old kitchen fireplace, as the freedom-seekers were, long ago. The museum also has a number of interactive displays, local artifacts, and information-packed posters to keep you well informed. Be sure to take a look at the reproduction of the box in which 34-year-old Henry "Box" Brown was shipped from

---

FAST FACT: The Kennett Underground Railroad Center documents over two dozen Underground Railroad sites within an eight-mile radius of Kennett Square—possibly the largest concentration of Underground Railroad stations in the nation.

> **I**f you have never been deprived of liberty as I was, you cannot realize the power of that hope of freedom."
> —Henry "Box" Brown, 1849

Richmond, Virginia, to Philadelphia in March 1849. Try to imagine how you might feel stuffed inside that box for 26 hours (with a few of those hours spent upside down).

Mary and I travel to the Chester County Visitor Center (300 Greenwood Road) just outside the main entrance to Longwood Gardens in Kennett Square. This building is the former Longwood Progressive Friends Meeting House. It was originally constructed in 1855 by radical Quakers who had been kicked out of their worship community. While all Quakers denounced slavery, not all Quakers approved of the Underground Railroad. Divisions arose with some members advocating a more passionate involvement in the anti-slavery movement. As the issue of slavery became more intense, schisms formed and relationships became strained within the Society of Friends.

In 1854 local abolitionists in the area initiated a new Progressive Friends Meeting. A year later they constructed their own meetinghouse—the Longwood Meeting of Progressive Friends and the current visitor center. Mary shows me the impressive bulletin board in one of the original rooms. Here are newspaper clippings, articles, and a panoply of photos illustrating the early years of this formidable site and the role it played in local politics—particularly the politics of the anti-slavery movement. It was here that some of the most well-known speakers of the day came to share their views and philosophies with rapt audiences: Frederick Douglass, Lucretia Mott, and Sojourner Truth.

Directly across from the visitor center is the Longwood Cemetery. If you have the time, the visitor center will provide you with a detailed map of all the markers in the cemetery as well as a self-guided walking tour that will direct you to the locations of the graves of prominent people in the Underground Railroad movement. The guide also lists background information on the work of these individuals within the anti-slavery movement, including Eusebius Barnard (Lot C-20) and John and Hannah Cox (Lot C-12).

The Coxes played a pivotal role in the Underground Railroad and originally owned the land on which the cemetery is located. Their home, Longwood, was an ideal location since it was on the main road to Philadelphia from points south and west. In addition, since Maryland was considered a southern state, this part

The former Longwood Meeting of Progressive Friends

of southern Pennsylvania was one of the first places escaping slaves could safely visit after crossing the Mason-Dixon Line. Slaves passing through the area were often transported to the Cox home where they were sheltered, fed, and clothed. John Cox was president of the Anti-Slavery Society and he and his wife entertained many well-known abolitionists of the day. It has been said that author Harriett Beecher Stowe visited the Coxes and was inspired to use several events of the visit in her book *Uncle Tom's Cabin*.

After you depart the cemetery, travel .2 miles north on US 1. On the right side of the road you will find the **Cox house**. At the time of my visit the house was mothballed and boarded up. However, you can pull into the driveway that encir-

The former Cox House—another station on the Underground Railroad

cles the house and get a sense of what this structure must have looked like more than two centuries ago when it was first constructed (early 1800s) by two of the most ardent abolitionists of the time. Walk around the house and try to view it without all the traffic in the background. Imagine this as an area without trucks or cars, strip malls or donut shops, but as a rural outpost on a long path to freedom.

Continue on your journey westward along US 1. When you come to the intersection with PA 41 head north for several miles until you come to the small Lancaster County town of Christiana. Make your way to the **Christiana Underground Railroad Center at Historic Zercher Hotel** at the corner of Slokom and Green Streets.

As you enter the museum (it's free and there are no tour guides), you'll quickly notice that it is confined to a single room. Don't let the lack of space fool you—this may well be one of the most significant places along the entire Underground Railroad tour. For many historians this place may have had much to do with the onset of the Civil War as did any other location in our country.

In the early 1800s the Christiana area was the confluence of the main lines of the Underground Railroad through Lancaster County. Since Pennsylvania had abolished slavery in 1780, many freedom seekers saw this region as "safe territory." There is a notebook on the center display in the museum that lists the locations of more than 20 "stations" in the immediate area. Although many used these farms and homes as a passage to other points east and north, a significant number of freedom seekers remained in the region. There arose a sizeable set-

The Cristiana Underground Railroad Center at Historic Zercher Hotel

tlement of free African Americans who often lived in partnership with white farmers, many of them Quakers active in the Underground Railroad.

With the support of the local population, many former slaves were able to secure employment, a new place to live, and a renewed sense of personal freedom. Many stayed to raise their families and contribute to the local economy. However, not everything was "peaches and cream." That's because slave catchers frequently roamed the area capturing people of color irrespective of whether they were free or not.

The Fugitive Slave Law (originally passed in 1793) and the Compromise of 1850 stated unequivocally that any escaped slave could be returned to his or her owner whether the slave had been captured in a free state or not. The law also stipulated that local citizens were required to assist in the capture of slaves under penalty of law. The law also granted slave catchers national immunity in their pursuit of runaway slaves. To many, the Fugitive Slave Law was a de facto embrace of nationally sanctioned slavery.

The William Parker farm was about two miles southeast of Christiana. In 1851, a local slave catcher, William Padgett, thought he recognized some of the people there as former slaves from the Maryland plantation of Edward Gorsuch. After notifying Gorsuch, both Padgett and Gorsuch, along with a party of slave catchers, journeyed to the Parker farm on September 11, 1851.

Although the facts at this point are not entirely clear, the meeting between Gorsuch and Parker was less than friendly. A fight broke out and in its aftermath Gorsuch was killed. His son, Dickenson, and several others were wounded. The federal government immediately dispatched Edward Ingraham, who set up his office in Zercher's Hotel. Ingraham declared martial law and U.S. Marines were brought in to arrest four white men and 37 African Americans. Each of the 41 people was formerly charged with treason against the U.S. government.

The body of Edward Gorsuch was brought to Zercher's Hotel where an inquest was held to determine the cause of death. At the same time, the group accused of treason were held in the attic of Zercher's Hotel until they could be transported to Moymensing Prison in Philadelphia where they were held for trial.

The trial began on November 24, 1851, on the second floor of Independence Hall in Philadelphia. The first person brought before the jury was Castor Hanley, a local Christiana miller. On December 11, after about 10 minutes of deliberation the jury found Hanley not guilty. Since it was apparent that the jury was not going to convict the other defendants, the prosecution declined to bring them to trial. The accused were turned over local authorities in Lancaster County. It was the belief of the court that the prisoners would be effectively charged and convicted of murder in the local

FAST FACT: The 41 people charged were the largest number of Americans to be charged with treason in the history of our country.

court. Yet because of local opposition to slavery, all the remaining defendants were subsequently released from custody. The result: no one was ever held accountable for the death of Edward Gorsuch.

As I read the posters, documents, and clippings I learned that the William Parker farm where the confrontation took place is no longer standing. It was torn down in 1899 and is unavailable for viewing.

Zercher's Hotel may appear unassuming and undistinguished from the outside—but its place in history is anything but. For many, the hotel and events that happened here remain as one of the most significant catalysts to spark the Civil War. It was a mighty fulcrum that nudged the nation into that great battle and the eternal question of state's rights.

CONTACTS

Mother Bethel African Methodist Episcopal Church, 419 S. Sixth St., Philadelphia, PA 19147; (215) 925-0616; www.motherbethel.org.

Belmont Mansion, 2000 Belmont Mansion Dr., Philadelphia, PA 19131; (215) 878-8844; www.belmontmansion.org.

Johnson House, 6306 Germantown Ave., Philadelphia, PA 19144; (215) 438-1768; johnsonhouse.org.

Kennett Square Underground Railroad Center, P.O. Box 202, Kennett Square, PA 19348; (610) 347-2237; undergroundrr.kennett.net.

Christiana Underground Railroad Center, 11 Green St., Christiana, PA 17509; (610) 593-5340; www.zerchershotel.com.

The Conrad Weiser House just outside Womelsdorf

4 Somebody Slept Here

Estimated length: 102 miles

Estimated time: 1–2 days

Combine this tour with: Chapter 2

Getting there: We'll begin in Morrisville—about as far east as you can get in Pennsylvania without being in New Jersey. For much of the tour, we'll be confined to major thoroughfares as we hopscotch westward following the general path of the Pennsylvania Turnpike. The vistas between the sites is limited, but the locations of each of these homes are not.

Highlights: If you're a fan of HGTV, then this is your tour. You'll see some of the state's most amazing architecture—from stately homes to frontier outposts. The tour starts in the countryside of far eastern Pennsylvania and sweeps westward through some colonial masterpieces and ends up with two rustic yet historically important dwellings. By the time you're done, you'll want to begin redecorating (or possibly relocating) your own humble abode.

Americans have always had a love affair with their houses. From the simplest dwellings to the most ornate mansions, we love the immense variety of architectural styles that can be found in every corner of this country.

This tour covers some of Pennsylvania's finest, most historic, and most representative homes. They are classic in the sense that they played a part in the history of the state as well as the history of the people who helped build the state.

Our first is the reconstructed 17th-century home of William Penn, founder and first governor of Pennsylvania. **Pennsbury** is one of those gorgeous homes and locations that should be on the itinerary of every visitor to the state. If you

FAST FACT: The White House is the most-visited house in the country with 1.25 million visitors annually. It is also the only house in the country protected by the Norwegian Advanced Surface to Air Missile System (NASAMS).

love old houses and the well-manicured grounds that typically surround them, you will have an instant love affair with Pennsbury. Pennsbury was the place William Penn selected as his summer retreat, his "home away from home," his escape after attending to all the administrative and political details of the new colony while in Philadelphia. On these 8,400 acres 26 miles north of the city, he could reflect and relax. As he wrote his first wife, Gulielma: "Of cities and towns of concourse beware; . . . a country life and estate I like best for my children."

As the house was under construction in 1682, Penn directed that hundreds of trees be planted throughout the grounds. Four thousand fruit trees, including cherry, plum, and peach, were arranged in neat orchards on the grounds. One of the first environmentalists, Penn made sure the main house was provided with natural foods including parsnips, lettuce, carrots, asparagus, peas, cabbages, artichokes, and herbs from the large garden. Horses, cows, and other livestock grazed in nearby meadows. He also had a formal flower garden installed in front of the house.

Unfortunately, a succession of political storms forced Penn to return to his native England in 1701 to tend to matters both political and financial. He was unable to return to his beloved estate and it slowly began to deteriorate. Penn died in 1718 and his descendants sold the property in 1792.

Today, the house and surrounding grounds have been restored to their original condition. The masterfully reconstructed clapboard manor house is surrounded by an array of outbuildings and beautiful gardens spread across 43 acres of the original estate. Pennsbury has an incredible collection of 17th-century furnishings including items of pewter, ceramics, textiles, and wicker. Walk across the grounds and you may encounter a horse, cow, or gaggle of geese meandering across the grass. You'll certainly enjoy the gardens full of 17th-century flowers.

Pennsbury is a living history museum—an opportunity to see "history in action." The historic buildings are shown only on guided tours and feature an audiovisual introduction along with a 90-minute hour tour. Begin your journey into the past at the **visitors center** where you will be able to dole out the appropriate fees and see the "William Penn: Seed of a Nation" exhibit.

As you are led about the grounds you will be able to examine some of the structures Penn included on this estate (many re-constructed). You will have an opportunity to see the **Manor House**, the beautiful home that was Penn's delight. It was here that Penn was able to escape the oppressive heat and noise of Philadelphia and enjoy the natural beauty of the tranquil surroundings.

Separate from the main house is the **Kitchen House**. As was the custom in the day, the kitchen building was physically detached from the main building in order to prevent the spread of any potential fires that might break out (far better to destroy the kitchen than the entire manor). It was in this building that basic household chores such as baking, food preparation, cooking, food preservation, beer brewing, and basic laundry work took place.

Near the Kitchen House is the **Kitchen Garden**, where the help was able to grow a wide variety of foods for use in the house. You'll also be able to view a **Worker's Cottage** and get a feel for how a middle-class family

Statue of William Penn outside Pennsbury Manor

FAST FACT: William Penn only lived in Pennsylvania for a total of four years (1682–1684 and 1699–1701).

might have lived in the 1700s. Near the garden is the **Crozier House,** which was originally built on the foundations of Penn's house. If you have time, walk down

The Graeme Park Mansion—an elegant country estate

to the **Boat House** and see the reproduction of a barge Penn would have used to travel from Philadelphia to Pennsbury (the roads in the area were much too rudimentary and water travel was so much gentler on the bones).

I made my initial visit to Pennsbury on a late summer's day. The colors were vibrant, the air clear and the scenery just short of incredible. As I stood looking at the grounds I was taken by the solemnity of the environment as much as I was wrapped in the wondrous sights before me. When you journey here, you too, will get a sense of why Penn selected this particular location. Even more than 300 years later, this estate still holds its natural charm and vibrant luster.

After you leave Pennsbury turn left onto Bordertown Road. After about 5.1

miles turn onto US 13 south (Bristol Pike). Travel for about 2 miles and get on the Pennsylvania Turnpike (I-276) and head west. After approximately 14.8 miles take exit 342 and merge onto PA 611 north (Easton Road) toward Doylestown. Drive for an additional 3.9 miles and make a left turn onto County Line Road (just after the Naval Air Station). Drive for about 1 mile and turn left into Graeme State Park. Park your car in the small parking area and walk over to the barn—where the visitors center is located.

The **Graeme Park Mansion** is the only surviving residence of a colonial Pennsylvania governor—Sir William Keith. Keith was the provincial governor of Pennsylvania from 1717 to 1726. His brand of government was based on a "power to the people" principle. As you might imagine, his egalitarian beliefs did not endear him to many of his contemporaries.

Keith secured 1,200 acres of land outside the town of Horsham and promptly began constructing "Fountain Low"—so-called because of the many natural springs on the property. This was Keith's summer residence—a way to escape the heat of Philadelphia and retire to a more genteel environment each year. Besides the main house, he also built a "long house" for his servants, a malt shop, a barn, and several smaller structures.

In 1726 Keith was forcefully removed from office and traveled to England in hopes of securing a government position. He died before he could return and the house was eventually sold to his son-in-law Dr. Thomas Graeme in 1739. It was renamed Graeme Park and remodeled into a county estate in 1750. Graeme added elaborate paneling in several rooms as well as imported ceramic delft tiles around the fireplaces. As you might imagine, this was the place to be in the mid-18th century and many parties and formal events were held here during those years.

Upon the death of Dr. Graeme in 1772, the house and grounds passed to his daughter Elizabeth Graeme Fergusson. A few years later Elizabeth was accused of being a traitor and the property was confiscated by the colonial government. However, with the help of some influential friends she was able to clear her name and regain ownership of the property. Unfortunately, her finances suffered greatly and she was ultimately forced to sell Graeme Park.

A succession of owners lived on and worked the land around the house. They each maintained the property in its original condition until it was eventually turned over to the state of Pennsylvania in 1958. It is one of the finest examples of colonial architecture you may ever visit.

FAST FACT: In Colonial America, itinerant painters roamed the countryside, each carrying a unique set of pigments. These pigments were then mixed with a farmer's or household's own milk and lime to create paints for the house.

As you tour this house take notice of some of its distinctive features and classic styling. Entering the mansion through the southern door you will come into Dr. Graeme's office. Take notice of the high ceilings—a typical feature of many summer homes of the day. The dining room is next—even though it was originally a kitchen when the house was first constructed. The closet here has a spiral staircase that was used to access the upper floors.

For formal entertaining, the parlor room was the most elaborately furnished room in the house. The paint on the walls is original to the room and to the house. Proceed to the master bed chamber and you'll discover that this particular room had two uses—it was used as the usual sleeping quarters, but also served as an extra entertainment center. The paint on the fireplace wall is also original to the house.

This home features a number of bedrooms (or bed chambers as they were often called). There is a small bed chamber with a fireplace that was used by guests to the house. Another bed chamber was used by Elizabeth Graeme prior to her inheritance of the house. Next there is a third-floor bed chamber that was used by Graeme's children. The design here is much simpler than in other rooms. Finally, there is the nursery with portions of the chimneys. This feature assured that the room would be particularly warm for the youngest members of the family.

This is a house that will spark your imagination. You can literally close your eyes and hear the clop-clop of horse hooves as they tug carriages past the stone gateposts on their approach to the house. Keep your eyes closed and you will be able to transport yourself along the carriage path and past the formal gardens that accentuated the magnificent architecture of this estate. Classical chamber music echoes across the grounds, visitors in high-button shoes and flowing dresses pass by, and the gentility of the estate permeates the summer air. This is indeed a time long past—but a time to remember. Getting back in your car will be a sober reminder of what has passed those many years ago.

Hope Lodge, on the outskirts of Philadelphia

Depart Graeme Park Mansion and make a right turn onto County Line Road. Drive to PA 611 and make another right turn. Travel down PA 611 for about 4 miles and merge onto the Pennsylvania Turnpike (I-276) headed west. Travel for about 4.7 miles and take exit 339 toward PA 309/Fort Washington/Ambler. After .2 mile merge onto Pennsylvania Turnpike Apr. Travel for .6 miles and continue straight onto Pennsylvania Avenue. After another .6 mile turn left onto South Bethlehem Pike. Drive for about 1 mile and **Hope Lodge** will be on your left.

Hope Lodge (it wasn't given that name until later) was built between 1743 and 1748 by Samuel Morris, a prosperous Quaker entrepreneur. Morris wore many hats—farmer, ship owner, miller, ironmaster, shop owner, and mill owner.

FAST FACT: Hope Lodge is the *only* house museum in Pennsylvania devoted to two historic time periods side by side. Some rooms in the mansion are furnished in the Colonial style (1743–1770) while other rooms are shown in the Colonial Revival style (1922–1953).

When the house was first constructed it served as an excellent example of early Georgian architecture in the gently rolling Pennsylvania countryside.

The estate was lovingly maintained by Morris until his death in 1770. It was then inherited by his brother Joshua. Joshua in turn sold the property and dwelling to another Philadelphia merchant, William West.

The Wests lived at Hope Lodge from 1776 to 1782. The house was then known as Whitemarsh Farms and Whitemarsh Estate. It was during this time that the estate gained historical fame when the Continental Army encamped in the surrounding fields for six weeks immediately after the Battle of Germantown and before encamping at Valley Forge in the winter of 1777. It was during this time (the Whitemarsh Encampment) that the house was used as a headquarters by George Washington's Surgeon General, John Cochran.

After West's death, the house was sold to Henry Hope, a wealthy English banker whose family later gave its name to the famous Hope Diamond. Hope had purchased the property as a wedding gift for his ward, James Watmough. It was the Watmoughs who were responsible for naming the site Hope Lodge, in honor of their benefactor.

Two generations of Watmoughs owned Hope Lodge before it was sold to Jacob Wentz, their tenant farmer, in 1832. The Wentz family lived at the house for nearly 90 years and were the first owners to concentrate their attention on farming the property. As farmers, they were financially unable to add interior improvements to the house (such as indoor plumbing and gas lighting) and thus retained the 18th-century integrity of the house.

In 1921 the Wentzes sold the property to a development company who were intent on demolishing the structure and expanding a nearby limestone quarry. Fortunately, William and Alice Degn, historic preservationists, stepped in and purchased the property in 1922. They painstakingly restored the house, created a rose garden, and added their own collection of 18th- and early 19th-century furnishings.

After the Degns passed away, ownership of the house was transferred to the Hope Lodge Foundation, and in 1957 to the Commonwealth of Pennsylvania. Today, Hope Lodge is administered by the Pennsylvania Historical and Museum Commission with the Friends of Hope Lodge, a nonprofit support group.

NOTE: At the time of my visit, public tours of Hope Lodge were unavailable due to severe state cutbacks. However, the site is not closed. You are welcome to stroll around the Colonial Revival gardens, walk the grounds, and marvel at the handsome symmetry of this Georgian mansion. Hopefully, by the time you read this, state funding will have increased sufficiently to reopen the architecturally delightful home so that new generations of visitors may marvel at its design, grace and beauty.

After you depart Hope Lodge head back north on South Bethlehem Pike. When you get to the intersection with Pennsylvania Avenue turn right and then continue on Pennsylvania Turnpike Apr. Take the Pennsylvania Turnpike (I-276 west) on-ramp to Harrisburg. After about 11.8 miles take exit 326 to merge onto I-76 east toward Valley Forge/US 202. Take exit 328A for US 202 south/US 422 west. Keep right at the fork to continue toward US 422 W. Drive for .4 mile, keep left at the fork, and follow signs for US 422 west/Pottstown. Merge onto US 422 west and travel for approximately 29.7 miles. Turn right onto Daniel Boone Road and after about .7 mile turn left onto Old Daniel Boone Road. Follow the road around to the visitors center for the **Daniel Boone Homestead**.

When I was growing up in the '50s and '60s, my heroes were rugged and incredibly daring frontiersmen such as Davy Crockett ("King of the Wild Frontier") and Daniel Boone. I read their stories and consumed books about their adventures on the American frontier. I was an incurable fan.

The exploits of these early pioneers solidified my interest in the history of the American West (although Daniel never made it across the Mississippi River) and carved an indelible image in my mind of the values of fierce determinism and rugged individualism. They were heroes, not just to me and my friends, but to an entire country who relied on them to make things right—regardless of the odds.

When I was provided the opportunity to literally walk back in time—to the ancestral home of one of those heroes—I grabbed it with gusto. For it was Daniel Boone whose name was forever linked with the story of the American frontier just as much as it was branded onto my own mind as a youngster.

Daniel's father, Squire Boone, was an English Quaker who immigrated to

FAST FACT: Daniel Boone was also a militia officer in the Revolutionary War (1775–1783).

Pennsylvania in 1717. He lived in a number of different places in and around the Philadelphia area until he eventually purchased 250 acres in the Oley Valley (near Reading). Squire and his wife Sarah settled down to a comfortable rural life and had 11 children, of which Daniel was the sixth. Born on November 2, 1734, Daniel grew up with an appreciation for the ruggedness of his surroundings and he quickly honed his frontier skills across the hills and dales of south-central Pennsylvania.

In 1750 the Boones picked up their lives and moved to the Yadkin Valley in North Carolina. It was there that Daniel met and married Rebecca Bryan with whom he raised 10 children. In 1773 he struck out for Kentucky (then the extent of the American frontier), but was unsuccessful in settling the new land. However, he returned to North Carolina two years later and established the town of Booneborough. Over the course of the next decades, Boone was instrumental in helping settle other parts of this frontier in addition to dealing with Native Americans in the area.

Boone was able to return to his boyhood home in Pennsylvania on two separate occasions—once in 1781 and again in 1788. On both occasions he was hailed as a hero and a man of honor. In spite of his status, his personal finances suffered greatly. He departed Kentucky and moved further west into Missouri where, for a time, he worked for the Spanish government. He died near St. Louis on September 26, 1820.

After the Boones left Pennsylvania in 1750, the Pennsylvania estate passed to a cousin—one William Maugridge. After Maugridge's death in 1766 the property was bought by John and Elizabeth DeTurk and remained in their family until the 1820s. It was eventually turned over to the Pennsylvania Historical and Museum Commission in 1938.

Walking the grounds of the Daniel Boone Homestead, particularly in the spring and fall months will give you a sense of the quiet beauty of this region. The din of trucks pounding over pavements and automobiles zipping along highways are nonexistent here. You will listen to many of the same sounds as did young Daniel Boone as you stroll over portions of this 579-acre historic site.

One of the first buildings you will want to visit is the **Boone House**. Be aware,

The Boone House in the Oley Valley

however, that the house you will tour is completely unlike the one Daniel grew up in. That's because generations of the Maugridge and DeTurk families have added, subtracted, modified, and re-designed portions of the home so that it is quite unlike the original log structure. Walls were replaced, a porch was added, and stones were used to expand sections of the home. The house is, nevertheless, representative of many farmhouses that dotted the landscape during the early 1800s.

What is original, and what young Mr. Boone was well acquainted with, lies beneath the main structure in the cellar. Here you will see the actual cellar that Daniel may have played in. Look over to the south wall and you'll see the home's original spring that flows through a trough in the floor. Note the archway that

FAST FACT: On hunting trips, Daniel Boone read the Bible and *Gulliver's Travels*. As one of the most literate members of any group, Boone would frequently read these books to his hunting companions.

supported the home's original fireplace, as well as the stone walls that were part of the home's original foundation. This cellar also served as a food storage area for the Boones and the other families who occupied this home.

Stroll over to the **Smokehouse**, which was constructed sometime in the early 1800s. Here meats were cured, preserved, and smoked. The loft above was used as a meat storage area.

You'll want to look at the **Blacksmith Shop,** which would have been very similar to the one Squire Boone used in his trade as a blacksmith. While the current structure is very similar to the one used by Squire Boone (it dates from 1769), it is originally from the nearby town of Amityville.

The **Homestead Barn** has several portions that are original to the one used by the DeTurks in the late 1700s. Note the distinctive construction with a southern orientation in order to take advantage of winter sunlight to warm the stables along with the steeply sloping bank to protect the inhabitants from fierce winter winds.

Walk on over to the **Bertolet House** and the **Bertolet Bake House**. These two structures are not original to the property, but were moved here in 1968 in order to demonstrate typical 18th-century structures. These buildings use Pennsylvania German log architecture such as a centrally located fireplace, two rooms behind the fireplace (for heat), and the steeply pitched roof.

The site has a number of other buildings used for recreational and private events throughout the year. When you visit, plan to take a slow casual walk around the property and soak up all the years that were spent here by one of America's great heroes. Consider how this property shaped and influenced a young Daniel Boone in the years prior to his explorations of the 18th-century frontier.

After departing the Daniel Boone Homestead, return to US 422 west. Make a right turn and stay on US 422 west for about 24 miles. You'll drive through the town of Robesonia on the other side of Reading. Before you get to the burg of Womelsdorf, make a left turn onto Weiser Drive (there's a small sign on the side of the road), travel for about .25 mile and then make a right on Weiser Lane and the parking area. You're now at the **Conrad Weiser Homestead**.

"Who was Conrad Weiser?" you might ask. How does he rate a home administered by the Pennsylvania Historical and Museum Commission? The answer is simple: he was a well-respected mediator between Pennsylvania and the powerful Iroquois Nation in the early 1700s.

But first, we need to tramp back into some early history. Weiser was born in Germany on November 2, 1696. When Conrad turned 13 his father decided it was time to immigrate to America and so the family settled on the New York frontier. In the following years young Conrad took up with neighboring Mohawks, learning the language of the Iroquois and acting as a go-between for the growing German community. He subsequently became quite adept with the customs, traditions, language, and heritage of the Iroquois Confederacy.

In 1723, a large segment of the German community traveled 400 miles south along the Susquehanna River to south-central Pennsylvania into what is now Berks and Lebanon counties. Conrad's father and mother were able to acquire 200 acres of prime real estate near the present-day town of Womelsdorf. The Weisers were not only productive farmers, they were equally productive parents, raising a total of 14 children.

Conrad, with his extensive knowledge of Iroquois life, was frequently employed to help shape new policies and treaties as more settlers poured into the region. He was involved in treaty negotiations, land purchases, and travels throughout the Iroquois territory on behalf of both state and national interests. His efforts, particularly his command of Native American languages, helped ensure a level of peace and tranquility between whites and Native Americans. As a result, Pennsylvania remained fairly stable in what was a turbulent time for many other sections of the new country.

Although he briefly assumed a

FAST FACT: When Weiser passed away, one Iroquois Indian noted, "We are at a great loss and sit in darkness…as since his death we cannot so well understand one another."

commission of lieutenant colonel in the provincial militia, he was deeply committed to maintaining peace at all costs. He kept close ties with the local community and was instrumental in founding the city of Reading in 1748 and helping establish the county of Berks in 1752. He was a pivotal figure in many political offices as well as in his own business operations. At the time of his death on July 13, 1760, he owned several thousand acres of farmland in the region.

You can take a brief walk back to those times with a visit to the Conrad Weiser Homestead just outside Womelsdorf. After stopping in at the **Visitor Center** (a 1834 structure constructed by John Scheetz who purchased the Weiser farm), stroll over to the **Conrad Weiser House**. This structure was originally believed to be Weiser's second home on the property; however, recent architectural research seems to indicate that the date of construction may be in question. It is known that a portion of the house was built in the 1700s, but an actual date cannot be accurately determined. A series of misfortunes (tornado, fire) destroyed portions of the house so that most of the original woodwork is gone. However, what is not gone is the classic Germanic design of a typical family home.

Walk over to the adjacent **Spring House**—a 19th-century structure that served as both a springhouse as well as a bake house. Look carefully, and you'll note an oven constructed off the gable wall.

Walk on over to the circle in the middle of the property. Here in the middle is the **Weiser Gravesite**. This is where Conrad is buried. It is believed that seven of his children are also interred here, along with members of Iroquois negotiating parties. The person missing from this gravesite is Weiser's wife, Anna Eve. Her final resting place is unknown.

Right behind the gravesite is the **Conrad Weiser Monument**—the tall structure with the cement ball on top. This was constructed in 1909 and placed in the borough of Womelsdorf. It was later moved to its present site (in 1926) by the Patriotic Order Sons of America.

This site is small and can easily be traversed in an hour or two. Although your visit may be short, please note that the influence of the man celebrated here was indeed grand. Weiser had a propensity for bringing two disparate sides together and engaging them in common conversation. He was a pivotal figure in the early settlement of Pennsylvania—a settlement that was respectful of the original inhabitants and mindful of the expansionist needs of a growing new country. That he was able to keep the two sides in constant and peaceful negotiations is a testament to his enormous political skills.

CONTACTS

Pennsbury Manor, 400 Pennsbury Memorial Rd., Morrisville, PA 19067; (215) 946-0400; www.pennsburymanor.org.

Graeme Park, 859 County Line Rd., Horsham, PA 19044; (215) 343-0965; www.graemepark.org.

Hope Lodge, 553 South Bethlehem Pike, Fort Washington, PA 19034; (215) 646-1595; www.ushistory.org/hope.

Daniel Boone Homestead, 400 Daniel Boone Rd., Birdsboro, PA 19508; (610) 582-4900; www.danielboonehomestead.org.

Conrad Weiser Homestead, 28 Weiser Lane, Womelsdorf, PA 19567; (610) 589-2934; conradweiserhomestead.org.

Coal mining: "Another day older and deeper in debt"

5 Where Anthracite Was King

Estimated length: 131 miles

Estimated time: 1–2 days

Combine this tour with: Chapter 6

Getting there: This tour begins in McDade Park on the outskirts of Scranton. After viewing the Anthracite Heritage Museum and taking the Lackawanna Coal Mine Tour, we'll journey down to Weatherly to visit one of the most distinctive "museums" you'll ever see. Then it's down along PA 93 to beautiful Jim Thorpe—a classic Pennsylvania coal town. Then we'll meander along US 209 through some of the roughest and toughest mining country in the state. We'll finish up in Ashland and then Centralia—a true Pennsylvania's ghost town.

Highlights: This is a trip based on a single commodity—anthracite coal. Not only will you discover what this critical ore is, but you'll learn about the lives (and deaths) of the people who were consumed with its mining. This journey is as much a history of Pennsylvania as any trip through Philadelphia or Lancaster. This is a journey of vast riches and devastating losses—both financial as well as personal.

In 1749 the Proprietary Government of Pennsylvania purchased from the Indians of the Six Nations a section of land about 125 miles long by 35 miles wide for the sum of 500 pounds (about $2,500). Although unknown at the time, this section of land comprised about all of the anthracite coal fields.

According to legend, it was a hunter, one Neco Alan, who in 1790 accidentally ignited an outcropping of hard coal near the present-day town of Pottsville. Then another hunter, Philip Ginter, found a small vein of "black stones" near Summit Hill the following year.

FAST FACT: Formed over 300 million years ago, 98 percent of anthracite coal found in the United States lies under 484 square miles in northeastern Pennsylvania.

The discovery of anthracite coal was both advantageous as well as frustrating. The American Industrial Revolution was in its infancy in the late 1700s and early 1800s and wood and charcoal were the primary fuels that powered the young nation. But the "manufacture" of those fuels was entirely dependent on the lumber industry. Anthracite coal, on the other hand, was recognized as a potential "solution" to satisfying the young country's demand for fuel simply because of its apparent abundance.

It was actually the War of 1812 that was the stimulus for the use of anthracite coal. The depletion of American forests slowly but predictably increased the cost of firewood as a fuel source. As a result, industry slowly began to rely on large amounts of bituminous (soft) coal imported from England. But the British blockade during the War forced Americans to turn to other fuel sources—primarily anthracite (hard) coal.

However, the anthracite coal fields of Pennsylvania lay at least 90 miles away from the large industrial centers of the East Coast. The mountainous terrain hindered the transport of coal and made the journey much too expensive. Initially canals (which we'll examine in Chapters 9 and 10) were the first step capitalists implemented to get the coal to eastern markets. Eventually, it was the railroads that proved to be the transportation "solution." Railroads were much more efficient and economical in their ability to transport coal from distant Pennsylvania coal fields to large eastern markets. By 1863 there were more than 1,000 miles of track across the region providing an efficient means of reaching Philadelphia, New York, and Baltimore.

The increased availability of coal spearheaded the demand for cheap labor— the miners, laborers, drivers, pickers, and unskilled laborers who were needed to get the coal out of the ground and into the country's expanding transportation system. Waves of European workers, mostly unskilled, arrived to live and labor in isolated coal towns and do the "dirty work" necessary to extract the coal. Initially it was German and Welsh workers who arrived, then the Irish, and eventually Italian, Polish, and Lithuanian workers. Most immigrated to company towns where every aspect of their lives—from the home they lived in, to the food they

ate, to the schools their children at-
tended—was all directed by a coal mining company. Their lives were anything
but ideal—living conditions were substandard, discrimination was rampant,
and wages were deplorable. But for
most, this was the American Dream—a

FAST FACT: More than
10,000 deaths were
recorded in the anthracite
mining industry between
1869 and 1900.

noble, if not ideal, way to escape the political and social conditions of 19th- and
early 20th-century Europe and build a new life. The fact that that life was demanding, dangerous, and sociologically crushing did not diminish the optimism
those early immigrants brought to these shores.

Coal mining in the late 1800s and early 1900s was among the most dangerous occupations in the world. One of the major accomplishments of a miner's
typical work day was to be able to complete his shift (often 12 hours) without in-

Living conditions for miners were rudimentary at best.

> **F**AST FACT: A miner in 1902 made about $2.75 a day or 21 cents per hour.

jury or death. Albeit, safety was not a priority for the mine owners—getting as much coal out of the ground in the most efficient manner possible was the ultimate goal. Mine collapses, fires, explosions, oxygen deprivation, and faulty equipment were constants in most mines. Rare was the miner who completed a career underground without some disability or disfigurement.

Mining wages were substandard and conditions always favored the mine owners. For example, workers had to pay for their own blasting powder, tools, and lamp oil. Rent, groceries, and doctor's fees were also deducted. It was not unusual for all the deductions to equal the amount of the wages. In those cases, a miner would receive a "bobtail check"—a check equaling $0.00. Many wound up in debt—often permanent debt—to the company.

The Great Depression signaled the beginning of the end for anthracite mining in Pennsylvania. Cheaper and easily obtained fuel alternatives such as electricity, oil, and natural gas meant that anthracite coal was less desirable, both from an economic and a practicality standpoint. Whereas an amazing 100 million tons of anthracite coal was mined in Pennsylvania in 1917, that total dropped to 46 million tons in 1938. The mines began to empty, as did the mining towns on the surface. Workers sought employment in other industries, and a significant chapter in both the history of Pennsylvania and the industrial history of the country began to slowly close. The industry still exists today, though it employs fewer than 2,000 workers, in contrast to the nearly 175,000 workers in the early 1900s.

Our tour begins at the informative **Anthracite Heritage Museum** in Mc-Dade Park on the outskirts of Scranton. This unique museum is dedicated to preserving and interpreting the rich legacy of anthracite coal and the region in which it was mined.

The theme in the first exhibit room is **The Region Emerges**. This portion of the museum focuses directly on the coal region of northeastern Pennsylvania. Included are relief maps that illustrate the ruggedness of the region, charts that diagram the location of selected anthracite seams and diagrams of coal mining regions throughout this exclusive region of the country.

The **Anthracite People** exhibit room tracks the history of this region from the first native Americans who inhabited this region thousands of years ago to the

The Anthracite Heritage Museum in Scranton

Europeans who flocked to this isolated piece of geography to seek new opportunities. There are displays on the economic transition of the area including the development of transportations in concert with increasing demands for coal. Included is an array of documents and artifacts from the various ethnic groups that emigrated to this area in the 19th century.

A Lifetime of Work is an exhibit that illustrates the tools, machines, and implements used by anthracite coal miners as they clawed their way through underground mines. The procedures miners used to not only obtain the coal, but to process it once it reached the surface are also highlighted. As technology became more sophisticated, the need for menial jobs slowly disappeared and lives were literally changed overnight. Even more critical, and the focus of several exhibits here, were the safety and health issues faced by many miners.

Women at Work focuses on the sacrifices women had to make in order to hold the family together, ensure a basic level of living, and support their husbands while they were away from home. Many women supplemented the family income by tending gardens, raising livestock, picking coal, and preparing rooms for boarders. Raising children became a primary responsibility of women since, when the men weren't working their 12-hours shifts, they were most likely asleep or spending time at the local saloon complaining about their working conditions.

The museum has three typical life centers on display. These include a cutaway replica of a company home with some of the furnishings typical of the early 20th century. There is also a replica of a church interior—often the center of all the social activities in a coal town and a place where friends and family could gather for celebrations such as weddings and baptisms. There's also a cutaway replica of a tavern—another social gathering place that figured prominently in the lives of the workers. This was a place to exchange gossip, play cards or shoot darts. Although saloons were required to close on Sundays, many bars had signs on their doors that proclaimed, "Sundays We Are Closed, Go Around Back"—a reflection of the importance of this institution in the lives of miners.

The final exhibit room, **The Region Matures**, is devoted to four interconnected themes: the mechanization of mining, the response to economic dislocation, individual success, and cultural maintenance. Here, visitors get to see some of the actual mine equipment as it was used throughout the industry. Also included is information about the Ku Klux Klan, which was a presence in many mining communities—a social backlash to the many immigrants, principally from Ireland, Italy, and Slavic countries, who lived in the region. A few success stories (very few) are also displayed along with the ways in which various ethnic groups were able to maintain their identity and culture.

For first-time visitors to this region, the museum is an excellent first step in getting to know the people who worked here, the lives they led, and the power of an industry whose power was much more than economic. The museum does a fine job of examining the forces and conditions that impacted miners and their families in addition to outlining the rough and tumble work done each day below ground.

After departing the museum, walk down the short hill to the **Lackawanna**

The Lackawanna Coal Mine Tour takes you deep into the daily lives of miners.

Coal Mine Tour. Separate from the Anthracite Heritage Museum, but sharing the same grounds in McDade Park, the Lackawanna Coal Mine Tour is a must-see experience that will bring the daily trials and tribulations of mining to life. Here, you will be able to travel 300 feet below the surface in actual man-cars. You'll journey through three separate veins of anthracite coal and then you'll be taken on a guided tour along the floor of this once bustling mine. It is a tour you will not soon forget.

On my visit to the mine, I was accompanied by a random collection of families, all of whom had taken a perfect summer day to travel into the bowels of the earth to spend over an hour in almost complete darkness. As Scott, our tour guide, loaded us into the cars to begin the 10-minute descent down through the main tunnel it quickly became apparent that this was not a tour (or working conditions) for claustrophobics or those who require the constant company of a solar sphere in the sky. We were each decked out in a jacket (made available by the tour operators), since the temperature in the mine is a constant 53 degrees year round.

Upon reaching the bottom, Scott admonished us to keep an eye on where we were walking. The floors were wet with the constant drip of water seeping down from the surface and the ceiling overhead was crusted with all manner of outcroppings ideal for any author 5 feet, 11 inches tall to conk his noggin.

Scott's patter was sincere and descriptive and he provided the dozen or so visitors with mind-altering data and real-life stories that brought a true sense of reality to the displays and artifacts in the museum. We learned that the anthracite coal veins of the Lackawanna Valley are the remains of subtropical trees that flourished here over 300 million years ago. As the plants died, they were covered by muddy water and decomposed to form peat. In the course of millions of years, silt buried the decaying swamp. Under the weight of the sediment deposits water and gases were squeezed from the peat beds to form low-grade coal. These horizontal beds of coal and sedimentary rock—subjected to immense pressure— folded and reformed at the same time the Appalachian Mountains were rising in Pennsylvania. This compression transformed the low-grade coal to anthracite or hard coal that surrounded us in this mine.

As we wended our way into dead-end tunnels and past rudimentary mining equipment and random veins of coal, Scott described the "day-in, day-out" life of an anthracite miner who spent 12 hours every day (but Sunday) in his subterranean "office." We learned that miners only got paid when they brought the coal out of the ground. They didn't get paid for drilling the holes (used for blasting powder)—a three- to four-hour task that had to be done before any coal could be extracted. Neither were they paid for their travels through the mine, or anything else not directly related to getting a large quantity of underground coal to the surface. What made this process even more demanding was the fact that for every ton of coal removed, miners had to remove 10 tons of rock. Miners

FAST FACT: A 66-foot layer of peat is needed to form a five-foot deep vein of anthracite.

typically had a quota of 15 tons of coal per person per day. Anything less would be a deduction from their pay. Miners couldn't include any rock or other debris— that would also be a deduction from their pay.

As we strolled through the mine, our passage was illuminated by light bulbs hanging overhead. This would have been a luxury for coal miners, according to our guide. Each miner was equipped with only a small head lamp, which he had to purchase himself, to pierce the darkness.

We learned that there were two animals kept by miners—both of which were essential to their jobs. Canaries were kept in small cages hanging down from the ceiling. Particularly sensitive to deadly gases, these birds were used to detect the presence of noxious fumes and, ultimately, the need for miners to beat a hasty re- treat in the other direction. The other animal—a favorite pet of the miners—were rats. They could easily tolerate the conditions deep under the ground, required very little care, and were constant companions for those working in a very dark environment for long stretches of time. Rats, just like canaries, were also sen- tinels for any potential dangers that might occur underground.

We ducked in and out of short shafts, traversed winding tunnels, slid past massive wooden doors and faced the rudimentary working conditions prevalent more than a century ago as we walked into and out of the caverns that comprise this anthracite coal mine. I was particularly touched by the stories of 10- to 12- year-old boys who spent 12 hours a day sitting in absolutely pitch-black tunnels occasionally opening and closing massive wooden doors for the passage of coal cars through the recesses of the mine...all for 11 cents per hour.

The tour takes about 75 minutes and gives you a real feel for life under- ground—a life of isolation, eternal blackness, constant danger, and subsistence wages. After exiting the mine you come away with a newfound appreciation for the miners, the daily dangers they faced, and the tenacity they needed to survive. If you are at all interested in the impact of anthracite coal in this country's his- tory, then you must take this tour. You will not forget it.

After returning to the sunlit world, get in your car and exit McDade Park. Wind your way through Scranton streets to I-476 south toward Wilkes-Barre. Drive for approximately 27 miles and take exit 95 toward PA 940/I-80. Keep right at the fork and merge

FAST FACT: Anthracite is the second cleanest burning fuel after natural gas.

Eckley Miners' Village provides a look into miners' lives.

onto I-80 west. Take exit 273 for PA 940 toward PA 437/White Haven. Turn left onto PA 940 west/Church Street and travel for about 7.1 miles. Turn left onto Highland Road/SR 2053. Continue straight onto Buck Mountain Road/SR 2051. After .5 mile continue on SR 2053, turn left onto Main Street and you'll be at **Eckley Miners' Village**. The drive from Scranton will take approximately one hour.

Eckley Miners' Village is another must-see on your journey through Pennsylvania's coal history. It's an example of a "living history museum"—where artifacts are not locked up behind glass barriers or roped off exhibits, but one where you can literally stroll through the lives of those who lived in this world.

As you enter the **visitor center** and pay your admission fee, it quickly becomes apparent that this is a museum unlike any other. Here, you can view an orientation film and get a sense of what daily life was like for anthracite miners and their families. You learn that coal was formed millions of years ago as the leaves, branches, and fallen tree trunks of pre-historic forests accumulated on the floor of coastal swamps. Moisture and bacteria converted the plants into peat—the first step in the formation of coal. Mud and sand sealed off the peat from the air preventing further decay and pressing moisture and gases from

> **F**AST FACT: Geologists estimate that approximately 8 to 12 feet of compressed vegetable matter was required to form one foot of coal.

the peat. This pressure, plus heat from the earth's core and from shifting land masses altered the amounts of carbon, oxygen and hydrogen in the peat. The peat slowly changed into lignite, then to coal.

Signs and displays demonstrate how anthracite and bituminous coal were formed during the same geologic period. The difference in their composition is due to the additional heat and pressure resulting from the upheavals that formed the mountains of eastern Pennsylvania. Anthracite has a higher carbon content and is heavier and more compact than bituminous coal. Because it contains fewer impurities anthracite burns cleaner and longer than does bituminous coal.

The small museum is well worth the time. It's a good overview of daily life—not just what the men had to do, but also what the women and other family members had to do to survive in this very demanding line of work. This is a well-done exhibit illustrating a typical life of hundreds of thousands of miners' families.

Now you're on your own for a self-guided tour of a typical company mining town. This particular town sprang up in 1854 and was built near the colliery where coal was mined and processed, providing housing for miners and their families. In addition to the houses, it also had stores, schools, and churches that provided the economic, educational and religious needs of the villagers.

The village was populated by a succession of immigrants from several European countries. Seeking economic opportunities, workers from Ireland, England, Wales, Germany, as well as numerous ethnic groups from southern and eastern Europe, settled in the town. Their heritage is reflected in the furnishings of these houses as well as the social activities they maintained while living here. Walk through this village and you walk through the lives of those who worked and lived here—a village, a community, and a neighborhood completely unlike the tract homes and suburban developments that now dominate the American landscape.

Begin your walk at stop #5—the **Laborers' Double Dwellings**. These were

1854 homes assigned to the colliery's unskilled workers. Each family was assigned four rooms and a shallow stone cellar in these frame and plank houses. Stop #7 is another 1854 cottage, which only provided three rooms per family and was considerably smaller than the laborers' houses on Main Street.

Stop #10 is a **Miners' Double Dwelling**, a typical house occupied by first-class or contract miners. There were two downstairs rooms and two upstairs rooms in addition to a summer kitchen. Stop #15 is a single family dwelling, a large single house that would have been occupied by a mine boss, a colliery superintendent, or a mine foreman. At Stop #18 you can see the foundation of the **Eckley Hotel** (1857), which had the only barroom in the village. This was the center of many social celebrations in the village including St. Patrick's Day banquets and oyster dinners.

Stop #19 is the **Doctor's Office** where accident victims were brought to be treated by the village doctor. But it is Stop #21 that will dazzle you. This is the **Mine Owner's House**, the largest and most opulent house in the village. It was

Skilled colliery workers occupied these larger houses.

The mine owner lived in the largest and most fashionable house.

strategically located away from the other houses in the village and represented the wealth and social standing of its occupants.

There are several other stops throughout this unique and historic coal mining village. Several of the stops (#9—**Eckley Social and Sports Club**, #12—**Mule Barn**, #13—**Company Store**, and #14—**Breaker**) were constructed as movie props for the film *The Molly Maguires* (1970) starring Sean Connery and Richard Harris.

Simply put—Eckley's Miner's Village is cool! A stroll through this town (2 miles round trip) offers you every opportunity to see and feel what life in a mining village must have been like. You'll discover houses sorted according to rank

Molly Maguires Pub & Steakhouse in Jim Thorpe

and how much money a miner made. You'll see a range of structures critical to the survival of the village as well as each mining family. And you'll discover a part of Americana you'll never experience in a history book. While I opted to take the self-guided tour through this village, you may elect to do a guided tour—an opportunity to further examine these unique lives and their village.

We'll leave Eckley Miners' Village and head south toward another mining town—**Jim Thorpe**—a community still vibrant with the pulse of its singular history. After you exit the parking area, head northeast on Main Street toward SR 2051. Turn right to stay on Main Street and then turn right onto SR 2051/SR 2053. This road has several name changes—it is first Valley Road, then it changes to SR 2051, and it eventually becomes Freeland Road. After 2.7 miles make a sharp right onto Buck Mountain Road. After 3.6 miles turn right onto Evergreen Avenue, turn right onto East Main Street, turn left onto Hudsondale Street, and continue onto Brenkman Drive. After 1.5 miles turn left onto PA 93 south/Hudson Drive and continue for about 5.8 miles. Turn left onto PA 209 north and continue for approximately 3.5 miles. At the train station the road will bend around to the right. When you come to the traffic signal note the **Molly Maguires Pub and Steakhouse** to your right (a great place to dine). Go straight through the intersection and find a parking space in the historic downtown area.

The town of Jim Thorpe, tucked between several steep mountains, looks much the way it did 150 years ago when it was a thriving and bustling coal town. Walk around this self-designated "Switzerland of America" and you'll be able to see Victorian architecture and quaint streets filled with galleries, shops, and merchants as diverse as the town.

Formerly saddled with the uninspiring name of Coalville, this town began its life in the early 1800s as a cluster of buildings for coal miners and mill workers. It eventually grew into the much larger burg of Mauch Chunk, the Native American term for "sleeping bear." When the Lehigh Coal and Navigation Company and the Switchback Gravity railroad were established to transport anthracite coal from the mines north of town to the big cities south of town, thousands came to the area to work in the coal industry. Along with all those workers came merchants and entrepreneurs who established hotels, breweries, and other necessary businesses that powered the town's economy.

The town went through tough times during the mid-1800s, including a series of devastating fires and floods. But a major re-building and construction boom helped turn this once-thriving coal town into an equally thriving tourist town. By the end of the 19th century, large mansions were built on the outskirts of town and numerous attractions fueled a robust economy. Business people with very large egos

FAST FACT: Jim Thorpe never lived in, or visited, the town that now bears his name.

built very large homes—each trying to outdo the other in terms of square footage, opulence, and neo-European facades and interiors. For the most part, though, the town was primarily a middle-class community peopled by an assortment of merchants, factory workers, businesspeople, laborers and, of course, miners.

The town's current name—Jim Thorpe—is in honor of one of the greatest athletes this country has ever known. Thorpe accomplished the unique feat of winning both the pentathlon and decathlon at the 1912 Stockholm Olympics. Not only was he an Olympic champion, he also played major league baseball for more than six years and was a standout football player at the Carlisle School in Carlisle, Pennsylvania.

After his death in 1953, his wife Patricia was upset when the government of Oklahoma, Thorpe's native state, refused to erect a monument to honor him. So she began a search for a proper tribute for this all-American hero. When she learned about the boroughs of Mauch Chunk and East Mauch Chunk and their efforts to attract business she contacted them. In quick order the two towns merged, the new municipality was named in Jim Thorpe's honor, and the athlete's remains were re-buried in a monument on the 1400 block of North Street on the east end of town. The memorial also includes two statues of Thorpe in athletic poses.

The Jim Thorpe area is packed with all sorts of things to do, including whitewater rafting excursions, long biking trails, a coal mine tour, a train ride, mansion tours, ghost walks, vineyards, museums, jails, opera houses, and a varied collection of shops and restaurants that will fill up a weekend. The **Inn at Jim Thorpe**, built in 1849, is a unique combination of old world charm and modern conveniences in the heart of town. It has hosted a number of dignitaries, including General Ulysses S. Grant, President William H. Taft, Buffalo Bill, Thomas Edison, and John D. Rockefeller.

Now it's time to visit some of the coal towns that distinguish Pennsylvania as a coal-mining state. This route will take us through several of those towns on a 28.5-mile journey into both the past as well as the present. As you depart Jim Thorpe follow US 209 south and stay on this road until you arrive in Pottsville (PA 61).

The first coal town we encounter on this journey is Nesquehoning. This town has a sprinkling of Victorian architecture with several interesting housing de-

The Inn at Jim Thorpe—a cozy place to stay

signs. In fact, there is a delightful assortment of architectural styles along both sides of the road.

The highway next passes through the blue-collar community of Lansford. It almost seems as though a white-paint salesman came through here years ago because almost every house in Lansford is painted white (with the occasional gray and yellow). Notice how the town is built on a series of hills and keep an eye

FAST FACT: Geologists estimate that before coal mining began in this country there were 65 billion tons of anthracite coal available in Pennsylvania. After 200 years of mining, Pennsylvania still has 25 billion tons remaining.

out for the distinctive church spires on the left side of the road.

The road quickly passes through the tiny town of Coaldale. This burg seems to be a tired town with its houses hanging on the side of the road. As you drive through, notice how many of the houses are perched up on the hill beside the road.

The next town is the somewhat larger coal town of Tamaqua (population 7,107). The houses here are somewhat larger than those encountered earlier and the town has been able to maintain a significant number of trees along the road. Notice the varied architecture—particularly the large number of duplexes. Tamaqua is a town that has grown up around coal, but it has also been able to adapt to modern times and modern life. The downtown area is thriving, traffic is robust, and the architecture reflects both the town's Victorian roots and modern development.

As you drive south of Tamaqua, take a look around and imagine traveling down this road 100 to 150 years ago. Imagine how isolated this part of the country would have seemed to immigrants and others who had just come here from abroad. The countryside is undeniably picturesque, but it would have been quite isolated in the 1800s.

You will next pass through several old mining towns including New Philadelphia (established 1868), Cumbola, and Port Carbon. For many of these once-proud communities, economic and social conditions have conspired to paint these towns in tones of days gone by. Some of the buildings look tired, others look ignored, and many houses are just hanging on. Coal was a cruel master for many of these villages and burgs. Once the industry began to evaporate, so too did the towns that supported it.

You'll eventually come into the city of Pottsville. Make a right turn on PA 61 north and drive for approximately 15.5 miles (you'll pass I-81), through the town of Frackville and into the town of Ashland. Ashland is another classic coal town. Pay particular attention to how the houses hug the street with one right after the other. As is the case with many towns in this coal mining region, Ashland is built on a hill.

Travel through town until you come to South 20th Street. Make a left turn and go to the end of the road. Make another left and you'll find yourself at the **Pioneer Tunnel Coal Mine**. If the kids are begging you to go someplace that is dark, damp and full of danger, then this is where to go. The Pioneer Tunnel is a horizontal drift mine that runs 1,800 feet straight into the side of a mountain.

Visitors ride in open mine cars into a 52-degree mine. There, a tour guide explains how the mining operation worked and describes the various features found in a typical mine. There are storyboards and displays illustrating various methods of underground coal mining.

Return to PA 61 and make a left turn. PA 61 makes a sharp right turn at North Memorial Boulevard. Turn right and drive for about 2.1 miles until you arrive in the town (or what once was the town) of **Centralia**. Centralia, you see, is a ghost town.

Let's be honest—there's absolutely nothing to see in Centralia. Roads go nowhere. Streets are empty. Houses are nonexistent. And weeds are everywhere. Centralia is, in many respects, a sad punctuation mark on the coal industry—a once-prosperous industry that has succumbed to the ravages of economic and technological changes that, once mighty, is now emaciated.

The town got its start in 1841 when a tavern was established in the area. Streets were eventually laid out and the site acquired an official name—Centreville. However, since there was another Centreville nearby, the town was renamed Centralia.

Incorporated as a borough in 1866 it quickly became wedded to the anthracite coal industry—the major employer in the community. The coal industry lasted for nearly a century, when many of the companies, for economic reasons, pulled up stakes and moved away. The borough's population reached its peak in 1890 with 2,761 residents recorded. Since then, the population has declined precipitously; by 1980, there were only 1,012 residents remaining.

Its history—or, more appropriately, its fate—was sealed on May 26, 1962. It was on that day that a trash hauler dumped either hot ash or hot coals into an open trash pit at the edge of town. The hot coals penetrated a vein of coal underneath the pit and ignited a subterranean fire. That fire continued burning underground and eventually spread into several abandoned coal mines beneath the town. All attempts to extinguish the fire were unsuccessful.

The fires continued to burn under the town well into the 1970s and 1980s.

FAST FACT: The U.S. Postal Service revoked Centralia's ZIP code (17927) in 2002.

Increased levels of carbon monoxide and carbon dioxide as well as lower levels of oxygen were constantly reported. The incident reached crisis proportions when, in 1981, a 12-year-old child fell into a sinkhole four feet wide and 150 feet deep that had suddenly opened up beneath his feet in his back yard. Fast action by his 14-year-old cousin saved the young man's life. It was quickly apparent that this was more than a short-lived crisis—this was a perpetual disaster.

The residents of the town were given buyout offers and relocation money if they would move out and into other communities (efforts to extinguish the underground fire were unsuccessful). Most of the families accepted these offers; however, a few refused to budge in spite of all the health hazards and government warnings. Pennsylvania Governor Bob Casey invoked eminent domain in 1992, essentially condemning all the buildings in town. In 2009, then-Governor Ed Rendell began the formal eviction of remaining Centralia residents.

Little remains of a once-vibrant town. There are still about 10 residents remaining, but you would hardly know it as you drive these deserted streets. Most of the abandoned buildings have been demolished and the wide and empty streets are completely devoid of any houses or buildings. On my most recent visit to this town I drove past a single home—ghostly in appearance—on a lonely street with absolutely nothing around it save for an wide expanse of weeds and the silence of the breeze blowing through the trees.

FAST FACT: According to at least one estimate, the underground fire should continue to burn for at least another 250 years.

The town is haunting—an eerie quiet is settled over the lonely street corners and roads that lead to nowhere. I drove my car to the pit where the fire originally started and looked out over…nothing. There was not a person, an animal, or another vehicle in sight. This is a town of death and desolation.

In a strange reminder of what was, the four cemeteries in town are still in operation, but there are no new additions. Yet the fire continues to burn—occasionally smoke and steam can be seen seeping from a few cracks and crevasses in and around the now deceased town.

I drove a few of the empty streets and stopped to take some photos. As I stood on the hill by one of the cemeteries I glanced off to the east and noticed a series of large wind turbines. Here was a modern form of energy production hovering over a town that had died as a result of an ancient form of energy—coal. It was a surrealistic exclamation mark for the town and for the journey.

After touring Centralia, turn around and retrace your trip along PA 61 South. Travel back through Ashland and then Frackville and eventually to I-81. At this point you need to make a decision—turn north and travel back to Scranton or turn south and head toward Harrisburg and further adventures.

CONTACTS

Anthracite Heritage Museum, 22 Bald Mountain Rd., McDade Park, Scranton, PA 18504; (570) 963-4804; www.anthracitemuseum.org.

Lackawanna Coal Mine Tour, 22 Bald Mountain Rd., McDade Park, Scranton, PA 18504; (570) 963-6463; www.lackawannacounty.org/attractions_coal.asp.

Eckley Miners' Village, 2 Eckley Main St., Weatherly, PA 18255; (570) 636-2070; www.eckleyminersvillagemuseum.com.

Jim Thorpe Chamber of Commerce, P.O. Box 164, Jim Thorpe, PA 18229; (888) 546-8467; www.jimthorpe.org.

Pioneer Tunnel Coal Mine, 19th and Oak Streets, Ashland, PA 17921; (570) 875-3850; www.pioneertunnel.com.

LODGING

The Inn at Jim Thorpe, 24 Broadway, Jim Thorpe, PA 18229; (800) 329-2599; www.innjt.com.

DINING

Molly Maguires Pub and Steakhouse, 5 Hazard Square, Jim Thorpe, PA 18229; (570) 325-4563; www.mollymaguiresrestaurant.com.

The Enslow Bridge is a photographer's dream.

6 Through Covered Bridges

Estimated length: 62 miles (Columbia County); 56 miles (Perry County)
Estimated time: Half day (Columbia County); half day (Perry County)
Combine these tours with: Chapters 5 and 14

Getting there: You'll begin your Columbia County covered bridge tour in Bloomsburg. The journey will take you through beautiful scenery along country roads and out-of-the-way places in a circuitous route through the county. Your tour through Perry County—beginning in Carlisle—is equally dramatic with an abundance of farmland and sweeping vistas.

Highlights: Both of these tours have been designed to provide you with the best in Pennsylvania's covered bridges. You'll see bridges found nowhere else in the country, along with equally distinctive scenery. You will be far off the beaten path, but you will always remember these landmarks of the Pennsylvania countryside.

Travel through almost any part of eastern Pennsylvania, and you'll likely come across one of the most iconic features on the landscape—a covered bridge. These distinctive architectural buildings are certainly not unique to eastern Pennsylvania, but they are so ubiquitous that they are often associated with the region as one of its most recognizable structures.

Records show that the first covered bridge in the United States was constructed by one Timothy Palmer in 1805. This lengthy structure was located on Market Street in Philadelphia and spanned the Schuylkill River. Shortly thereafter, another covered bridge was built by Theodore Burr over the Delaware River between Morrisville, Pennsylvania, and Trenton, New Jersey. This enormous structure was 1,008 feet in length—one of the longest covered bridges ever built.

Soon thereafter, covered bridge-building took off with a vengeance. In the

FAST FACT: At one time, 64 of Pennsylvania's 67 counties had at least one covered bridge in use.

years between 1820 and 1900, approximately 1,500 covered bridges were built throughout Pennsylvania using a variety of styles, designs, sizes, and construction techniques. The question that often arises when people see these bridges is why were so many of them built. The answer is one of practicality as well as pragmatism.

One of the features early Pennsylvania settlers discovered was an abundance of swift flowing streams and rivers. Being practical people, they quickly saw not only a water source, but a source of energy that could be used to power all sorts of mills and other industries. As the mills were constructed, villages and farming communities grew up in the general vicinity. To access those communities and to take advantage of an immediate source of lumber, it was necessary to cross over the numerous streams. The abundance of old growth lumber provided a ready resource for the bridges needed to span those waterways.

It soon became evident that a bridge left to the elements would disintegrate quickly. As a result, it seemed necessary to protect a bridge's wooden beam and surface area. The most practical solution was the construction of walls and a roof over the bridge to ensure its longevity and preservation. The result was the covered bridge…or more appropriately, many covered bridges over many different waterways. To help the bridges last longer the original uncovered construction received a roof and became known as the Permanent Bridge.

One of the most distinguishing features of these bridges is that their construction was so professional that many of them have survived for 100 years or more. Bridges were normally constructed by local bridge builders, which is why construction styles vary throughout the state. Today, there are approximately 220 bridges still in existence, and the fact that so many of them have survived is a salute to the people who built them so long ago.

Cut down two trees, lay them parallel to each other across a river or stream, and nail a series of flat boards

FAST FACT: Covered bridges are also known as "kissing bridges." Tradition holds that if you kiss your sweetheart while traveling through a covered bridge you will have good luck.

across the two trees from end to end and you basically have a bridge. The only problem is this structure is subject to the elements and the eventual deterioration that results from years of rain, snow, and wind. However, by covering the bridge with a supporting framework you can effectively protect

FAST FACT: At one time in Pennsylvania there were at least 1,526 covered bridges. Today only about 200 remain, which is still more than any other U.S. state.

your structure from those elements. That framework is often called a truss, and it not only protects the bridge, but also supports the crossing load on the deck of the bridge.

Ever since 1805, there have been as many as 18 different truss designs used for covered bridges in the United States. In Pennsylvania only about seven of those designs have been used, with three designs predominating. These include:

Kingpost Truss—Used primarily for short spans (20 to 30 feet), this design is one of the oldest used in bridge construction. Basically it consists of a bottom piece (called a stringer), a vertical bean (Kingpost), and two diagonal beams from the top of the Kingpost down to the stringer.

Queenpost Truss—The Queenpost design is an extension of the Kingpost truss and was used for longer covered bridges of up to 75 feet in length. The center of this design is a Kingpost design with additional segments (each an equilateral triangle) added on to each side to expand the stability of the bridge.

The Kingpost Truss

Burr Truss—Invented by Theodore Burr, who constructed a bridge over the Hudson River in 1804 with this design, it is the most "popular" bridge design used in Pennsylvania's covered bridges. Basically it used the design of the Queenpost Truss (a series of triangles) and added two long arches—each of which rested on the abutments on either side of the bridge.

The Queenpost Truss

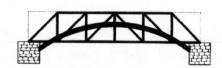

The Burr Truss

The longest covered bridge in the world spanned the mile-wide Susquehanna River between Columbia and Wrightsville. It was 5,960 feet in length and not only long, but versatile as well. It included railroad tracks, a towpath for canal boats, and a carriage/wagon/pedestrian road. This bridge was burned on June 28, 1863, by Union soldiers to prevent Confederate troops from using it as they moved eastward from Gettysburg. A new covered bridge, constructed in wood, replaced the original, but it was demolished in a windstorm a few years later. The original bridge still exists today across the Susquehanna, but it is no longer covered.

This section could have focused on many different counties throughout eastern Pennsylvania. I choose Columbia and Perry counties because they get fewer visitors, yet are endowed with some of the most spectacular bridges in the state. Although other Pennsylvania counties have more covered bridges, I wanted to provide you with some new possibilities and new views to enhance your visit to this part of the state. The bridges you will see on the two featured tours in this chapter will amaze, delight, and engage you. You'll see parts of the country not often featured in traditional tourist guides and you'll get a true sense of the significance of these bridges in the settlement and exploration of these wild areas.

TOUR 1—COLUMBIA COUNTY

Begin your drive in the college town of Bloomsburg. Drive north on SR 42 (if you are traveling on I-80, you can also take exit 232 off the highway and head north on SR 42). In a short while you'll see a mall on the right side of the road. Soon afterward, SR 42 comes to a T at a traffic light. Make a left turn at the traffic light (now Millville Road) and continue on SR 42 north. Drive about .7 mi. and make a right turn onto Covered Bridge Road (TR 493), and after .2 miles you will come to the

Wanich Bridge—This well-preserved bridge was originally constructed in 1884 by George Russell at a cost of $500. It is a Burr truss design with stone-and-mortar abutments and wingwalls. It was named for a local farmer, John Wanich, who resided nearby. Notice the two windows—one on the south side and one on the north side. These windows allow anyone walking inside the bridge to look for approaching traffic.

Drive through Wanich Bridge, make a U-turn, and drive back through the bridge. Return to SR 42 north. Turn right and drive for another 8 miles and when

The Wanich Bridge on Little Fishing Creek in Columbia County

you get to the town of Iola, bear left onto SR 442 west. After about 1 mile, make a left turn onto Chestnut Lane (TR 621), where you will see the

Shoemaker Bridge—This bridge, which spans the West Branch Run, was built in 1881 by T.S. Christian at a cost of $322. It was named for Joseph Shoemaker, a local lumberman and farmer. This bridge uses the Queenpost design and is approximately 48 feet in length. One of its distinguishing features is a narrow window at the end where the road curves. This window, as in the Wanich bridge, offers a view of oncoming traffic.

You won't be able to drive through this bridge. After viewing the bridge return to SR 442 and turn right. Drive for about 1 mile back down this road and then

---

FAST FACT: Each year the Governor of Pennsylvania signs a proclamation to encourage all Pennsylvanians to visit covered bridges. **"See Pennsylvania's Covered Bridges" Week** usually begins the first Saturday after the first Sunday in May up to and including the third Sunday of May.

---

turn left back onto SR 42 north. Continue driving for approximately 1.2 miles and make a right turn onto Serano Road (SR 4031). Drive for approximately 2.5 miles (this road turns into a dirt/gravel road along the way). On the left will be the

Sam Eckman Bridge—Bridging Little Fishing Creek, this 65-foot long bridge was constructed in 1876 by Joseph Redline at a cost of $498. It was named for Samuel Eckman, a well-to-do businessman with several enterprises including a shingle mill, a farm, a birch oil factory, and the Millville Creamery. This bridge is distinguished by the fact that the west-end abutment is made of stone and mortar, while the east end is built on poured concrete.

Continue driving on Serano Road (SR 4031) for 1.4 mile until you come to a T. Make a right turn and continue on Serano Road (SR 4031). In .5 mile and on the right (Arden's Hill Road/TR 685) is

Jud Christian Bridge—This bridge also crosses Little Fishing Creek and was constructed in 1876 by William L. Manning for $239. The bridge has a Queenpost design, along with board and batten siding and a sheet metal roof. It was named for Jud Christian, a farmer and lumberman living nearby.

Drive through the bridge, make a U-turn, and drive back through. Make a right turn back onto Serrano Road (SR 4031). Continue driving on Serano Road for another .6 mile until you come to a stop sign at the intersection of Serano Road and Austin Trail. Continue straight on Austin Trail (SR 4039). In about .8 mile make a slight left down to

Creasyville Bridge—A Queenpost bridge that also spans Little Fishing Creek, the Creaseyville Bridge was built by T.S. Christian (the same builder of Shoemaker Bridge) in 1881 for a total cost of $301.25. Since it was located near Iram Derr's sawmill, it may have also been known as the Derr Bridge. It is one of the shortest bridges (44 feet, 7 inches) in Columbia County and in relatively good condition.

Drive through the bridge, make a U-turn, drive back through the bridge and return to Austin Trail. Make a right and retrace your route back to the intersection of Serano Road and Austin Trail. When you come to the intersection make a left turn and drive up and over the hill to the stop sign. Make a right turn and then a very quick left (you are still on Austin Trail (SR 4039). Continue for about 4.4 miles until you come to SR 254. Make a left turn at the stop sign (onto SR 254) and in about .3 mile make a right turn at the stop sign onto Rohrsburg Road (SR 4041). Drive for about .7 mile and make a right turn onto Utt Road (SR 456). Drive for about .5 mile and make a left onto Turkeypath Road (SR 572). Just down the road is

Kramer Bridge—Constructed in 1881 by C.W. Eves for $414.50, this bridge was named for Alexander Kramer, a local farmer. It seems as though Mr. Kramer was one of the bidders for the construction, but lost out to Mr. Eves. The bridge crosses Mud Run and is a Queenpost structure with the original shake roof (now covered with sheet metal).

After viewing Kramer Bridge, make a U-turn and return to the stop sign (at the intersection of Turkeypath Road (SR 572) and Utt Road (SR 456). Make a right turn back onto Utt Road and return to Rohrsburg Road (SR 4041). Turn right onto Rohrsburg Road (SR 4041) and travel for one mile and at Hartman Hollow Road (TR 575) you'll come upon

Patterson Bridge—This bridge gets lots of vehicular traffic and has held up quite well since its original construction in 1875 by Frank Derr at a cost of $804 (its stone-and-mortar abutments have been reinforced with concrete in recent years). It spans Green Creek and was named for Patterson's sawmill, which was located nearby. This is another bridge with side windows used to view oncoming traffic.

Drive through the bridge, make a U-turn, drive back through the bridge and return to Rohrsburg Road (SR4041). Make a right turn back onto Rohrsburg Road (SR 4041) and travel for 1.7 mile to the junction with SR 487. Turn left at the stop sign. Travel north for about 2.9 miles. Make a right turn onto Winding Road (SR 1020) at the open grate steel bridge (You will note a sign on the right side of the road for Twin Covered Bridges). Drive for .3 mile and you will come to

East and West Paden (Twin Covered Bridges)—The East and West Paden (Twin) covered bridges were originally built over Huntington Creek in 1884 by W.C. Pennington for $720 (Some publications give the date of construction as

The East and West Paden Bridges are the only twin bridges in the U.S.

1850, but recent research indicates the 1884 date is accurate.). They were originally named for John Paden, who operated a nearby sawmill.

They are called twin bridges simply because of their close proximity to one
another. In reality, they are not twins—West Paden Bridge is 100 feet in length
and of the Burr Arch truss construction. East Paden Bridge is 72 feet, 8 inches in
length and of Queenpost construction. The bridges were bypassed in 1963 and
have been converted into public pavilions in the Twin Bridges County Park.

Exit the small parking area and turn right back onto Winding Road (SR 1020).
After one mile make a quick left turn down a short road (there will be a sign) to
the

Josiah Hess Bridge—This is one of my favorite bridges simply because of
all the incredible photo opportunities it offers. It's off the main road, closed to

vehicular traffic, and in a bucolic setting (over a bubbling stream) that is ideal for snapping a succession of shots perfect for any self-published calendar or office poster.

This bridge spans Huntington Creek and was originally constructed in 1875 by Joseph Redline at a cost of $1,349.50, considerably more than many other bridges. It got its name from the Hess family who lived nearby and ran a saw mill and farm in the area. Although closed to cars, you can easily walk under or through this bridge to get a glimpse of the delightful views.

After viewing the Hess Bridge, turn around and return to Winding Road (SR 1020). Make a right turn and drive back past the Twin Bridges and return to SR 487. Make a right turn on SR 487 north (toward Benton) and drive 3.2 miles to the steel bridge in the village of Stillwater. Just before the steel bridge make a right

The Josiah Hess Bridge offers incredible photo opportunities.

The Fowlersville Bridge cost less than $400 to build.

turn onto Wesley Street—it comes up very quickly just before the steel bridge. In front of you is the

Stillwater Bridge—This is another bridge that was more expensive to build than others in the area. It cost James McHenry $1,124 to build in 1849 using high Burr arches sandwiching a multiple kingpost truss. It was named for the borough of Stillwater and spans Big Fishing Creek. Unfortunately, it is not possible to drive or walk across this bridge as it is barricaded on both sides. The bridge has also seen considerable deterioration and weathering over the years.

Turn around and return to SR 487. Make a left turn back onto SR 487 south and drive for approximately 11 miles. When you come to the town of Orangeville make a left turn onto SR 93 south. Drive for an additional 6.7 miles until you come to the intersection of SR 93 S and Lake Road (SR 1017). Make a left turn onto Lake Road (SR 1017) (the Old Stone Church is on the corner) and drive for .3 mile. Turn right at the stop sign and drive .4 mile to the entrance of Briar Creek Park. Make a right turn into the park and follow the road for about .7 miles until you come to a gravel parking area and the

Fowlersville Bridge—This bridge is not in its original location, which was the West Branch of Briar Creek near Fowlersville. It cost $397 to build in 1886 and was named for the Fowler family, who had settled in the area after the Revolutionary War. Constructed by Charles Krug, it was one of the last bridges built in Columbia County. After a new bridge was constructed over Briar Creek, this 40-foot bridge was moved to Briar Creek Park in 1986.

After seeing the Fowlersville Bridge, retrace your steps back into Orangeville. At Orangeville, make a left turn back onto SR 487. Travel down SR 487 until you get to exit 236 of I-80. Head west on I-80 and travel 4 miles to exit 232 and back into Bloomsburg.

TOUR 2—PERRY COUNTY

This tour is slightly shorter than the previous one—but no less dramatic. You'll get everything on this trip—from freshly spruced-up bridges that sparkle in dazzling reds all the way to bridges that have seen better times and yet are still standing against the ravages of nature.

This is a tour you can easily complete in a half-day and one filled with an incredible variety of photo opportunities.

Begin your journey in beautiful downtown Carlisle (you can begin in this quaint college town or start off in Harrisburg and journey westward to Carlisle). From Dickinson College in the center of town, head north on PA 74 north. You'll go up and over scenic Waggoner's Gap (as you near the top be sure to glance over to your left to observe the vistas). After 14.6 miles you'll arrive in the tiny town of Alinda. Make a left turn at the stop sign and head west on PA 850 west toward Landisburg. After 1.3 miles you'll come to a stop sign. Turn left on Carlisle Street, then a right onto Kennedy Valley Road. After .4 mile you'll arrive at

Rice's Bridge—This is a handsome bridge with an unusual design. Originally constructed in 1869 it crosses Sherman's Creek just outside of Landisville (the bridge is sometimes referred to as the Rice/Landisville Bridge). The design is single Burr arches sandwiching a multiple kingpost design that stretches along the length of this 132-foot structure. There are also queenpost trusses that overlay the kingpost truss—making it appear as though there are two trusses. You'll also notice the windows on each side of the bridge near the end where the road bends.

After viewing the bridge, drive through it, make a U-turn, and travel back through the bridge and back into Landisburg. At the stop sign, continue straight ahead on PA 850 west (toward Loysville). Drive for 3.2 miles (go through the town of Loysville) and travel to the junction of PA 274 and PA 850. Stay on PA 850 west for an additional 4.1 miles. When you come to the stop sign make a right turn onto PA 17. Travel for 3.7 miles and make a right turn onto Fritz Road. After .2 mile you'll come to

Kockenderfer Bridge—This bridge was one of the later bridges built in Pennsylvania. It was constructed in 1919 by the Adair Brothers and crosses over Big Buffalo Creek. The structure is primarily a multiple kingpost that is overlaid with a queenpost truss. The bridge is privately owned and is closed to all vehicle traffic.

After viewing this bridge, drive over the adjacent concrete bridge, turn around, and return to PA 17. Make a right turn on PA 17 and then a quick left onto Covered Bridge Road. After .9 miles you will arrive at

Saville Bridge—This bridge was constructed in 1903 and used the Burr truss to span Big Buffalo Creek. The builder was L.M. Wentzel and it is currently owned by the state of Pennsylvania. This bridge is in some degree of deterioration, although it is still open to vehicle traffic. Some improvements have been made in recent years and the bridge retains much of its earlier charm and character.

After traveling through this bridge, make a U-turn, and drive back through the bridge on Covered Bridge Road to PA 17. Make a right turn onto PA 17 and drive for 3.8 miles to the stop sign. At the stop sign make a left turn onto PA 850 east. After 1.6 miles, turn right onto Emory Green Road. Travel for 2.2 miles until you arrive at PA 274 (also known as Sherman's Valley Road). Make a right turn and drive for .3 mile and then turn left onto Lyons Road. After .3 mile you'll arrive at a stop sign. Make a left and directly in front of you will be

Adairs Bridge—This is one of the longest covered bridges in the state—extending to a total length of 160 feet. It was constructed in 1864 and used the Burr

The Bistline Bridge in Perry County

truss. Situated between Tuscarora Mountain and Blue Mountain, this bridge is a photographer's dream, thanks to its picturesque setting and structural and exterior improvements made over the years. Make sure you add it to your list of classic Pennsylvania sites.

Travel through the bridge, make a U-turn, and return to the intersection (Lyons Road). Bear left (follow the large arrow) onto SR 3008 until you get to PA 274. Turn left on PA 274 west and travel for .7 mile. Turn left onto Madison (SR 3005). Drive for 2.5 miles and bear left at the "Y." Directly ahead is

Bistline Bridge—This 106-foot bridge has been completely restored over the years, making it among the most photogenic of covered bridges. Originally

FAST FACT: One of the oldest covered bridges in Europe is the Holzbrücke, which was constructed over the river Rhine from Bad Säckingen, Germany, to Stein, Switzerland. It was first built before 1272 and has been destroyed and rebuilt many times.

built in 1871 with the Burr truss design, it is open to vehicular traffic. Like many of the covered bridges in Perry County, it crosses over Sherman's Creek and is flanked by beautiful country scenery.

Make a U-turn, and return through the bridge. At the intersection make a left turn onto Red Rock Road. Travel for 1.6 miles and make a left turn onto Adams Grove Road. After another 1.6 miles you'll arrive at

Enslow Bridge—Another picture-postcard setting makes this bridge one you will thoroughly enjoy. It too spans Sherman's Creek and is 116 feet in length. Constructed in 1904 it employs the Burr truss design—although the original builder is unknown. It is also known as the Turkey Tail Bridge—a moniker I could not verify in available records.

After taking photographs, drive through the bridge, make a U-turn, and return back through the bridge. Drive back along Adams Grove Road for 1.2 miles. When you get to the stop sign, turn left onto Sherman's Valley Road. Drive for an additional 2.2 miles and make a left turn onto SR 3003 (Springer Road). After .2 mile you will be at

Book's Bridge—This is a bridge with three different names. It is variously known as either Book's Bridge, Books Bridge, or Kaufman Bridge. Constructed in 1884, it uses the Burr truss design. This was a bridge that was on the verge of tumbling into Sherman's Creek—it had deteriorated to the point of almost complete destruction. At the last minute, it was rescued by the state and considerable improvements have been made on its exterior and interior to the point where it is now a picture-perfect covered bridge that begs visitors to stay a spell and have a picnic lunch nearby.

Make a U-turn and drive back through the bridge. Drive back to Sherman's Valley Road and make a left turn. Continue for 1.3 miles and make a left turn onto Mt. Pleasant Road. At the intersection with Cauffman Lane, bear left and .2 mile ahead will be

Mt. Pleasant Bridge—Here's another classic bridge that will command your attention and a plethora of photographic memories. If you visit on a Sunday afternoon you are likely to see several Amish buggies passing through this bridge—a scene directly out of any Pennsylvania calendar or brochure from the Pennsylvania Department of Tourism.

Built in 1918 by L.M. Wentzel, the bridge uses a Queenpost design with a Kingpost truss. As with many of the previous bridges, it crosses Sherman's Creek and is about 73 feet long. The bridge has been renovated with new concrete abutments and paint.

Drive through the bridge, make a U-turn, and return to Sherman's Valley Road. Turn left onto Sherman's Valley Road (now called Big Spring Road/PA 274) and in 1.8 mile make a left turn onto Lower Buck Ridge Road in the village of New Germantown. Drive for .2 miles and you'll arrive at

Book's Bridge—a classic "kissing bridge"

The New Germantown Bridge graces many a painting.

New Germantown Bridge—This is another of my favorite bridges. The setting is so picturesque and so classic that it literally begs you to stay a while. My wife, a professional artist, has used this bridge and the surrounding rural countryside as a focal point for one of her best-known paintings.

Constructed in 1891 by John W. Fry, this bridge uses a multiple Kingpost truss structure sandwiched between two Queenpost trusses. It is both handsome in design and appearance. Please don't miss this one.

After you've spent some time at this bridge, drive through, make a U-turn, and return to PA 274. The tour is over, but you still have one more decision to make—turn right and return to your starting point in Carlisle, or turn left and travel another one of Pennsylvania's eye-opening scenic routes (PA 274 to PA 75) and link up with the Pennsylvania Turnpike at Willow Hill.

CONTACTS

Columbia-Montour Visitors Bureau, 121 Papermill Rd., Bloomsburg, PA 17815; (570)784-8279 or (800) 847-4810; www.itourcolumbiamontour.com.

Perry County Tourism; pavisitorsnetwork.com/perry.

The Susquehanna River near Harrisburg

7 Down the Susquehanna

Estimated length: 90 miles
Estimated time: 1 day
Combine this tour with: Chapter 14

Getting there: Start in Williamsport and wend your way down the eastern side of the Susquehanna River. Slide by dozens of small towns and scores of photo opportunities as you watch the river course its way southward between high palisades and long acres of forests. By the time you arrive in Harrisburg, you'll understand the draw of this river on those of us fortunate enough to live in its wake.

Highlights: This drive is perfect for those lazy summer days when you just want to get out and see something new. You'll be coursing down the historic Susquehanna along narrow-lane roads (and a few freeways) that pass some of the most majestic scenery in the state. You'll walk with millionaires, fight alongside colonial soldiers, eat with a former president, and take a tranquil journey beside a most incredible river.

In so many ways, the Susquehanna River defines Pennsylvania. It is an integral part of the state's history as much as it is an integral part of the geography of the land. For those not familiar with the Susquehanna, it may seem like a minor geographical feature flowing from New York down through Pennsylvania and emptying into the Chesapeake Bay in Maryland. But consider that this river is the longest river (more than 464 miles in length) on the American East Coast draining into the Atlantic seacoast.

The Susquehanna River consists of two main branches. The north, or main, branch begins in upstate New York at Oswego Lake. The west branch, which be-

FAST FACT: The Susque-hanna has the distinc-tion of being the longest non-navigable river in the United States. That is, it is the longest U.S. river without reg-ular commercial boat traffic.

gins in western Pennsylvania, joins up with the main branch near the small town of Northumberland in central Pennsylvania and becomes part of the Susquehanna. In all, this river has a 27,500-square-mile watershed and empties approximately 18 million gal-lons of fresh water into the Chesa-peake Bay every minute.

Interestingly, the river has its roots in prehistoric times. The basin through which it flows was well-established during the Mesozoic era (250 to 265 million years ago). In fact, the river is considerably older than the mountains through which it now flows—mountains that were formed primarily during the uplift events of the early Cenozoic era (65 million years ago) when the early Ap-palachians were being developed.

Native Americans occupied the regions through which the Susquehanna flows approximately 5,000 years ago. However, it was not until the early 1600s that the first Europeans visited this region. It was Captain John Smith who jour-neyed from Virginia up the Susquehanna in 1608 and made initial contacts with the Susquehanna tribe. Later, the French and Swedes used the river as a primary egress into the frontier during their explorations of the mid-Atlantic region. In the 1800s a significant migration of German immigrants settled along both sides of the river and established farming communities that are still being tended to this day.

Prior to the arrival of Europeans, areas of the river basin in present-day Maryland and Pennsylvania were occupied by the Susquehannock tribe of Native Americans. This designation was first reported by John Smith on a map drawn in 1612. The map used the spelling "Sasquesahanough." Other scholars have de-bated this origin, saying that the name could have come from one of several Al-gonquian languages spoken in the region.

The Susquehanna River was also a significant geographical feature for William Penn as he set about to define the limits of his new colony in the 18th century. Penn negotiated with the Lenape Indians of the region to permit white settlement between the Delaware River in the eastern portion of the colony and the Susquehanna River in the central portion of the colony. This negotiation allowed for increased settlement of the region as well as the establishment of trading routes and transportation corridors that encouraged additional settlement. The river became not just a boundary, but a defining geographical feature that facilitated discovery and commerce.

Although the river proved frustrating in terms of a north-south transportation corridor, it did encourage the initial establishment of forts, towns, and villages along its length. Although the Susquehanna never fulfilled its promise as a navigational route, it did allow for the growth of several industrial centers and towns throughout the 19th century.

The river, though non-navigable, played a significant role in the development of transportation during the early history of the country. Because boats could not use the river to transport cargo up and down the river, ferries were employed to

"Roaring Bull II" Ferry at Millersburg

FAST FACT: More than 200 bridges cross the Susquehanna throughout its length, but there is only one remaining ferry (in Millersburg).

carry goods back and forth across the river (we'll travel on one of those ferries later). Several dams were built on the river in order to allow the ferries sufficient water depth to operate.

It was later that two separate canal systems were constructed on the lower Susquehanna in order to handle increased transportation needs. The first canal—the Susquehanna Canal—was initially completed in 1802. The second canal—the Susquehanna and Tidewater Canal—was considerably longer and more successful. Just as with the ferries, the canals necessitated the need for additional dams in order to provide sufficient water depth.

As the industrialization of Pennsylvania continued throughout the 1800s, the ferries were eventually replaced by bridges and the canals were replaced by railroads. Many of those bridges and railroads followed the identical routes of the earlier ferries and canals.

At this point, let's leave the Susquehanna for a few minutes and consider one of Pennsylvania's greatest natural resources—timber. When William Penn arrived in what is now America in 1682, it is estimated that 90 percent of the over 20 million acres now comprising Pennsylvania, were covered with dense stands of white pine, Eastern hemlock, and mixed hardwoods.

As settlers arrived in this new land, the forests were haphazardly cleared in order to create sustainable farms and to supply necessary construction materials. As the frontier expanded and more people moved into the interior, the demand for wood products increased. By the time of the American Revolution, lumbering had spread well into the center of Pennsylvania.

As the need for more timber increased, so did the need for transporting it ef-

FAST FACT: According to the U.S. Department of Energy, there is an average of 700 trees per acre of land (depending on the species). Eighteen million acres of trees would equate to approximately 12.6 billion trees.

The Dayton House with its classic mansard roof

ficiently from the interior to centers of industry and commerce. As a result, rivers such as the Delaware, Susquehanna, and Schuylkill were crowded with freshly cut logs on their way downstream to lumber mills. As more and more lumber was extracted from Pennsylvania's interior, the need for lumber products was also mushrooming. Much of that lumber was used for major construction products such as homes, buildings, ships, and boats. However, the forests also furnished fuel, potash, tanbark, wood for furniture and coopering, rifle stocks, shingles, household utensils, and charcoal. Lumber also became a significant export, particularly if it could be efficiently transported to large seaports such as New York, Boston, Philadelphia, and Baltimore.

FAST FACT: At one time, Williamsport had more millionaires per capita than anywhere else in the world.

The rise of the lumber industry increased dramatically in the mid-1800s. Not only was the country on the cusp of the Industrial Revolution, but lumber was also a valuable commodity during the years of the Civil War. Technology also advanced the timber industry with the introduction of steam-driven machinery in combination with the use of the circular saw blade. During the period between 1850 and 1870, the center of the lumber industry increasingly shifted into northern and central Pennsylvania.

In the late 1800s, the central Pennsylvania town of Williamsport, with 29 sawmills, became known as "the Lumber Capital of the World." (Today, it is better known as the birthplace and headquarters of Little League Baseball.) Its great mills, strategically located on the Susquehanna River, were supplied by logs floated downriver from tributary streams to the north. The log boom, operated by the Susquehanna Boom Company, stretched for seven miles along Williamsport's riverfront and was credited with a holding capacity of over 250 million board feet of lumber. During the late 19th century, Pennsylvania became the greatest lumber producing state in the nation—thanks in large part to the Susquehanna River.

As a result, many people became incredibly rich.

Many of those rich people built elaborate and ornate houses in a section of Williamsport that was to become affectionately known as Millionaire's Row (now Millionaire's Row Historic District). Several of the 263 buildings in this district date from 1855, but all are emblematic of the incredible wealth that came out of the timber industry, primarily during the 19th century. To say there were vast riches in this area would be a gross understatement—one trip through this neighborhood will underscore the wealth that was distributed among a bevy of entrepreneurs who sought to take advantage of this great natural resource.

My visit to Millionaire's Row was through two imposing stone pillars—as though I were entering an exclusive gated community off limits to the common man. But the houses I encountered left absolutely nothing to the imagination—they were spectacular beyond description. While I won't be able to describe each one, I do want to give you a flavor for the variety of opulence and range of design in this once-exclusive community—a community built by lumber and sustained,

The Peter Herdic House on Millionaire's Row

at least temporarily, by the vibrant economic forces of the late 1800s and early 1900s.

You may want to choose one of two ways to see these spectacular homes. You may opt to drive slowly down West Fourth Street in Williamsport and ogle each home on both sides of the street. Or you may wish to take your time and walk down one side of West Fourth Street and then back up the other side to take in the splendid architecture of all the dwellings on this tree-lined boulevard.

Begin your journey, as I did, at the intersection of West Fourth and Elmira streets. If you are driving, please note that West Fourth Street is one way (east to west) and that, for the most part, you'll be traveling through a residential district.

The J. N. Kline House with distinctive Ionic columns

Each of the numbers listed below represents the house number of a selected dwelling on West Fourth Street, so you will be able to easily locate each home (the numbers will be on both sides of the road).

The Peter Herdic House (#407). This classic and quite famous home, constructed in 1855, was once slated for demolition. It is now listed in the National Register. It features a flat roof, wide eaves, and a cupola. Note the eyebrow window trims.

Ulman House (#411). Built in 1880, this home has both Romanesque and Queen Anne influences. It is distinguished by a set of double doors, a tower, and a stained-glass window on the second floor.

Dayton House (#427). Another 1880 home, this one features a mansard roof and beautifully decorated windows. It originally had a tower that was later removed.

Cross over Center Street.

Lewis Jamison House (#508). Built in 1875, this home exhibits both a mansard and gabled roof. Arched windows and a gingerbread trim complement the architecture, which is a combination of both Queen Anne and Gothic.

J. N. Kline House (#519). One of the later houses to be constructed on this street, this 1910 home is an example of neoclassical architecture. Pay particular attention to the decorative chimneys.

Hiram Rhoads House (#522). What an impressive residence—note the stained glass in the front double doors and the multi-gabled roof. Rose stone lentils and red slate combine to make the colors of this home quite striking. This was the first home in the area to get a telephone.

Cross over Locust Street.

Lamade House (#610). I've always been enamored of houses with wraparound porches, and this one is a good example. The home was built in 1890 and features a tower on the southwest corner and several brick columns.

Walton Bowman House (#619). Here's another house with a wraparound porch. This 1894 masterpiece also features a multi-gabled roof and impressive chimneys. If you are on a walking tour you may be able to notice the carriage house in the back.

Cross over Walnut Street.

Rowly House Museum (#707). Here's yet another example of a Queen Anne home. Pay particular attention to the patterned slates on the roof, as well as the tile insets in the brick. The house dates to 1888.

Deemer/Maneval House (#711). I particularly enjoyed the decorative chimneys on this 1880 structure. With its wraparound porches and gabled roof, this home is indeed a standout.

LaRue Munson House (#747). This home is now Finks Decorating Center, but it dates from 1888 (long before the advent of decorating centers). Pay attention to the fish-scale trim on the roof dormers and the stained-glass window on the east side.

Cross over Campbell Street.

The Berkshire (#801). Here is a most impressive four-story structure that was constructed in 1905. It features two protruding bays and stone lentils. Note the columns and railings on the upper floor.

Emery House (#835). Here's another house with a tower and lots of stained glass. It was originally a wedding present for Mary While Gamble Emery. The building now serves as the McCormick Law Firm. As the story goes, the inside of the house was used for target practice by reservists during World War II (giving coronaries to every preservationist in town).

Hinckley House (#870). This house is distinguished by the fact that it employs a wide variety of building materials—everything from brick to tile to wood. Constructed in 1880, it is also distinguished by a multi-gabled slate roof.

Go past Maynard Street.

Harrar House (#915). This is not my style of house, but it is impressive

The Rowley House on Millionaire's Row

nonetheless. It was built in 1870 and featured ornate brick walls. Note that the first floor windows are flat on top, while the second floor windows are rounded. This, too, was a wedding present from one rich person to another.

FAST FACT: The Susquehanna River drains almost one-half of the total land area of Pennsylvania.

Gleason House (#925). Notice the very large door on this 1890 home. The house also features a tower along with curved window glass.

Go past Third Avenue.

Foresman-Cleveden House (#949/951). Believe it or not, this mansion has 50 rooms. After a devastating fire in 1885, a third story was added to the original structure. There is lots of decorative wood along with beautifully arched stained-glass windows.

The Stonehurst (#967). This is one of the few homes in the area that was constructed with brownstone. Built in 1868, it has Greek Revival and Italianate features along with decorative arches on the front porch.

Go past Park Street.

Goodrich/Weightman/Cochran House (#1005). Here's another Wow! House. In the 1880s it was owned by Annie Weightman-Walker-Penfield, who, at one time, was one of the world's wealthiest women. Notice all the gables on the roof as well as the Tudor chimneys.

Mussina House (#1022). This 1883 house features lots of stained glass. Pay particular attention to the decorative railings and protruding bay on the right side of the house.

Reading House (#1025). One of the few homes in the neighborhood with a mansard roof, this 1865 dwelling also features cast-iron cresting along the roof.

Howard House (#1051). This is another one of my favorites, although it has now been turned into student apartments. Built in 1885, this brick mansion features an abundance of window styles including stained glass, leaded, bull's eye, and French-plated.

Emerson House (#1062). This simple brick house was built in 1880 with a multi-gabled roof. It has a large porch with a protruding bay on the first floor.

You have just been through one of the most distinctive neighborhoods in the country. While your tour has placed an emphasis on the exteriors of these wonderfully expansive homes, be assured that the occupants spent as much on the in-

> **F**AST FACT: The athletic teams at Williamsport Area High School are known as the "Millionaires."

teriors (hand-carved staircases, mahogany floors, priceless works of art) as they did on the exteriors. In an obvious attempt to flaunt their wealth and impress neighbors, the lumber barons of the day left no architectural stone unturned in their desire to show off (financially speaking, that is). This must have been an incredible neighborhood in the late 18th and early 19th centuries. You will find yourself placing your imaginary self on the porches and balconies of these ornate mansions long after you leave Williamsport.

After you depart Millionaire's Row, drive south one block until you come to West Third Street. Make a left turn on West Third Street and drive east until you come to the intersection of US 15 (North Market Street). Make a right turn on US 15 and drive across the bridge spanning the Susquehanna River.

As you head down US 15 (and if you are traveling during the summer) you'll see lots of greenery on both sides of the road. You'll also experience the rolling hills of this region as the road tends to go up and down. Drive for approximately 5.8 miles and make a left turn onto PA-54 east (toward Montgomery). Stay on PA 54 east for about 3 miles and pass through the little town of Montgomery (watch your speed limit—it's 35 miles per hour…then drops to 25). When you get to the end of town turn right onto PA 405 south. Just after you cross the Susquehanna River, the speed limit picks up to 55 miles per hour and the road is completely encircled by trees.

Continue driving for about 15.5 miles and when you arrive at the intersection of PA 405 south and PA 45 west, you'll have to make a decision. If all that ogling at the grand homes of Millionaire's Row has left you hungry, plan to turn right and travel a very short distance west along PA 45 into the charming village of Lewisburg and the **Lewisburg Hotel** (136 Market Street). Established in 1834, this hotel has been a prominent feature of Lewisburg's Main Street ever since. The hotel had easy access to the Pennsylvania Canal, the Old East-West Turnpike, and two major railroads and quickly became an important way-stop for thousands of travelers in the 1800s. Besides its Victorian elegance, the hotel has provided accommodations for generations of travelers including such notables as President James Buchanan, Jim Thorpe, Walt Whitman, Marion Anderson, and most of the Big Bands of the thirties, forties, and fifties.

The Goodrich/Weightman/Cochran House has a carriage house in the back.

Extensively restored and remodeled in the late 1990s, the hotel has been returned to its former elegance and grace. Walk through the door and you will be met by plush carpeting and polished brass that reflect the grandeur of a different era. But you are here for the food. The main dining facility, the Governor's Room, provides a well-appointed Victorian atmosphere for any repast from simple to expansive. You'll return to the road with renewed energy and a deeper appreciation for "the good old days."

Depart the hotel, head east on PA 45 and return across the bridge back to PA 405 south and turn right. At this point, PA 405 follows the curves of the west

The Joseph Priestley House in Northumberland

branch of the Susquehanna. If you're traveling in the summer, notice all the green around you—rolling hills, small patches of corn fields, long stands of trees, and a beautiful countryside.

At the end of PA 405, the road changes over to PA 147 south (you'll be staying on this almost all the way to Harrisburg.). After an additional 4.6 miles you'll come into the town of Northumberland. Make a left turn onto PA 11 (Water Street) , make a right on Wallace Street and a left on Priestly Avenue. The **Joseph Priestley House** will be on your right.

While Joseph Priestley was a pioneer in the world of chemistry, he was also known as a theologian, an educator, and a political philosopher. He was originally from England, having been born in Fieldhead on March 13, 1733. In 1755 he began a small ministry and in 1762 he married Mary Wilkinson.

Priestley, ever the passionate learner, taught himself science in his early thirties. By 1767 he had discovered a way to produce carbonated water by mixing it with carbon dioxide. He called this "fixed air" and we have been using it in much the same way in the intervening years since that discovery.

But it was on August 1, 1774, that Priestley made his most famous discovery—oxygen. By carefully focusing the rays of the sun on a known quantity of mercuric oxide, Priestly was able to collect a sample of a certain "air" in a pneumatic trough. When he placed a burning candle in this "air" he noticed that it burned "with remarkable vigor." He also subjected a mouse to this "air" and discovered that the creature lived twice as long as it would have in a normal environment.

Priestley was also a politician and ardent supporter of both the American

> **F**AST FACT: The first name Priestley gave to oxygen was "dephlogisticated air."

Revolution and the French Revolution. He was increasingly being persecuted for his political views and in 1791 a group of rioters destroyed his house, laboratory, and library. He and his wife decided that an escape to America, where their three sons had emigrated, would be the better course of action. Priestley's destination was a proposed colony for English dissenters to be settled near Northumberland, Pennsylvania. Although the colony did not become a reality, Priestley continued advocating his religious and political beliefs, held Sunday services in his house, and provided support for the Unitarian Church in Philadelphia.

His home in Northumberland, where he lived from 1794 until his death in 1804, was one of approximately 100 houses in this remote yet picturesque spot on the north bank of the Susquehanna. Priestly once wrote that each fork of the river was "as large as the Thames in London, bounded by rocks and hanging woods...." Priestly is buried in Northumberland's Riverview Cemetery along with other members of the family.

When you visit the Priestly House you will note that it is a re-creation of an English gentleman's estate. While the main house is simple in its architecture—serene and sedate—it has a historical charm unlike any other dwelling in the surrounding area. The exterior of the house is Georgian along with additional features primarily in the Federal style. You'll quickly notice how "balanced" the house is—there is deep attention to the symmetry of the structure. There is a balustraded deck on the roof and semi-circular fanlights over the main entrance.

Construction on the house took three years and was accomplished by workers and carpenters hired in Philadelphia. After its completion, Priestly (now a widower) lived here with his oldest son, Joseph, and Joseph's family until his passing on February 6, 1804.

Begin your tour of the house in the **visitors center** and former carriage barn. You'll be able to view an orientation film and an introductory exhibit about the life and achievements of Joseph Priestley, as well as obtain tour tickets for the house.

As you tour the house you will notice that it has been decorated with period furnishings from the late 18th and early 19th centuries. A central hallway bisects the living area and also includes a library. Pay particular attention to the large windows in the parlor—each of which has a solid wooden apron made from a tree with a 40-inch diameter.

The laboratory, located in the south end of the house, has a collection of equipment similar to what Priestley would have used. Note the model of the large burning glass that Priestley used to discover oxygen and writing desk.

The house and the surrounding grounds evokes a peaceful atmosphere—one isolated from all the hustle and bustle of big city life or of the urban discord Priestley tried to escape in his native England. This was certainly a place conducive to experimentation and reflection—two traits Priestley valued immensely.

After your visit, return to PA 147 south. You'll cross over the Susquehanna again and enter the town of Sunbury. Just across the bridge PA 147 makes a sharp right turn (it's also known as North Front Street). Just after you pass Nittany Lion Drive on your left will be the **Northumberland County Historical Society** and old **Fort Augusta** (the fort is no longer

Fort Augusta historical marker

there). Pull into the driveway (careful, it's easy to miss) and park behind the building.

Fort Augusta was originally constructed in 1756. It was built as a way for the British to defend themselves from French and Indian raids initiated in the upper Allegheny region. Later, the fort was taken over by American forces during the American Revolution, serving as a fortress to protect settlers of the upper Susquehanna River from British forces. The fort was eventually dismantled in 1794.

The only remnant of the fort is an underground powder magazine. Where the fort once stood is now the headquarters of the Northumberland County Historical Society. The building is now known as **Hunter House**, in which is located a small museum. Within the museum's collection are several historical and archeological artifacts recovered from Fort Augusta, as well as selected items of local interest. Please note that the museum has limited operating hours (when I stopped by they were only open for three hours one day a week).

After your visit, exit the parking area and make a left turn back onto PA 147 south. We'll be traveling down this road for about 29.3 miles to Millersburg. For the most part, this section of the road follows the meandering Susquehanna River and is a very pleasant, relaxing drive. You'll weave your way through corridors of trees on a mostly rural road. Imagine traveling this road by wagon or horse 100 or 200 years ago. The serenity and quietude are almost overpowering, the rustic beauty exhilarating.

After about 40 minutes of driving and dreaming and staring you'll come into the quaint river town of Millersburg (the speed limit is 25 miles per hour). Look for the Ferry sign and make a right turn on North Street. Go to the bottom of the hill and cross over River Street (the river will be directly in front of you). Stop at the top of the ramp and if no ferry is waiting there, note the most unusual way of signaling the captain (who, is most likely, on the other side) that you would like some transportation across the river.

Ever since the early 1800s, ferries have been crossing the Susquehanna River. The earliest ferries were known as pole ferries and propelled by men using long poles to push a ferry and its goods across the river. Sometime around 1873, the pole ferries were replaced by steam-powered ferries. While these boats were considerably more efficient, they also brought some new challenges to those trying to get from one side of the river to the other. For one, their increased weight re-

A ride back in time on the Millersburg Ferry

quired considerably deeper water in order to get across. Since the Susquehanna is mostly a shallow-water river, it was necessary to artificially raise the water level. This was done by constructing ferry walls or dams from one shore to the other. These blocked the flow of water and raised the water level so a ferry could easily cross. The ferry walls are still in use today and a primary reason why the **Millersburg Ferry** has been designated as a Registered Historic Place.

From approximately 1866 to 1956 the Millersburg Ferry was a critical cog in the transportation system of the central Susquehanna Valley. The ferry was necessary for farmers and other businesspeople to transport their goods from the western side of the river to the lucrative markets in Harrisburg and Lancaster and eventually on to Philadelphia. Folks on the eastern side of the river found that the ferry was an easy way to access the recreational opportunities of the western shore. The railroad that eventually came to Millersburg also increased the need for a reliable transportation system across the Susquehanna.

The Millersburg Ferry transported a wide variety of goods across the river, in-

Sign for the Millersburg Ferry

FAST FACT: The Millersburg Ferry is believed to be the last "wooden double stern-wheel paddleboat" operating in the United States.

cluding cattle, livestock, produce, lumber, construction materials, motor vehicles, and people. The operation began with four boats, but the economic impact of the Depression seriously reduced the fleet. Today, there are still two boats—*The Roaring Bull V* and *The Falcon*—crossing the river, primarily during the summer.

As with every great technological innovation there is also the inevitability of technological obsolescence. This was certainly true for all the ferries that once crossed the river. The construction of auto bridges was the proverbial death knell for the ferries. Today, the Millersburg Ferry remains as the only ferry still operating on the river and the only way to cross the river for the 40 miles between Duncannon to the south to Sunbury in the north.

My wife and I like to drive our car onto the ferry on a lazy summer afternoon and float across the Susquehanna watching the eddies along the banks, the shimmering reflections of a late summer sun on the water or a rising flock of birds arc its way over the river. This is life in the *very* slow lane, life as it was more than a hundred years ago—long before supersonic airliners and instant messaging. To listen to the chug-chug-chug of the ferry engine and to chat with the captain is one of life's great pleasures.

The Millersburg Ferry, which operates between April and October, should be on every itinerary to eastern Pennsylvania. The journey from shore to shore takes about 20 minutes and you can travel in your car or leave your vehicle behind and come aboard as a foot passenger. The fares are reasonable, the journey memorable, and the time invaluable.

After your trip, return to PA 147 and head south. After about six miles turn right onto PA 225 south (South Fourth Street) and drive for 9.1 miles. Keep left at the fork and follow the signs for US 22 east/US 322 east/Harrisburg and merge onto US 22 east/US 322 east. Drive for 2.1 miles and take the exit toward PA 443/Fishing Creek/Rockville. Continue straight on North Front Street/River Road for about 1 mile and **Fort Hunter Mansion** will be on your right. Turn into the parking area and park your car.

You've now arrived at beautiful Fort Hunter. It was here in 1725 that Ben-

The Mansion at Fort Hunter

jamin Chambers established a small settlement. His brother-in-law, Samuel Hunter inherited the property and expanded it considerably.

But the French and Indian War was on the horizon and the British needed a series of fortifications along this perilous river. One of those forts was Fort Augusta, another was Fort Hunter. Fort Hunter was relatively small as forts go—it was a ten-by-fourteen-foot log blockhouse surrounded by a stockade and manned by volunteer soldiers.

After the defeat of the Indian Nations in 1763 the fort was left to the elements. Then in 1787 Captain Archibald McAllister purchased the property. McAllister developed a self-sufficient community that included a grist mill, country store, school, shops, tavern, blacksmith shop, and distillery. The location was ideal and trade flourished. When the Pennsylvania canal opened in 1834, the site blossomed financially.

In 1870 the property was purchased by Daniel Dick Boas who later willed it to his daughter and son-in-law. The Reilys maintained a successful dairy farm on the site and the home became a significant social center for the citizens of Harrisburg. The property eventually came into the possession of Margaret Wister Meigs, one of the nieces of the Reilys. She eventually established the **Fort Hunter Museum and Fort Hunter Park**.

In addition to the mansion, other sites to see include the tavern house, centennial barn, covered bridge, conservancy, and the Heckton Church. But it is that mansion that will sweep you back into the 1800s with its graceful charm and echoes of a bygone era.

This mansion, built in the Federal style on the site of the old Fort Hunter, was constructed in three sections. Archibald McAllister built the front two sections with local quarry stone. The middle "cabin" section was constructed in 1786 and designed at the initial McAllister house. The grand front mansion was created in 1814. The section on the rear of the house was added by Daniel Dick Boas in 1870.

As you enter this impressive building you will find yourself gaping at every detail. The entrance hall is handsome in every respect and the furnishings are authentic down to the last chair leg. You'll feel as though you have been ushered into a 19th-century home of a prominent Harrisburg family (which you have) awaiting your introduction to the master of the house. Your guided tour will take you into each of these beautifully appointed rooms; observe the elliptical staircase, the rich furnishings and the well-tended artifacts.

The Fort Hunter mansion is not only a beautiful structure on the inside, it is equally beautiful on the exterior as it overlooks the flow of the Susquehanna River. You can easily understand why this location was ideal as a wartime fortification, as well as a distinguished place for the mansion that followed. The atmosphere is transformative and the history is grand.

If you have the time, you may elect to wander the grounds of this delightful estate. Obtain a printed walking guide and plan an extended visit to view the Ice House, Flower Garden, Dairy, Heckton Church, Stone Arch Bridge, Centennial Barn, Spring House, Tavern House, Stone Stable, and Pennsylvania Canal. What you will discover is a most delightful Victorian estate that has now become a treasured museum and recreational park. You may want to sit on one of the benches along the edge of this estate—the Susquehanna River in full view—and simply dream. With the mighty river churning by, the well-manicured grounds all around, and the historic buildings sprinkled across the landscape it is indeed a most pleasant and relaxing picture-postcard scene.

CONTACTS

Lycoming County Visitors Bureau, 210 William St., Williamsport, PA 17701; (800) 358-9900; www.vacationpa.com/contact.aspx.

Joseph Priestly House, 472 Priestley Ave., Northumberland, PA 17857; (570) 473-9474; www.josephpriestleyhouse.org.

Fort Augusta, 1150 North Front St., Sunbury, PA 17801; (570) 286-4083; www.northumberlandcountyhistoricalsociety.org/index.htm.

Millersburg Ferry Boat Association, P.O. Box 93, Millersburg, PA 17061; (717) 692-2442; www.millersburgferry.org/2001.html.

Fort Hunter Mansion and Park, 5300 North Front Street, Harrisburg, PA 17110; (717) 599-5791; forthunter.org.

DINING

The Lewisburg Hotel, 136 Market St., Lewisburg, PA 17837; (570) 523-7800; www.lewisburghotel.com.

A Pennsylvania hex barn

8 The Pennsylvania Dutch Tour

Estimated length: 72 miles

Estimated time: 1 day

Combine this tour with: Chapters 11 and 12

Getting there: This trip begins in the beautiful country town of Kutztown and takes you along some rural country roads to see some of the finest hex barns anywhere. Afterward, you'll head down US 222 and turn off into the quaint town of Ephrata. From there, it's onto PA 272 and the former farming community of Landis Valley.

Highlights: Explore the heart of the Pennsylvania Dutch country with this tour. You'll experience the classic town of Kutztown, plus back country roads and seldom-traveled byways to discover some of the classic icons of the region—hex barns. Then you'll experience life long ago at Ephrata Cloister and Landis Valley Farm.

When most people think of rural Pennsylvania they envision long rolling hills sprinkled with towering trees or verdant stretches of rich green grass. The image often has a large red barn with a few cows calmly chewing their cud or milling about a small earthen pond. There may be fields of corn or soybeans along the side of the road and a tractor plowing the fertile earth for the next crop.

This vision is not far from the truth—in fact, it still exists in the Pennsylvania Dutch country. This tour is actually a trip backward—a trip back in time to rustic and decorative buildings, life in the early settlements of the westward expansion, and a peek into the religious freedom promulgated vigorously by

FAST FACT: The Penn-sylvania Dutch are of German heritage, not Dutch. Despite commercialization of the term, they were not origi-nally from Holland.

William Penn. You'll see parts of Penn-sylvania as they were a century or more ago. No arcades, amusement parks, or neon signs will be found on this journey—this is history as it was… and still is.

Among other sights, a trip through the land of the Pennsylvania Dutch will take you through fertile countryside where century-old German bank barns are decorated with a unique folk art design, often known as hex signs. This art is dis-tinctive to the area—reflecting both culture and tradition.

The first major immigration of Germans to America took place in the latter 17th century, many of whom settled in northwest Philadelphia County. It wasn't until the early 18th century that a mass migration of immigrants left Germany and settled in Pennsylvania. These settlers came to take advantage of the reli-gious freedom offered by William Penn. They included settlers of plain dress—Amish and Mennonites—and others of more "worldly" dress—Lutherans and other Reformed groups.

Over time, the various dialects spoken by these immigrants fused into a unique dialect known as Pennsylvania Dutch or Pennsylvania German. At one time, over a third of Pennsylvania's population spoke this language, which also had an impact on the local dialect of English. To this day, German Americans re-main the largest ancestry group in Pennsylvania.

The Pennsylvania Dutch live primarily in southeastern and south-central Pennsylvania in the area stretching in an arc from Bethlehem and Allentown through Reading, Lebanon, and Lancaster to York and Chambersburg. Like other immigrants, they brought their old world language, traditions, and art to their new home. Mystical bird and floral designs graced their birth and marriage certifi-cates, family Bibles, quilts, and some furniture. Some farmers decorated their large German-style bank barns, not with fancy ornamentation, which was pro-hibited, but rather with geometric patterns reflecting pride, heritage, and tradi-tion. Six-pointed star designs were very popular. The German word for six, "sechs," sounded like hex to their English-speaking neighbors. In time these "hex" patterns became commonly called hex signs.

Historians have discovered four-foot wooden stars set into stone walls on the gable ends of barns built as far back as the late 1700s—what we would now call the first hex signs. Interestingly, prior to the 1830s, the high cost of paint

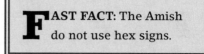

FAST FACT: The Amish do not use hex signs.

meant that most barns were left unpainted and unadorned. As paint became affordable, the Pennsylvania Germans began to decorate their barns much like they decorated items in their home (clothing, furniture). Barn decorating reached its peak in the early 20th century, at which time there were many artists who specialized in decorating barns with hex signs. Drawing from a large repertoire of folk designs, barn painters combined many elements in their decorations—many with roots in the artistry and symbolism of medieval Europe.

These colorful designs had interpretations or legends associated with them. Families often selected a hex sign for their barn based on design and meaning. Some of the more popular symbols included hearts for love, birds (called distelfinks) for luck and happiness, tulips for faith, and stars for good luck.

Here are some of the current interpretations of selected hex symbols:

PATTERN/SYMBOL	INTERPRETATION(S)
Scallop border	Tranquility, smooth sailing
Closed circle border	Eternity triangle, Trinity
Dove	Friendship, camaraderie, peace, purity, and happiness
Crescent moons	The four seasons
Wheat	Abundance and good will
Oak leaf	Long life, strength, endurance
Tulips	Faith, hope, charity, and trust in mankind
Pineapple	Welcome and hospitality
Rosettes	Good luck
Raindrops	Water, crop abundance, fertility
Eagle	Strength, courage, clarity of vision
4-pointed star	Good luck

This drive begins in Kutztown, a delightful small college town in Berks County. The town was founded in 1779 and formally incorporated in 1815. It was initially settled by Germans, primarily from the Palatinate region of southwest Germany. Even today the town retains much of its original heritage (over 91 percent of the residents can claim German ancestry).

Spend a little time here and you're likely to hear vestiges of the Pennsylva-

FAST FACT: Kutztown is the second-oldest borough in Berks County. The city of Reading was the first.

nia Dutch language from those who cling to their traditions and sayings. For a true Pennsylvania Dutch experience, plan your visit for late June/early July and visit the annual Kutztown Folk Festival—a 10-day celebration of traditional crafts, food, music, and folk life.

The first part of the tour provides you with an opportunity to see some of the best in authentic folk art—hex barn art. Begin in the center of Kutztown at the intersection of Main Street and PA 737. Head southwest toward Kutztown University. The road passes between several academic buildings in this charming former teacher's college and then out of town. About 2 miles from your starting point you'll come to Crystal Cave Road. Make a right hand turn, go over US 222 and at the 2.8-mile mark turn left onto Eagle Road. Stay on Eagle Road for another 2.5 miles. You'll go over a one-lane bridge and immediately come to a fork in the road. Bear right, go to the stop sign, then head straight on PA 662 north.

After .5 mile there will be a simple barn (Barn #1) on your right with four hex

Barn #1

Barn #7

signs (all the same) on the side facing the road. Stay on PA 662 north for 3.8 miles and you'll see a red barn (Barn #2) on your left with three hex signs on it. Shortly thereafter, make a right turn onto Windsor Castle Road and in .3 miles you'll see Barn #3 on the right with four hex signs. Directly across the road, on the left, will be another small building with two painted signs.

Travel for 1.5 miles and make a right turn on Virginville Road. Immediately after making the turn you'll see a white barn (Barn #4) on your left with three hex signs displayed near the top. Get ready, because this road will have several hex barns—all in close proximity to each other. Continue down Virginville Road for .2 mile and there will be another white barn (Barn #5) on the left. This is the Epting Farm and its barn will have some small hex signs along with three additional murals on the side. Go for another .1 mile and you'll come to the Adam Farm on the left and its white barn (Barn #6) with two hex signs and two pictures. Then, .7 mile further along will be the Miller Farm's white barn (Barn #7) with four hex signs and two murals. There's also an additional smaller building with two hex signs and one mural.

Continue along Virginville Road for .2 miles and again on the left will be a Miller Farm barn (Barn #8). This, too, will be white and will have two murals on the side. Then, .2 miles further along will be Barn #9—another Miller Farm barn, except this one is red with two murals on the side.

Watch your odometer, and 1.5 miles after Barn #9 you'll come to a stop sign. Make a left turn onto PA 143 north and travel for .3 mile. On the left will be the Sunday Farm hex barn (Barn #10)—a white structure with three hex signs on its side. About .5 mile further along the road, also on the left side will be another hex barn (Barn #11)—the Leiby Farm red barn with four hex signs on its side.

After Barn #11 travel 1.2 miles farther on PA 143 north. On your right will be Dreibelbis Station Bridge—a red covered bridge that was originally built in 1869. Make a right turn and slowly drive through the bridge. Try to imagine the various vehicles that traveled through this covered bridge long before the invention of the internal combustion engine. Once on the other side of the bridge, go up to the stop sign (.1 mile), make a U-turn and return through the bridge and back to PA 143. Make a left turn and head south on PA 143. From the bridge it will be 2.1 miles to the next stop sign. Bear left at the stop sign and continue on PA 143 south. After .4 mile you'll find yourself in the quaint and picturesque town of Virginville (note the distinctive rural architecture). About .5 mile further along the road you'll see Barn #12—a white barn on the left side of the road with three hex signs (you may have to look behind you). Travel for another .5 miles and you'll come up to one of the few barns (Barn #13) on the right side of the road. This will be a red barn with two hex signs.

You've just seen 13 authentic examples of hex barn art. These barns exemplify the variety of decorative art work that is characteristic of the region. You'll also get a sense of the ruralness of this region as well as the austere lives led by some of the people who live in this region. This is Pennsylvania as it was…and still is.

FAST FACT: No one is sure how Virginville got its name, but there are two theories. Some say Virginville was named for the untouched beauty of the countryside; others attribute the name to the honor of Comte de Vergennes, a foreign minister to France's Louis XVI.

Dreibelbis Station Bridge

After Barn #13, travel for 1.2 miles until you get to the intersection with PA 662 South (You may recognize this intersection from earlier). Turn left onto PA 662 south. Travel for 1.4 mile and you'll now be at the intersection of PA 662 and US 222 (the Moselem Springs Inn will be on your left). Your total travel time from Kutztown to this point (allowing for time to slow down and admire all the barns) will be about 1.5 hours. Now make a right turn onto US 222 and head south.

You're now traveling through some scenery that is less than spectacular. Warehouses and lots of industrial development line the road. Vistas are few and far between—mostly you'll be gazing at long stretches of concrete and asphalt. But you're on your way to an incredible place.

When you make that right turn onto US 222 south (after the hex barn tour), check your odometer. You'll be traveling exclusively on US 222 for about 31.9 miles to US 322—a journey that will take about 35 minutes. After you pass the

> **F**AST FACT: The town of Ephrata is named after Ephrath, a biblical town in what is now Israel.

exit for the Pennsylvania Turnpike you'll want to keep your eyes open for the US 322 exit. After taking the US 322 exit on the right, follow the off ramp for another .3 mile to the stop sign (US 322 west or Main Street). Make a right turn and drive for 2.4 miles. The entrance to the **Ephrata Cloister** will be on your left. Turn into the parking area, and amble your way over to the visitors center. Pay your admission and then take your time roaming around this incredible site.

The founder of Ephrata Cloister, Conrad Beissel, was born in Germany in 1691. As a young man, he apprenticed as a baker and traveled throughout the German countryside to perfect his skills. Along the way, he encountered Pietism, a movement to reform the state sanctioned Protestant churches. However, as a

Saron (Sister's house) at Ephrata Cloister

pietist, Beissel was found to be in conflict with the church. He was ultimately
banished from his homeland and immigrated to Pennsylvania in 1720 to
enjoy the religious freedom advocated
by William Penn.

FAST FACT: When Beis-
sel first arrived in Pennsylvania in 1720, he planned
to join a commune of hermits.

Beissel eventually found his way to an area just east of present-day Lancaster
and affiliated himself with the Brethren, an Anabaptist group. In 1724 he was appointed leader of the newly formed Conestoga Brethren Congregation. Beissel
had some radical ideas for the group, including Saturday worship and celibacy. In
1732 he broke away from the group and, along with several followers, established
a site along the banks of the Cocalico Creek in northern Lancaster County—now
known as Ephrata Cloister.

What began as a hermitage for a small group of devoted individuals grew into
a thriving community of nearly 80 celibate members supported by an estimated
200 family members from the region at its zenith in the mid-18th century. The
community became known for its self-composed a cappella music, Germanic cal-
ligraphy known as *Frakturschriften,* and a complete publishing center, which included a paper mill, printing office, and book bindery.

During the period from 1735 to 1746, the community constructed no less than
eight major structures. These included dormitories and meetinghouses, as well as
a number of smaller dwellings, workshops, and mills.

With the death of Beissel in 1768 the society quickly declined. Peter Miller,
successor to Beissel, recognized that the monastic life was no longer attractive to
new generations. By 1813 the last of the celibate members died, and the following year the remaining members of the married congregation formed the German
Seventh Day Baptist Church. Poorer members of the church moved into many of
the buildings on the cloister property and altered the spaces to suit their needs.

By 1929 the remaining church members living at the cloister had a major dis-
agreement on the disposition of the site and its artifacts. In 1934 the court system
revoked the incorporation charter for the church at Ephrata. The property was
placed under the care of a court-appointed receiver who in 1941 sold the remaining 28 acres to the Commonwealth of Pennsylvania.

Today, this National Historic Landmark is administered by the Pennsylvania
Historical and Museum Commission. Daily tours, special programs, and ongoing

Classic cloister structures

research continue to educate visitors about Ephrata's surviving legacy and the people who built it.

Stop in to the **Visitors Center**, where you can take a look at several exhibits and an introductory film. Then set out on the grounds, either by yourself or as a member of a guided tour, to roam around.

You'll want to stop by **Conrad Beissel's House** (#2) — an original surviving structure that dates from the early 1700s. Equally impressive is the **Saron or Sisters' House** (#3), which was originally built in 1743 for couples who left their dwellings to live as celibate Brothers and Sisters. The experiment was brief and the building was remodeled to accommodate the Sisterhood. Nearby is **The Saal** (#4) — a worship hall constructed in 1741.

The Bakery (#8) was a busy place in 18th-century Ephrata since each individual at the cloister consumed about a pound of bread each day. Nearby is **The**

Physician's House (#10), where minimally trained doctors would use a combination of herbs and tonics to provide for some relief from diseases and various ailments. As I looked around the place I got the immediate sense that health issues were not a primary concern of the community.

> **F**AST FACT: At the zenith of the community in the 1740s and 1750s, about 300 members worked and worshiped at the Cloister.

Other significant buildings on the grounds include **The Printing Office** (#14), the **Carpenter's House** (#16), the **Workshop** (#20) and the **Stable** (#20). But what truly impresses visitors is the austerity and simpleness of both the structures and the ways in which they were used. This was a different time—a time of plain living and devotion—and your tour of these grounds will open your eyes to a lifestyle and a passion quite different from our own.

After your visit, exit the parking lot by making a left turn back onto US 322

The Physician's House and Bake House at Ephrata Cloister

FAST FACT: Loaves of bread baked in the cloister bakery were enormous—each weighed about four pounds.

west. Travel for a mere .1 mile, go under the overpass, make a right turn onto the access ramp and then head south on PA 272. Travel for 9.1 miles on PA 272 south and turn right onto Landis Valley Road (Look for the prominent sign and make sure you turn on Landis Valley Road, not Valley Road). Travel for .2 miles and make a right turn into the large parking area for the **Landis Valley Museum**. This part of your journey, from Ephrata to Landis Valley, will take about 16 minutes to complete.

Landis Valley Village and Farm Museum currently encompasses over 100 acres. In the 19th century, it was a crossroads village—existing as an intersection of important Lancaster County byways when a hotel was built here in 1856. The community that grew up around the hotel became known as Landis Valley.

The village and museum offer visitors a slice of time—it's a living history vil-

Landis Valley House Hotel

lage and farm that collects, preserves and interprets the history and material culture of the Pennsylvania German rural community from 1740 to 1940. The site also enhances visitors' understanding and appreciation of Pennsylvania German practices, interactions with others, and their impact on the state and nation.

It's interesting to note that the museum contains the nation's largest collection of Pennsylvania German artifacts and presents them in authentic farm village surroundings. As you walk through the grounds you'll see that the unique open-air setting includes several examples of industrial life from the era, craft demonstrations, and agriculture with animals, plants and implements authentic to the period.

Begin your visit at the **Visitor Center,** which includes an exhibit gallery and introductory film on the village. Afterward, you can amble over to the **Log Farm** (#3) and see several re-created structures representative of a Pennsylvania German farmstead from about 1750 to 1800. **The Brick Farmstead** (#4) is an original 1830s building where Jacob and Elizabeth Landis, a Mennonite family, lived and farmed. They also operated a blacksmith shop on this main road.

The Log Farm (plus sentry) at Landis Valley Village and Farm Museum

> **F**AST FACT: In 1790, Pennsylvania Germans made up 40 percent of the southeastern Pennsylvania population.

Duck into the **Farm Machinery and Tool Barn** (#6) and get a feel for Pennsylvania German farm machinery and tools from the colonial era to the 20th cen-

A classic hex barn

tury. **The Landis Valley House Hotel** (#7) is a 1856 structure in its original location and furnished to depict life in the late 19th and early 20th century. **The
Maple Grove Schoolhouse** (#8) is a 1890 Amish schoolhouse with all its original furnishings. Stop by the authentic **Country Store** (#10) and see how their
merchandise compares with those in your local department store.

    The Erisman House (#16) is a circa-1820 log house representative of sim-
ilar homes in the early 19th century. Be sure to stop in the **Tavern** (#17) and see
what a typical public house and tavern must have looked like in the early 1800s.
There are several other buildings on site that will give you glimpses of life and living as practiced by Pennsylvania Germans in the mid-19th century.

    It wasn't until 1925, when brothers Henry and George Landis opened the
grounds as a private museum, that the culture and heritage of early Pennsylvania settlers became known to the general public. In 1953 the Commonwealth of
Pennsylvania acquired the museum and greatly expanded the operation. With
more than 50 buildings and about 100,000 objects, this is one of the largest living

history museums in America. It is a wonderful opportunity for visitors of all ages to lean about a distinctive culture and the contributions they made to the American experience.

CONTACTS:

Berks County Hex Barns, Greater Reading Visitors Center, 201 Washington St., Reading, PA 19601; (800) 443-6610; www.readingberkspa.com.

Ephrata Cloister, 632 West Main St., Ephrata, PA 17522; (717) 733-6600; www.ephratacloister.org.

Landis Valley Village and Farm Museum, 2451 Kissel Hill Rd., Lancaster, PA 17601; (717) 569-0401; www.landisvalleymuseum.org.

The Industrial Revolution was powered by many new machines.

9 Our Industrial Heritage–Part 1

Estimated length: 90 miles

Estimated time: 1–2 days

Combine this tour with: Chapter 10

Getting there: Begin in Easton and head down PA 611 to Doylestown. Depart Doylestown and drive west on PA 113, PA 422 and PA 345 to the tiny burg of Birdsboro. Proceed west on PA 422, US 222, and PA 183 to just outside the historic city of Reading.

Highlights: This tour starts in the industrial town of Easton and slides down a major thoroughfare to the suburbs of Philadelphia and the city of Doylestown. Sweeping vistas and bucolic scenery are not evident until you begin to wind your way through less-traveled areas of southeastern Pennsylvania, arriving in the rural outpost of Birdsboro. Then you'll whip around the southern perimeter of Reading, where the tour will end near Blue Marsh Lake.

The American Industrial Revolution was in reality several revolutions in one. There was the occupational revolution, the urban revolution, the economic opportunity revolution, the scientific and technological revolution, and the sociological revolution all wrapped up into one major force. The lives of ordinary Americans were forever altered and the pulse of the country was mechanized and accelerated as factories and industry (and the technology that spawned them) radiated out in every direction and into almost every American life.

That the Industrial Revolution changed our lives is a given; it is the various ways in which it did this that is the topic of this and the following chapter. We'll use these pages to delve into the products and consequences of that pivotal rev-

FAST FACT: Driving at 65 miles per hour means you are traveling at 95.3 feet per second. In other words, you are driving the height of a 10-story building each and every second.

olution in our country's history—primarily as it applies to eastern Pennsylvania. Let's begin with a pivotal element in the industrial north—transportation, or more precisely, the transportation of manufactured goods.

Our need to get from one place to another in the shortest amount of time is a given in our fast-paced lives. This fast-paced existence wasn't always the rule, however—especially in the 18th and 19th centuries. Horses that plodded along at four miles per hour, pulling wagons or carts over rough and difficult terrain, was not only the preferred means of transportation, but, quite simply, the only means of transportation as the new nation began its westward migration.

Not only did people have to get from one place to another, but the young national economy demanded that goods had to be moved from their place of manufacture or production to other points throughout the country. It was easy loading machinery or food items onto a wagon and sending it off into the wilderness. However, there were often those pesky things known as mountains that often made the journey quite difficult and quite demanding. Unfriendly folks in the interior and a deeply forested land also added to the challenges of moving goods across the frontier of "Penn's Woods."

To make the transportation of goods and people easier early pioneers looked back to Europe and quickly saw how canals effectively eliminated the "highs and lows" of the terrain and moved large bundles of goods from distant locations into urban areas and vice versa.

The Conewago Canal, initiated in 1790, was the first in the state. It helped transport goods via riverboats around the Conewago Falls on the Susquehanna River near the present town of York Haven. Like many of the early canals in the state it was dug by a gang of workers welding nothing more than shovels, picks and wheelbarrows. As you might imagine, the work was very difficult, the living conditions were primitive at best, and disease was often rampant. Pay was minimal and job security was nonexistent. But new frontiers were conquered and new transportation routes were established.

Encouraged by the success of the Erie Canal and its effectiveness in moving materials and people from the interior of New York State to the centers of population, the citizens of Pennsylvania began an ambitious campaign to construct hundreds of miles of canals throughout the early 1800s. A canal system generally consisted of canals, tow paths, locks, and dams along with the men, barges, and animals used to traverse along these "water highways." In 1824 the Pennsylvania Assembly added railroads to their definition of the state's canal system.

Canal building took off with a vengeance in the 1800s. Hundreds of miles of canals were constructed—primarily along the southern tier of the state as well as in the eastern highlands (principally to ferry lumber and coal to the large industrial cities of Philadelphia, New York and Pittsburgh). One of the earliest canals (and one we will visit in a later chapter) was the Union Canal, which connected the cities of Reading and Middletown. The Schuylkill Canal, linking Philadelphia with Port Carbon, was used to transport a variety of goods, primarily coal from the anthracite mines in northeastern Pennsylvania.

By the time 1834 rolled around, the Main Line of Public Works, a system of interlocking canals, railways and inclined planes, was moving significant numbers of passengers and materials between Pittsburgh and Philadelphia—a distance of approximately 391 miles.

As with any form of technology there is always newer technology just around the corner. So it was with the canals of Pennsylvania. By about the mid-1800s the railroads were increasing their lines and their influence over the landscape. They were faster, more convenient, and easier to maintain—particularly over long distances. When the Pennsylvania Railroad began offering rail service from the cities of Pittsburgh and Philadelphia in 1852 you could almost hear the death knell of the state's canal system. An iron spike was struck deep into the heart of the canal system when the railroad purchased the Main Line Canal from the state in 1857. By 1859 the totality of the state's canals had all been sold off and the canal system began a fast and unceremonious decline. It had very quickly outlived its usefulness. By 1900, the canals of Pennsylvania were essentially an extinct species.

We're going to start this tour in the

FAST FACT: At its peak (mid 1800s) Pennsylvania had 1,356 miles of working canals. That was more canals than any other state (At one time, the U.S. had more than 4,000 miles of canals.)

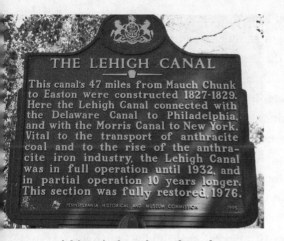

THE LEHIGH CANAL

This canal's 47 miles from Mauch Chunk to Easton were constructed 1827-1829. Here the Lehigh Canal connected with the Delaware Canal to Philadelphia, and with the Morris Canal to New York. Vital to the transport of anthracite coal and to the rise of the anthracite iron industry, the Lehigh Canal was in full operation until 1932, and in partial operation 10 years longer. This section was fully restored 1976.

PENNSYLVANIA HISTORICAL AND MUSEUM COMMISSION   1995

A historical marker—the only remnant of a bygone era

bustling town of Easton just across the Delaware River from New Jersey. Our beginning point will be Hugh Moore Park on the south side of the city—specifically the **National Canal Museum**. The museum is one of the few in the country dedicated to telling the story of America's historic towpath canals. The museum features numerous hands-on exhibits that offer insights and information about canals and the people and animals that worked them for more than a century.

As you tour this small but informative museum, you will be introduced to a variety of displays and exhibits on the history of the canal system, how canals were built, the different types of canal boats, how boats were loaded and unloaded, how the locks worked, what tools were used, how bridges were negotiated, and how tillers were used. Kids can even build their own canals and construct their own aqueducts.

One of the things you will learn here is that the barges on the canal were in essence floating boxes. Although they varied in size and shape, the early canal boats were all pulled by mules or horses along a towpath. The shape of these canal boats reflected the purpose for which they were built—to carry cargo. This meant they had rounded bows to maximize cargo space in the hull, which made them cheaper to build. Most of the boats used in Pennsylvania's canals ranged from 60 to 90 feet long and about 10 to 14 feet wide. Although most of the boats were designed for carrying cargo, others were designed for passengers. The passenger-carrying "packet boats" had a sharper bow—allowing it to cut through the water and give it greater speed.

There were even some boats especially crafted for traveling merchants and entertainers. These included "medicine shows" offering medical concoctions and remedies fortified with dubious claims of effectiveness. There was also the famous Spaulding and Rogers Floating Palace Circus—complete with clowns, trained ponies, and an aging lion.

The highlight of a visit here is an opportunity to ride on a mule-pulled canal boat (*The Josiah White II*) on a portion of the Lehigh Canal. The canal was originally constructed between 1827 and 1829 and extended 47 miles from Mauch Chunk (now Jim Thorpe) down to Easton. Here, the Lehigh Canal connected with the Delaware Canal to Philadelphia and with the Morris Canal to New York. This canal system was vital to the transport of anthracite coal and the rise of the anthracite iron industry. The canal was in operation for nearly a century; the section used for your ride was fully restored in 1976.

Mules are the preferred locomotion for these massive boats for one simple reason—mules are smarter than horses. It seems that horses have an inclination to go into the water, whereas mules do not. Thus, if you're walking some animals down a waterway and want to avoid stoppages, it's a good idea to use mules.

Shortly after I climb aboard the *Josiah White II*, the mules arrive and are

The *Josiah White II*

FAST FACT: A typical canal boat weighed in at 48 tons. It might carry up to 100 tons of coal.

hitched up to the boat. The single line tightens and we're off…at a top speed of 2 miles per hour. The two mules strain against the rope and slowly we inch away from the dock. Our captain holds the tiller firmly in his hands and gently guides the boat into the center of the canal. Our guide, Sarah, tells us that the mules' job is actually "a walk in the park." Mules, she tells us, can work for 18 hours a day, every day, for their entire lives. Pulling a barge is relatively easy work and one they do without complaint.

As I watch a family of geese slowly glide across our path I am reminded of how speed was not the primary consideration in "the good old days"; it was efficiency that took precedence. The opportunity to observe a quiet grove of trees, a

Approaching the locktender's house on the canal

squawking mallard, and a slow parade of people on the tow path is both refreshing and peaceful.

Before long, we arrive at the locktender's house. Visitors to the park can walk along the tow path from the museum and take a self-guided tour of this home. Here, you'll learn how a locktender's family tended to the various responsibilities of the lock seven days a week, 24 hours a day. It's a look into a life ruled by boats and water and one ruled, almost entirely, by the forces of commerce.

The boat is slowly turned around, the two mules are repositioned and, once again, we're off. Sarah fills us in on the various goods carried on the canal, some of the people who worked to ensure the continuous passage of traffic along these fluid arteries, and the historical place of canals in the evolving history of Pennsylvania. Scenes slowly pass by; the rushing world outside this little piece of real estate seems all the more distant. This is a voyage of tranquility—a step back in time that is at once refreshing and relaxing. You may discover that by the time you arrive back at the dock after this 45-minute nostalgic journey, you have a somewhat different view of the 65-mile-per-hour vehicle that will transport you back through the world outside.

Depart Hugh Moore Park and get on PA 611 south. Drive for about 11 miles until you come to the small village of Kintnersville. At this point, you will need to make a decision. If the family would like to see some more canals, you can make a left turn onto PA 32 south and head south to the town of New Hope. Along this gorgeous stretch of country road (quite narrow in spots) you can enjoy the beauty of the Delaware River (on your left) and the slowed-down pace of rural Pennsylvania. In summer, this can be a most magical journey as you slide through a sprinkling of small country towns with quaint B&Bs, rustic storefronts, and overarching stands of trees splaying sunlight across your windshield.

Along PA 32 south, the Delaware Division of the Pennsylvania Canal System has preserved a corridor of several canal locks—all part of the Delaware Canal State Park. The towpath trail is 59.3 miles long and the canal, with 24 locks, has been refurbished in several locations to look exactly like it did when it was commercially viable in the late 1800s and early 1900s. There are dozens of potential picnic spots along this vibrant stretch of history. When you arrive in the art colony of New Hope, the kids can jump on the New Hope Canal Boat Ride and get another mule-drawn barge ride along the Delaware Canal. There's also a locktender's house for public viewing.

What many canals look like today

If this is your journey, then leave New Hope, turn onto PA 179 south, drive for about 1.2 miles, then turn left onto US 202 south. Drive for about 9.5 miles into the town of Doylestown.

If you've had your fill of canals and waterways and mules and barges after departing Easton, then you should continue south on PA 611 south after you arrive in Kintersville. After approximately 18.7 miles you'll also arrive in Doylestown—home of the **Mercer Museum**—one of the most distinctive museums in the country.

Henry Chapman Mercer was a modern-day Renaissance man who was, among other things, a noted tile-maker, archaeologist, antiquarian, artist, and writer. In addition, he designed and built three poured concrete structures, one of which was the Mercer Museum.

Born in Doylestown in 1856, Mercer obtained his undergraduate degree from Harvard and a law degree from the University of Pennsylvania. After traveling extensively throughout Europe for eight years, he returned to Philadelphia and was appointed curator of American and prehistoric archaeology by the University of Pennsylvania in the early 1890s. Mercer devoted himself to finding old American artifacts and learning about German pottery. Mercer believed that American society was being destroyed by industrialism, which inspired his search for American artifacts. Mercer was known for his research and books about ancient tool-making, his ceramic tile creations, and his engineering and architecture. He wrote extensively on his interests, which included archaeology, early tool-making, German stove plates, and ceramics. His decorative tiles are installed in the Pennsylvania State Capitol building, Rockefeller's New York estate, Grauman's Chinese Theatre, the casino at Monte Carlo, and the St. Louis Public Library.

But he is most famously known for the Mercer Museum—a seven-story concrete castle with an eclectic display of more than 40,000 artifacts from early American society. Completed in 1916, the museum includes more than 60 early American crafts and displays—each in its own room, alcove, or display chamber on one of the seven floors. The museum is a paean to the ingenuity and creativity of American industry and technology. Displays on woodworking, metalworking, agricultural advancements, the textile trades, and the dairy industry are all faithfully collected and presented. Its core collection, however, is preindustrial tools and artifacts of everyday life—most of which predate the American Industrial Revolution. Viewing these tools and implements puts the concept of the Revolution into a proper perspective—one quickly gets an appreciation for the advent of technology in our everyday lives after having seen the artifacts displayed throughout this museum.

I begin my tour on the second floor, where I stroll in a circular pattern around the perimeter to gaze inside a variety of small rooms lining the walls. Here are

displays devoted to confectionary, glass blowing, printing, horn and tortoise working, kitchen utensils, fruit preservation, butter and cheese making, and bathtubs.
There's also a complete cider mill on display.

Moving up to the third floor, I roam the perimeter rooms to discover artifact
rooms as diverse as hat-making, engraving, decorated chests, animal husbandry,
leather working, harvesting, tinsmithing, wallpaper and pewter. It is on this floor
that I come across a sign that answers one of my most persistent questions about
this structure:

How were objects placed in the museum? — Most objects were moved
into the museum through the broad doorway on the east wall. Some
large pieces were disassembled and reconstructed inside. Others like
the cider press in room 24 were even placed in the building before it
was finished, then the structure completed around them. Workmen
hung large artifacts like the whale boat using scaffolding and block and
tackle. Iron hooks and other rigging hardware supported the weight.

The fourth floor showcases more crafts and skills such as shingle making,
basket and broom making, lumbering, brick making, healing arts, surveying and
navigation, spinning and weaving, wagon making, gunsmithing, nautical equipment, tobacco culture and mining. There's also an authentic Conestoga wagon
and an old whaling boat on display.

My eyes are straining from the visual overload, but I forge ahead to the fifth
floor to discover exhibits and displays on needlework, baking utensils, clocks and
watchmaking, woodworking, blacksmithing, musical instruments, laundering. I
also discover a fully fitted stagecoach and a complete mill.

I lug my bones up to the sixth floor of the castle. Here I view the Columbus
Gallery — a display of archeological and Native American exhibits. Also presented
is a display of stoveplates and firebacks.

Just one more floor to go — the seventh. Here is a display on solar salt making, a hearse and prisoner's dock, and the all-time favorite of kids — an authentic
hangman's gallows.

When you first enter this building you get the sense that you are entering a
medieval castle. The lighting is dimmed and the walls are festooned with all sorts
of knickknacks and brick-a-bracs. You almost feel as though you're in a Grade B
horror movie with a few vampires or ghosts about to appear out of a deep and

foreboding mist with bad organ music playing in the background. Fortunately, that's not going to happen.

What will happen is that your eyes will go on visual overload—you'll take in all the tools and equipment and technology that has been so much a part of America's Industrial Revolution from its earliest years to the present. The breadth of these holdings is staggering—you could easily spend an entire day here reading all the signage and perusing every tiny room and hidden alcove. On seven floors are all the tools of civilization—from ancient times to the present day.

After departing the museum, make a right turn on Green Street and then a slight right onto Main Street. Make a slight left onto North Easton Road and then turn left onto PA 113 west. Stay on PA 113 west for about 19.5 miles. Turn right on PA 73 west and drive for 1.7 miles, then turn right onto Main Street and turn left onto Game Farm Road. Drive for 3.4 miles, turn left onto Neiffer Road, turn right onto West Ridge Pike and then left onto Evergreen Road. After less than .5 mile make a slight right to merge onto PA 422 west toward Pottstown. Drive for about 5 miles and exit onto PA 100 south. Merge onto PA 724 west and drive for about 6.3 miles. Make a left onto Shed Road and drive for 3 miles until you come to PA 345 south. Turn left onto PA 345 south and then right onto Park Road. Take the first left on Mark Bird Lane and stay on this until you arrive at **Hopewell Furnace National Historic Site**. The journey from Doylestown will take you about 1.5 hours to complete and includes a mixture of rural roads and industrial complexes along the way.

Now you're in iron country.

Humans have been mining iron for centuries and smelting it since about 3500 B.C., when they first learned how to free iron from ore. The Iron Age in Europe (1200 B.C. to 400 A.D.) is an archeological period marked by expanded use of iron in a wide variety of implements, weapons, personal ornaments and pottery. The Chinese were the first to use cast iron and the use of this substance spread across Europe during the medieval period. Indeed, iron working and iron use is as ancient and sustaining as many civilizations. Yet in all that time the basic process of manufacturing iron has not changed much; it is the industry that surrounds this valuable substance that has changed the most—from industrially critical to barely influential.

The basic production cycle is fairly simple: heat iron oxide in an intense flame fed by a carbon fuel. The oxygen in the ore combines with carbon monoxide re-

> **F**AST FACT: Iron is basic to your survival. Without iron your blood would be unable to transport oxygen throughout your body.

leased from the fuel and is expelled as carbon dioxide. The remaining substance is iron. In ancient times this manufacturing process was crude and inexact and the resulting iron was less than satisfactory. As humans became more familiar with the chemistry involved in producing iron, they also became more sophisticated in how that iron was made. The use of tall blast furnaces was critical to the success of quality iron. The height of those blast furnaces allowed the rising gases to preheat the ore and offer the iron more distance to descend as it softens. As a result, it absorbs more carbon from the fuel. The addition of limestone helps in the removal of impurities in the ore. The result: better-quality iron.

As the procedures for making iron improved, so did the need for more iron. With greater demand, there was also an exponential rise in the need for more furnaces, which in domino fashion created the need for more workers and communities where those workers could live. Some historians refer to these small communities, forged and sustained by a single industry, as "iron plantations." Similar in many respects to European feudal estates where villages grew up around a land baron's castle, the life of an iron community was governed by its one and only industry. By the same token, it was a self-sustaining community that either rose or fell economically according to the prosperity of its single master—the iron furnace.

Hopewell Furnace was originally constructed in 1771 by Mark Bird. Ideally located with immediate access to the necessary raw materials and abundant natural resources, Hopewell began to flourish just as the American Revolution began to spread. The English thought they could limit the burgeoning iron industry by requiring the colonies to ship their raw pig iron to the mother country for production into viable goods that would then be sold back to the colonists at a tidy little profit. Americans, ever enterprising, quickly saw through these diversionary tactics and began to develop practices and procedures that would keep the entire operation on American shores.

The Revolutionary War not only created a need for more iron products, but it also helped spread the need for more furnaces and workers to tend them. Although Hopewell Furnace was a powerful cog in this vast industrial machine, its time was limited due to a succession of economic misfortunes. It was closed in 1808.

New ownership in 1816, however, brought Hopewell back into production. A succession of changing technologies and manufacturing procedures in the industry in the late 1800s eventually sealed the fate of Hopewell and it finally went out of service in the summer of 1883. Fortunately, the property and the 214 acres of land surrounding it were set aside in 1938 as a National Historic Site—one that will engage and inform you about a significant portion of our industrial heritage.

My first visit to Hopewell was on an early autumn afternoon. Golds and yellows and reds were sprinkled throughout the trees cascading up and over rolling hills. Armies of children and their parents were attempting to pull crisp apples from the orchards surrounding the well-maintained visitors center. A dog scur-

The Ironmaster's Mansion at Hopewell Furnace

> **F**AST FACT: Men known as "fillers" worked 12-hour shifts seven days a week entering 400 to 500 pounds of iron ore, 30 to 40 pounds of limestone and 15 bushels of charcoal every half hour into Hopewell's furnace to keep it in "blast."

ried here and there, squirrels darted across the parking lot, and the hum of insects could be heard from the open fields. This small rural community must have been quite a busy place in its day—the daily activities and chores must have taken on the same buzz that was currently echoing through this vibrant landscape.

When you visit, you will be greeted by an assembly of buildings that take you back in time; a collection of structures that was its own community—independent, self-sufficient, and sustaining. As you walk down the path from the **Visitors Center** you will initially be drawn to the massive **Ironmaster's Mansion**. This impressive home, originally constructed in the late 1700s, served not only as the primary dwelling for the manager of Hopewell Furnace and his family, it also served as the centerpiece for the whole village. Enter the home and you will get a sense of the furnishings and decorations of the early 1800s.

Walk over to the **Springhouse** and **Smokehouse** where the house servants would store and cure meats and other food items. Peek into the large barn, which housed up to 36 animals and enough feed to supply them for up to a year. Saunter over to the **Office Store** where workers could obtain household items and where those items were charged against their future work. Be sure to stroll through the **Cast House,** which surrounds the furnace stack. It was here that molders cast iron into a variety of products including stove plates and weaponry.

A host of other buildings and structures are spread out across this site. These include an assembly of tenant houses that were rented to families, a blacksmith's house that produced necessary hardware and horseshoes, a bridge house where workers carted the raw materials (charcoal, limestone, iron ore) used in the production process, and the charcoal hearths where colliers turned acres of wood each year into charcoal.

One feature that distinguishes

> **F**AST FACT: In 1822, Hopewell received an order for a stove from Joseph Bonaparte, brother of Napoleon and the former appointed King of Spain.

The office store at Hopewell Furnace

Hopewell Furnace from other historical sites is the inclusion of audio stations at 10 designated structures throughout the village ("the Voices of Hopewell"). Not only are these recordings narrated by imaginary inhabitants of Hopewell Furnace 200 years ago, each has been set up to stand alone, allowing you to take whatever path you wish through the village without missing a thing. Examples include Polly Kid, a hired girl who describes her feelings about her co-workers at the Ironmaster's Mansion, and Sam Houseman who talks about the work done at the Blacksmith Shop. These authentic re-creations provide visitors of any age with personal and dramatic stories about the human side of iron production.

Hopewell Furnace is a self-guided tour into the heart of the American Industrial Revolution. There are hiking trails, living history demonstrations, and a thriving vibrant village to experience. You can spend as little as an hour here or as much as an entire afternoon. However long your visit, you will come away with a deeper appreciation for the rough and demanding lives led by many of our ancestors—who forged much more than the most common element (by mass) forming the planet Earth.

Depart Hopewell Furnace on Mark Bird Lane. Turn right onto Park Road and continue onto PA 345 north. After a little more than 6 miles, turn left onto US 422 west and drive for about 11 miles. Continue onto US 222 north. After 2.5 miles make a right turn onto PA 183 toward Strausstown. Go straight through the traffic light and on the right side, immediately after the dairy farm, is Red Bridge Road. Turn right onto Red Ridge Road and the **Berks County Heritage Center** is straight ahead.

What a delight this place is! Here, you'll be able to experience the "simple life" of days gone by as well as the beginnings of the Industrial Revolution that were evolving in the 1800s. The Heritage Center is a collection of buildings as diverse as the times in which they existed—it's a walk backward in time, but a walk that will bring you face to face with a living museum—actually several museums—and the artifacts of an era that no longer is, but remains ever vibrant.

Start your visit at **the Reeser Farm House**, a 1774 stone house that now serves as the **Visitors Center**. This building, formerly constructed of logs and now wrapped in local stones, was a private home and farmhouse actively used by generations of Berks County families all the way up to 1978. It was here that I met my affable guide, Glenn Wenrich. Glenn is retired and his passion for things historic (especially canals) is palpable.

At the **Gruber Wagon Works**, Glenn led me through a three-story building that was the workplace for about 20 men who constructed wagons in the late 1800s and early 1900s. Box wagons and hay flats were the specialty of the house and I was able to see and touch the self-created machinery that was used to manufacture these ancient artifacts of transportation. The building and about 150 acres of land was originally purchased from William Penn for about $69—quite a real estate bargain.

Note the plethora of tools and machines used to construct wagons, along with the fine examples of wagons available for the buying public. The actual tools and shop conditions have been faithfully restored to their "turn-of-the-20th-century

> **F**AST FACT: Workers at the Gruber Wagon Works earned salaries according to the importance of the work they did. In the early 1900s apprentices made 15 cents an hour, wheelwrights (a person who builds or repairs wheels) earned 25 cents, and blacksmiths 35 cents.

exactness"—paint brushes are right where they were laid, machines are calibrated exactly as they were over a century ago, and tools are slipped into drawers in the exact positions they would have been a century ago. The building is just like it would be if, in some *Twilight Zone* episode, everybody was plucked right off the Earth.

The Gruber Wagon Works was in operation from about 1885 to 1972. The company produced approximately 100 wagons a year—most all for farmers and merchants. In 1917 a one-horse wagon sold for about $72 to $86, a two-horse wagon sold for $93 to $122, and a four-horse wagon sold for $106 to $148. Compare those prices to those today's merchants must pay for their business transportation needs.

The next stop on our tour is the **C. Howard Hiester Canal Center**. This exciting and dynamic museum, housed in an old barn, offers a realistic history of canal transportation with specific attention to the Union Canal and Schuylkill Navigation System and their contributions to the growth of Berks County. My guide was like a proud grandfather showing off his grandchild to a group of admirers. It is quickly apparent that if there is one thing Glenn knows—it's canals and their contribution to the industrialization of Pennsylvania.

After watching a short video on the history of canals in Pennsylvania and especially the history of canals in this part of the state, I was led through the scores of artifacts and battalions of implements associated with canal life, including the pilothouse of the icebreaker *Dolphin*, an authentic anchor, a pilot wheel and propeller, an actual windlass, and other displays that features the "tools of the trade" and the people who used them. Glenn pointed out the numerous displays that offer information about how two boats pass each other, the canals of the northeast, how boat yards operated, boatbuilding techniques, steam power, life on the canal, an actual canal lock, a locktender's shanty, and how locks were manufactured.

This is a museum that has something for everyone—one that encourages you

Opening a lock on the canal

to reach out and actively touch history and one that stimulates all your senses in a unique learning experience.

Other sites within the Heritage Center include **Wertz's (Red) Bridge**—the longest single-spanned covered bridge east of the Mississippi River, **Melcher's Grist Mill**—an 1888 water-powered farm mill used the grind cornmeal and grains into animal food, and the **Union Canal Towpath**—a 4.5-mile stretch of Tulpehocken Creek that includes remains of homes, mills, and an assortment of locks, aqueducts and other features prominent during the heyday of the Union Canal (a detailed map is available at the visitors center).

As Glenn reminded me, the canals no longer exist, but their impact and significance in the early years of the Industrial Revolution still do. Those canals, and businesses such as Gruber Wagon Works, stand as testimony to the dramatic changes that drove the American Industrial Revolution. Their power and significance may seem rudimentary when viewed through our 21st-century eyes, but their worth is no less important. They were harbingers of what we enjoy today, advances that moved this nation in a most vibrant direction.

CONTACTS

National Canal Museum and Hugh Moore Park, 2750 Hugh Moore Park Rd., Easton, PA; (610) 991-0503 ; www.canals.org.

Mercer Museum, 84 South Pine St., Doylestown, PA 18901; (215) 345-0210; www.mercermuseum.org.

Hopewell Furnace National Historic Site, 2 Mark Bird Lane, Elverson, PA 19520; (610) 582-8773; www.nps.gov/hofu.

Berks County Heritage Center, 2201 Tulpehocken Rd., Wyomissing, PA 19610; (610) 374-8839; www.countyofberks.com/parks.

Locomotive at the Pennsylvania Railroad Museum

10 Our Industrial Heritage–Part 2

Estimated length: 74 miles

Estimated time: 1–2 days

Combine this tour with: Chapters 9 and 13

Getting there: This journey begins in historic York. You'll drive across York County and into the quaint town of Columbia. Then it's down to bustling Strasburg for the Railroad Museum and then up to very rural Cornwall. You'll end this nostalgic sojourn at the Union Canal Tunnel just outside Lebanon.

Highlights: You'll see more industry in this journey than you ever thought possible—from farm equipment to a high-powered industrial complex, from mighty locomotives to the tiniest of timepieces that regulated the progress of this revolution. This will be an eye-opening experience as you visit some of the most distinctive museums in the state.

In the previous chapter, we visited the canals of eastern Pennsylvania, a most unusual museum, and a magnificent iron furnace that contributed mightily to the industrial transformation of eastern Pennsylvania and outdoor museum that captured all that industry at one site. In this chapter we'll continue our industrial journey and visit some equally important sites throughout the region.

We'll begin in the historic city of York (which I visit in greater detail in Chapter 13). Our first stop will be the **York County Heritage Trust's Agricultural and Industrial Museum**. This building, a former manufacturing plant, houses an array of tools, machines, implements, transportation, manufacturing, and industrial artifacts that transcend several decades (or centuries) of industrialization in Pennsylvania generally and York County specifically.

> **F**AST FACT: Even the earliest, and admittedly crude, McCormick reapers could do the work of five men.

Agricultural artifacts housed in the museum—those produced or used over three centuries include wagons, tractors, steam engines, and farm tools. Working industrial exhibits include a 72-ton A-frame ammonia compressor, once used to manufacture large blocks of ice and a three-story gristmill that was brought to the building by wagon. Exhibits on pottery, casket manufacturing, dental supplies, piano and organ manufacturing, as well as the county's industrial contribution to World War II are also featured. The exhibit, *Air, Land, & Water: Transporting People & Products,* housed in the transportation wing, includes York manufactured automobiles, an authentic Conestoga wagon, a horse and carriage, a trolley car (circa 1916), a couple of locomotives, a postman's wagon from 1898, and a 1937 Aeronca K airplane.

Here are some of the other displays:

- *Banking Artifacts:* Future safecrackers can try to access the "fortune" inside a 4-ton safe

- *Potato Farming:* This display showcases various potato farming implements, including a seed potato cutter, furrow plow, hiller, and potato plows.

- *Cigar Manufacture:* At the turn of the century, there were 500 cigar manufacturers in York. This exhibit demonstrates what a cigar manufacturing shop would have looked like in the early 20th century.

- *Automobiles: A*mong the vehicles on display is a Hart-Kraft light delivery truck—Model BXX—from 1911. There's also a Mayflower station wagon from 1906, a 1915 Sphinx Touring Car, and a 1922 Hanover Roadster.

- *Bicycles:* You'll get to see some of the bicycles of the 19th century, including the Victor High-Wheel bicycle from 1889.

This museum is full of all kinds of machines, technology, and exhibits that provide first-hand, hands-on opportunities to get a sense of where technology was 100 or 200 years ago and how far it has advanced since. You and your family can easily spend a most productive day wandering through the de-

> **F**AST FACT: A Conestoga Wagon could carry up to six tons, or 12,000 pounds, of freight.

A 19th-century mail wagon at the Agricultural and Industrial Museum

tailed exhibits and vibrant slices of the Industrial Revolution housed in this dramatic museum.

After departing the museum, direct your car over to US 30 east. Drive for approximately 15 miles until you cross the Susquehanna River. On the other side of the bridge, take the first exit on the right and head into the town of Columbia and the **National Watch and Clock Museum**.

Up until 1883 there was no such thing as time zones in America. Each city set its mechanical timepieces by where the sun was at high noon. That meant that people in cities only a few miles apart would have different times set on their watches and clocks. A businessperson going from Philadelphia to Harrisburg, for

The National Watch and Clock Museum in Columbia

example, would be traveling between two cities with two completely different ideas of what time nine o'clock was. Nine o'clock might mean just that in Philadelphia, yet at that same time, it might mean 8:44 in Harrisburg. Or could a passenger leaving Harrisburg on a train at three o'clock catch a connecting train to Washington, DC in Philadelphia at four o'clock Washington, DC time?

Confused? Then you definitely want to visit the next stop on our tour—**The National Watch and Clock Museum**. This is truly one of the most fascinating museums you'll ever see. Everything to do with time including timepieces, the history of time, how time was discovered, how time was used, and some of the mistakes we've made in gauging time are all on display. This is an incredible museum that will really put Chapters 9 and 10 in proper perspective.

You'll begin your journey in the **Ancient Timepieces** exhibit. Here sits one of the world's earliest clocks—an Egyptian clepsydra, or water clock. This is a timepiece that was first used around 1400 BC and relied on the flow of water to determine the passage of time. Here also are the first mechanical timekeepers, which were created in monasteries in the late 13th century. These gigantic clocks were often the official timepiece for an entire European village—although they could only indicate the approximate hour (not minutes) of the day.

Continue into the **Cabinetmaker's Workshop**, where you will witness the development of clockmaking in the United States—specifically in the later 18th century. Here you'll see some classic grandfather clocks as well as many exquisitely carved clocks that any antique dealer would die for. Also on display is an expansive collection of both European clocks as well as American clocks. The European varieties are noted for their elaborate woodcarvings, gold decorations, tortoise-shell trim, and exquisite design. American clocks, on the other hand, were more functional and considerably more practical.

For me, the most fascinating section of the museum is the **Railroad Station Office**. Here you will learn that up until the late 19th century this country did not have time zones—each town or region kept its own time. With the railroads spreading out across the country and more towns and cities becoming interconnected, there was a growing need for the standardization of equipment, train signals, ticketing procedures, and baggage handling, as well as the coordination of train signals.

The last item was the most complicated because of competing and contradictory times among cities in the same general region as well as those distant from one another. In short, everyone had his own time and seldom did two times match. Clocks and watches, often rudimentary and simplistic, were set by a sun dial or the position of the sun itself (the best reference point being high noon). Since there is a relationship between solar time and location as the earth rotates and the sun travels westward across the continent; in essence, high noon differs from point to point.

FAST FACT: As early as 4200 B.C., Egyptians noted that Sirius, the Dog Star, rose in the morning once a year directly in line with the sun. Counting the number of sunrises between these annual events they constructed a calendar with a year of 365 days. Our calendars of today can be traced to this fundamental idea.

FAST FACT: November 18, 1883, is known as "The Day of Two Noons." On that day, many communities observed their own noon, changed their clocks and watches to the newly implemented Standard Time, and then observed a second (now official) noon.

As the railroads brought the west closer to the east, confusion over what time it really was also expanded westward. While the concept of local time worked well when communities were fairly isolated, it became highly impractical as the railroad and the telegraph brought those isolated places closer and closer together. A standard time seemed to be the answer.

Standard time…that's a pretty radical thought. It's hard for us to believe today, but there was considerable opposition to the idea of a standard time, not just by the general public, but also by a corps of scientists, politicians, and industrialists. Many people believed that "natural time" or time told by the sun (and not dictated by railroad people) was the more normal course of action.

However, by the 1850s a number of railroads began subscribing to the time services offered by several American observatories—paying to have accurate astronomical time signals telegraphed to each station along their individual lines. Although this was a somewhat haphazard system, it did began to create a system (imperfect to be sure) of standardized time by the mid-1870s.

As a result, several scientific and professional societies devoted much thought to the concept of standard time. Plans were drafted, arguments were made, and eventually a system of time zones was proposed. However, it was not the government or a scientific organization that eventually settled on the time zone concept, but rather a group of railroad superintendents.

In October 1883 the General Time Convention approved a plan establishing five North American time zones—four in the U.S. and a fifth covering the easternmost provinces of Canada. A month later, standard railway time was put into effect. While many communities accepted the change as a sign of progress, others thought it unnatural and refused to use it. However, it did slowly gain acceptance and by the time Standard Time became the law of the land in 1918 most communities had already adopted it.

As you continue through the museum you'll come to the **Watchmaking Factory** where you'll learn the story of how watches became more accurate (railroad companies set the standards for watches carried by conductors) and how late 19th-century watches were periodically tested by certified watchmakers to ensure their reliability. In short order you'll slide over to a section on **Monumental Clocks,** which were more entertainment (pre-Nintendo) than timekeepers. You'll also see a unique collection of novelty clocks down through the ages.

Contrast the ancient water clocks of the Egyptians with today's timepieces that are controlled by the vibration of atoms and you will quickly see how the measurement of time has changed dramatically over the years. Just as important, this museum will provide you with a window into the influence and impact of time on everyday life and why we have become so fascinated by it and so dependent upon it. Time's influence on the Industrial Revolution in Pennsylvania

A true-to-life display at The National Watch and Clock Museum

and elsewhere is not to be dismissed lightly—it was critical in our rush into 21st-century technology—a fact that becomes more clear with each exhibit in this delightful museum.

One of the things you'll see here is an assortment of timepieces from throughout American history. You'll learn how watches, clocks, and other timepieces were constructed, how they became more simplified and smaller—large town clocks eventually evolving into the wristwatches we so commonly wear today. You will look at your wristwatch just a little differently after your visit.

From the Watch and Clock Museum, return to US 30 east. Drive for about 15.8 miles until you come to PA 896. Make a right turn on PA 896 and drive for 3.3 miles to PA 741. Make a left and drive for .3 mile. **The Railroad Museum of Pennsylvania** will be on your right.

That the railroads had a significant impact on the settlement of the American West is one of those facts that appears in every history textbook. But the impact

The Pennsylvania Railroad Museum

of railroads was much more than a simple linking of east and west coasts. Rail also transported manufactured goods from one part of the country to the other. In short, railroads expanded commerce exponentially, particularly in the 1800s.

While we don't know what railroad was the first in the country, we do know that there were several steam-powered locomotives that were chugging across select regions of the country by the 1830s. Merchants quickly saw the advantage of getting their goods from point A to point B quickly, efficiently, and in considerable quantities. As a result, the construction of rail lines expanded ten-fold. In the 20 years between 1840 and 1860, the United States went from 3,326 miles of railroad tracks to 30,600 miles. The more rail lines, the more goods could be shipped efficiently and priced lower. Unfortunately, the more people began to rely on railroads the less they began to rely on other forms of transportation such as horse and wagon and the canal systems in place throughout the east.

The burgeoning rail lines were owned by individual companies—hundreds of different enterprises—resulting in a complex web of different gauges for their tracks and little coordination of schedules (remember, time zones had not been "invented" yet). Getting a shipment of wheat, for example, across the country might mean using a dozen different rail lines, each with its own schedule and regulations.

It was the completion of the Transcontinental Railroad in 1869 that began to change all that. Finally railroad people began to see the need to standardize their tracks and standardize their schedules. And although this standardization took nearly 50 years to complete, it underscored the power of the Industrial Revolution for an entire country.

By 1920 there were more than 250,000 miles of railroad track in the country. A trip that may have taken several weeks in the past could now be completed in days. Goods and people could move almost anywhere in the country—almost everybody was linked. The railroads underscored and advanced American technology exponentially.

The Railroad Museum of Pennsylvania highlights the effect of railroads on the Industrial Revolution. Here you'll experience the power of trains as vehicles able to transport goods as well as ideas. The museum has more than 100 historic locomotives and vintage railcars preserved in its collection. Even a casual stroll through this enormous building will be sufficient for you to climb aboard these historical icons, don an engineer's hat, and sit in the cab of a 100-year old vehicle for a ride into the past. You'll feel as I did—dwarfed by the enormity of these transportation behemoths and awed by their complexity. You'll see classic wood-burners, massive steam and diesel engines, and electric-powered trains.

The museum also showcases railroad art, an interactive education center, and railroad artifacts. If you have the kids along they'll want to clamber aboard many of these classic vehicles (souvenir engineer hats are available in the Whistle Stop Shop). Also, if you have kids along you will probably discover that, like me, they may have an extreme reluctance to depart this iconic building and its equally iconic treasures.

Across the street from the museum is the famous **Strasburg Railroad** where you can climb aboard a working steam-powered railroad car for an incredible journey back in time. But it is the Railroad Museum that will put a significant punctuation point on the value of rail travel and transport in the 1800s and its in-fluence in powering a significant portion of the American Industrial Revolution.

When you leave the Railroad Museum, head west on PA 741. In the center of

"All Aboard!"

The Cornwell Iron Furnace in Lebanon County

Strasburg make a right turn back onto PA 896. Continue for 2.5 miles until you get to US 30. Make a left turn onto US 30 west and travel for about 8 miles. Make a slight left onto PA 283 and then exit onto PA 741 west. After about 1.5 miles, make a left onto PA 72. Drive for about 13.2 miles and turn onto PA 117 toward Mt. Gretna. Turn right onto Ironmaster Road, a left onto Burd Coleman Road and the first right onto Rexmont Road. In about .5 mile, the **Cornwall Iron Furnace** will appear on your right.

In the 18th and 19th centuries there were many iron furnaces across the Pennsylvania frontier. These furnaces were much more than factories for the production of iron—they evolved into vibrant communities that provided for the

> **F**AST FACT: At the height of the Industrial Revolution, Pennsylvania smelted one-seventh of the world's iron.

needs of workers and their families. Cornwell Furnace was no different—it was a self-sufficient working community (of about 10,000 acres) that was blessed with several natural resources: iron ore, limestone and wood for charcoal. This unique furnace is a testament to the once-thriving iron industry that helped to establish Pennsylvania as a major force during the Industrial Revolution.

Cornwell Iron Furnace came into being in 1742 when Peter Grubb established the site. He gave it the name Cornwell in honor of his father's birthplace in England. It quickly grew into a major industrial and residential site and joined other iron furnaces in helping make Pennsylvania a major producer of the world's iron.

When Peter Grubb passed away in 1754, his sons Curtiss and Peter inherited the property. They eventually sold the furnace to businessman Robert Coleman. Coleman obviously had a knack for iron smelting as he rose to become one of Pennsylvania's first millionaires. The Coleman family was able to maintain the operation of the furnace until 1883. It was about that time that newer and more efficient productions were in operation—making the Cornwall furnace virtually obsolete. The property was eventually donated by the great granddaughter of Robert Coleman, Margaret Buckingham, to the state of Pennsylvania in 1932. It has since been turned into a most informative tourist attraction—one that maintains the integrity of the past and underscores the vitality of this once-thriving industry.

Begin your tour at the **visitors center**, which is housed in the 19th-century charcoal barn. Besides the usual displays, books, and other knickknacks emblematic of many gift shops, there is a well-produced film that should be seen before you start your guided tour. The film provides a good overview of the iron industry with particular attention to the life and times in and around Cornwall Iron Furnace.

Your first stop on the tour is the

> **F**AST FACT: There were two shifts for the workers at Cornwall Iron Furnace: 6 AM to 6 PM and 6 PM to 6 AM. In other words, 12 hours on and 12 hours off.

A coal wagon used at The Cornwell Iron Furnace

Furnace Building. As you enter you'll notice several old wagons—each of which was used to haul iron ore to the furnace. This building was initially constructed in the mid-1800s during an expansion and remodeling process. It was here that charcoal, iron ore, and limestone were introduced into the furnace in the charging room on the upper level. Below is the blasting equipment, which provided air for the furnace (when the furnace was operating, one could hear its roar from as far away as 1 mile). Also on the bottom floor is the casting room where molten iron was cast into pig iron or other cast iron products.

Outside you can walk along the road that leads into the parking area. Here you will discover two unique structures. The first will be the **Roasting Oven**, where layers of iron ore and charcoal were placed in alternating layers. This arrangement allowed for the upward passage of air and eventually the elimination of sulfur from the ore. Sulfur would have a negative effect on the smelting process and was removed in order for the operation to continue smoothly.

The second structure is the **Coal Bins**. It was here that anthracite coal, used

F AST FACT: One acre of trees provided one day's supply of fuel (after it was turned into charcoal) for the furnace.

primarily to heat the homes of company workers as well as the ironmaster's mansion, was stored. The furnaces were not powered by this coal; rather, they relied entirely on charcoal fuel.

There are a few buildings not open to the public. These include the blacksmith shop, the wagon shop and the *abattoir* (smokehouse and butcher shop). However, you will definitely want to walk across Rexmont Road to see two other structures. The first is the **Paymaster's Office**. Although it wasn't built until 1875, this small building served as an important structure in the total operation of the Cornwall Iron Company.

Stroll down the road beside the Paymaster's Office until you come to the **Ironmaster's Mansion**. This is truly an example of how profitable the iron industry was—the opulence and architecture of this place will dazzle you (unfortunately, you won't be able to enter the building—it's now a private residence). Considering that this home was originally built in 1773 by Curtiss and Peter Grubb, it is a testament to what wealth can buy. The home was remodeled in 1865 by the Coleman family and today stands as a significant historical treasure.

As the final stop on this tour, we're going to travel a little north and a little west to visit one of the most picturesque and amazing canal sites in the state. After departing Cornwall Furnace, make your way back to PA 72 north. Make a right turn and drive north for about 6.5 miles (through the city of Lebanon). When you get to Maple Street, PA 72 makes a sharp left turn. Drive for 1.3 miles and when you arrive at the traffic signal make a slight left onto Tunnel Hill Road. Drive for about .5 mile and there will be a small paved parking area on the left side of the road. Pull into the parking area and walk down the steep paved path.

You will arrive at a most unique structure—the **Union Canal Tunnel**. Completed in 1826, it was the second canal tunnel in the country and is today maintained by the Lebanon County Historical Society as the "oldest tunnel in the United States."

The Union Canal was the first canal route ever surveyed in the United States and was designed to connect the Schuylkill River at Reading with the Susquehanna River at Middletown (near Harrisburg). Interestingly, the route for the canal was initially conceived by William Penn in 1690. It wasn't until 1792 that

The Union Canal Tunnel – the oldest in the U.S.

work on the canal was initiated, however. Raising sufficient funds was a constant challenge for the companies digging the canal and slowdown after slowdown plagued the effort. Eventually the state of Pennsylvania stepped in with some financial assistance and the canal was finally completed between 1821 and 1828— creating a water link between Philadelphia and the Susquehanna River.

The Union Canal was four feet deep and 36 feet wide. It was an amazing feat of engineering for its time—in a distance of 81 miles between Reading and Middletown it climbed 311 feet to the summit level of the canal at Lebanon and descended a total of 192 feet to the level of the Susquehanna River at the west end. Along its length it employed a total of 93 lift locks—each measuring 75 feet long and 8.5 feet wide. The 102 locks of the Union Canal were too small and could not accommodate larger boats. Refitting and enlargement of the locks began in the 1850s. Floods, water problems, and the completion of the Lebanon Valley Railroad, however, forced the Union Canal to close in 1885.

The tunnel you are now visiting was cut through solid rock using nothing more than hand picks, shovels and the most rudimentary of blasting techniques. It cut through a watershed ridge on the summit of the highest point between Reading and Middletown. The barges were poled through the tunnel while the mules were walked over the ridge to join the boat at the other end.

As you walk down the hill note the remnants of the canal in front of you. By turning 180 degrees to your left, you will be able to see the canal as it slices through the hill. Keep in mind that this tunnel is nearly 200 years old and would still be fully functional today if we were still using canals to transport our goods. You can, however, take a narrated boat tour on the canal and through the tunnel for a nominal fee every Sunday afternoon throughout the summer.

This would be an excellent place to bring a picnic. After a long day of touring and viewing various industrial sites, dinner at the little park beside the water would be perfect way to discuss what you've seen and take in the gorgeous scenery that surrounds this dramatic structure.

Today the clip-clop of canal mules is but a distant memory, the calls of the locktender across the water but faint echoes, and the passage of barges over (and through) long stretches of the Pennsylvania landscape are but brief paragraphs in history textbooks. But, the canals of Pennsylvania offer visitors and residents alike nostalgic journeys into distant times and long-ago memories.

CONTACTS

York County Heritage Trust's Agricultural and Industrial Museum, 217 West Princess St., York, PA; (717) 846-6452; www.yorkheritage.org.

The National Watch and Clock Museum, 514 Poplar St., Columbia, PA 17512; (717) 684-8261; www.nawcc.org.

Railroad Museum of Pennsylvania, P.O. Box 125, 300 Gap Rd., Strasburg, PA 17579; (717) 687-8628; www.rrmuseumpa.org.

Cornwall Iron Furnace, 94 Rexmont Rd., Cornwall, PA 17016; (717) 272-9711; www.cornwallironfurnace.org.

Lebanon County Historical Society, 924 Cumberland St., Lebanon, PA 17042; (717) 272-1473; lebanoncountyhistoricalsociety.org/canal-tunnel/union -canal-tunnel-park.

Lancaster Central Market

11 Around Lancaster County

Estimated length: 1–1.5 miles (walk); 62 miles (drive)

Estimated time: 1–2 days

Combine this tour with: Chapters 3 and 12

Getting there: You'll begin the tour on the streets of Lancaster. From here, you'll return to your car (fully loaded with goodies purchased at the historic Central Market) and set out to visit a church, a plantation, a birthplace, a presidential estate, and a colonial mansion. You'll log some miles, but also some memories.

Highlights: This walk and ride provides you with some of the most significant features of both Lancaster City and Lancaster County. The diversity of people, architecture, and history will all be evident in this journey. While there are hundreds of places you could visit in the county, this trip offers a selection of some of the most intriguing and delightful sites.

According to the Pennsylvania State Tourism Office, approximately 11 million visitors come to Lancaster County each year, and the county's total tourism economy is nearly $1.8 billion. As a result, travel and tourism is Lancaster County's second-largest industry, employing—directly and indirectly—more than 22,000 people. (Agriculture is first.)

What does this mean? Quite simply, it means that Lancaster County is a popular and fun place to visit and that there is a plethora of offerings here. From history to the arts and from amusement parks to covered bridges, the area is diverse and eclectic, engaging and consuming.

Nowhere is this more evident than when looking at all the history that has taken place in and around the 949 square miles of this diverse county. Combine

FAST FACT: Lancaster County has almost the same number of people as the entire state of Wyoming.

the tour featured in this chapter with the Amish journey of Chapter 12, toss in a couple of industrial sites, canals, a U.S. president, and several Underground Railroad sites for good measure, and you will have a living textbook that will out-history any other county in the state or the country.

Originally the area we now know as Lancaster County was inhabited by a number of Native American tribes including the Shawnee, Lenape (or Delaware), Gawanese, and Nanticoke peoples. Some of the earliest recorded inhabitants were the Susquehannocks, whose name meant "people of the muddy river" in Algonquin. They were also known by a more familiar name—the Conestoga, from their principal village, *Kanestoge*.

Lancaster County got its start back in 1681 when it was part of William Penn's original charter. The first recorded deed for a parcel of land in the county was issued in 1691 to one John Kennerly, although there seems to be evidence that people did not officially settle in the region until about 1710.

Lancaster County was originally part of Chester County—one of the original Pennsylvania counties. Then in May 1729, Lancaster County broke away and became its own entity. It was named after the city of Lancaster in the county of Lancashire in England. Interestingly, six other Pennsylvania counties were eventually carved from the expanse of land then known as Lancaster County.

The fertile farmlands of Lancaster County attracted many immigrants and settlers from overseas. These included families from Wales, England, Ireland, Germany, and other northern European countries. Lancaster County was also known as a haven for religious freedom and several religious sects found land and tolerance to be in abundance here. Mennonites, Moravians, the United Brethren in

FAST FACT: The Conestoga wagon, the famous broad-wheeled covered wagon of westward-bound travelers in the 18th and 19th centuries, was named after Conestoga Township in Lancaster County. The Conestoga wagon also started the American practice of driving on the right side of the road.

There's plenty going on at the Lancaster Central Market.

Christ, Methodists, Jews, and the Evangelical United Brethren all established firm roots in the county—primarily in the mid- to late 1700s.

If you live in Lancaster and want to meet someone for lunch, a social occasion, or just for fun, you would probably say, "Meet me at market." For decades, Lancasterians have used those four words to identify perhaps the most venerable institution in town—the **Lancaster Central Market**. People meet for a cup of coffee and a donut in the morning, a sausage sandwich and bowl of soup for lunch; they meet there for business appointments or just to "chew the fat," and they even meet there to purchase produce, meats, and other items for the family larder. To say that Central Market is an institution in this town is understating

The Yeates House, an example of 18th-century architecture

the obvious. It has been in this same place since 1730 and for more than 275 years it has been the place to meet and the place to buy.

Walk through the market and you'll feel like you've been transported to a European bazaar. Stands and booths overflow with an eclectic array of foods that will tantalize any palate and please any chef. Here you can discover meats, poultry, seafood, fruits, vegetables, candy, flowers, dairy products, bulk foods, baskets, household items bread, salads, homemade horseradish, Middle Eastern food, Greek food, German food, fresh ground coffee, bakery items, and organic products galore.

Our tour starts at the Central Market, but first you'll need a place to park. Two suggestions—the first is a small parking lot on West King Street right next to Central Market (keep in mind that King Street is one way—from west to east). The other is the super-sized Prince Street Garage at the corner of Prince Street and Orange Street. You'll always find a space here and it's only a half-block walk to Central Market.

After you've visited Central Market, walk east toward Penn Square. Make a right turn on South Queen Street and walk down to 24-26 South Queen Street. Here you'll see the **Yeates House** (now the Literacy Council of Lancaster-Lebanon Counties). This particular home was constructed in about 1765. Its owner, Jasper Yeates, was a delegate to the U.S. Constitutional Convention in 1787 and also served as a U.S. Supreme Court justice.

Cross the street and walk back up Queen Street to Penn Square and enter the **Marriott Hotel**. Proceed down the stairway or escalator and into the Lancaster County Convention Center. Near the back you'll come up to a bowed exterior wall directly across from Freedom Hall. This wall was once the rear wall of the **William Montgomery Mansion** constructed in 1804. Montgomery was a well-known lawyer in the early 1800s. Continue down the stairs and you'll come across buildings that are now part of the Convention Center. These buildings were once owned by Thaddeus Stevens—a prominent abolitionist, lawyer, and congressman who had a major influence on the passage of the 13th and 14th Amendments to the U.S. Constitution (He was also featured in the 2012 film, *Lincoln*—played by actor Tommy Lee Jones.). The one building on the corner was the **Kleiss Saloon**—a popular hangout in its day. Immediately next to it was **Stevens' house and law office**. Look carefully past the barricades and windows and you will note two cisterns, along with several artifacts discovered in them. There is considerable evidence to prove that these cisterns were used to hide runaway slaves along the Underground Railroad. When I visited, these sites were still being developed as part of an Underground Railroad museum.

Also part of this site is the **Lydia Hamilton Smith House**. Smith was a housekeeper who worked for Thaddeus Stevens. She kept his house and managed his business affairs. It is also suspected that she, too, was a conductor for the Underground Railroad—assisting Stevens in helping slaves seeking safe passage northward.

Walk back through the convention center and lobby of the Marriott. Exit the building, make a left turn, and stroll back down South Queen Street. Make a left turn on West Vine Street and head east on Vine. When you get to South Duke Street make a right turn and begin to wander. You are now in a part of Lancaster known as Old Town. Here are an amazing variety of homes dating from the mid-1700s into the early 1900s. Many of these classic homes are part of the City of Lancaster Historic District and scattered among tree-lined streets and brick sidewalks. You will see a wide variety of architectural styles representing almost two centuries of urban living. These private residences were scheduled for demolition in the 1970s, but through the efforts of many citizens were saved from the wrecker's ball.

After leaving Old Town walk north on South Duke Street. In half a block you'll come up to the **Evangelical Lutheran Church of the Holy Trinity** on your right. The congregation for this church was originally organized in 1730, although the church wasn't constructed until 1767. This particular church is the only one

FAST FACT: The weathervane topping the steeple on Evangelical Lutheran Church of the Holy Trinity incorporated the first commercial use of ball bearings in the United States.

in the city that has survived from colonial times. You can enter the church through the doors on Mifflin Street. When you do, note the façade of the organ on the balcony. This was the case of the original organ installed in 1774. You'll also note the stained glass window (*The Crucifixion*), which was created in 1913 by Louis Comfort Tiffany.

As you come up to the corner of King and Duke streets, look to your left and you will see the imposing **County Courthouse** on the northwest corner. It was originally built from 1852 to 1854.

Make a right onto East King Street. Immediately look for two residences (110 and 112). Note that these two homes were originally constructed in the early 1760s. Continue a short distance down King Street, and you'll come to one of the classic businesses in Lancaster—the **Demuth Tobacco Shop** (114 East King Street). This particular enterprise has been selling tobacco products since long before warnings were posted on some of those items. This shop has been in operation since 1770 and is the oldest operating tobacconist in America.

Make a U-turn on King Street and return to Duke Street. Make a right turn and head north on Duke. On the right-hand side of Duke (and across from the courthouse) you'll notice an array of law offices. Many of them are former colonial dwellings that have been put to quite another use. Pay particular attention to the **Muhlenberg House** (33 N. Duke Street). This particular building was a parsonage for Reverend Gotthilf Heinrich Ernst Muhlenberg, who was the pastor for Trinity Lutheran Church from 1780 to 1815.

Continue your walk up Duke Street. On the northeast corner of Duke and Orange Streets you'll see **St. James Episcopal Church**—a building erected in the 1820s. The church was originally founded in 1744 as the Anglican Church (Church of England). Before the onset of the American Revolution the rector of the church was Thomas Barton. Reverend Barton was a loyal subject of the King of England as well as of the church. Although there were many American patriots in his congregation, he could not openly condone their actions. So, he closed up the church and conducted church services in a secret location. Take a walk through the church cemetery and you will see the grave markers of a number of notable Lan-

The Muhlenberg House on Lawyer's Row

castrians. These include Edward Hand, surgeon to George Washington; Edward Shippen, father-in-law of Benedict Arnold; Robert Coleman, a delegate to the 1787 Constitutional Convention; and his daughter Ann Coleman, the one-time fiancée of President James Buchanan.

Make a right on Orange Street and head east. On the northwest corner of Orange and Lime Streets is the **Shippen House** (now the YMCA). Edward Shippen was a lawyer and a judge and lived in this house from 1751 to 1781. Shippen was

FAST FACT: Lancaster City was the nation's capital for one day, September 27, 1777, when the Continental Congress held a session at the courthouse. The city also served as the capital of Pennsylvania from 1799 to 1812.

the father of Margaret Shippen Arnold, the second wife of Benedict Arnold. The homes described below can all be found on East Orange Street.

Continue your walk to the **home of Dr. Thomas Bond** (#207). This home was constructed around 1780. Dr. Bond and Benjamin Franklin were instrumental in establishing the Pennsylvania Hospital.

The **Christopher Marshall Home** (#215) housed Marshall and his family from 1777 to 1797. Marshall moved here from Philadelphia specifically to avoid being captured by British armies roaming the City of Brotherly Love.

The **Timothy Matlock Home** (#222) housed the Matlock family from 1799 to 1812. Matlock was the clerk to the Continental Congress in 1776. It was he who penned the original copy of the *Declaration of Independence* that was signed by the members of Congress, now in the National Archives. He also penned several other federal documents and decrees, including George Washington's 1775 commission as commander-in-chief.

The **Baker-Stauffer House** (#235) was built around 1830 for noted coach maker John Baker. After it was purchased by David McNeely Stauffer in 1882 it was substantially enlarged.

The **Passmore House** (#247) was constructed sometime prior to 1760. It was the home of Lancaster's first mayor. Look closely and you'll notice an oversized front door. That's because His Honor was an oversized individual—by more than 400 pounds.

The **Andrew Jackson Steinman Mansion** (#301) sits at the corner of Orange and Shippen Streets. It was constructed in 1882 for newspaper magnate Andrew Jackson Steinman. One can only imagine that Mr. Steinman's ego was as large as his house.

From here, make a U-turn and return along Orange Street. Continue walking past Duke Street and then past Queen Street. At this point you will need to make a decision—do you want to return to your car right away or see one more structure? If the latter, then continue walking west on Orange Street until you come to

North Prince Street (if not, then turn left onto Market Street and back to Central Market). Make a right turn on North Prince and walk past the entrance for the Prince Street Garage. Shortly after you will see the **Sehner-Ellicott-von Hess House** (123 North Prince Street). This building (now the Historic Preservation Trust) was originally built about 1767. In 1800 it was the home of Andrew Ellicott, an engineer and surveyor. Ellicott was commissioned by President Thomas Jefferson to train Meriwether Lewis before he and William Clark set out on their exploration of the recently obtained Louisiana Purchase. This building also has a small museum open to the public.

After viewing the Sehner-Ellicott-von Hess House, make a U-turn and head south on Prince Street. When you come to Orange Street make a left turn and walk for about half a block. Turn right onto Market Street and soon you will be back at Central Market. Retrieve your car and you're off to some additional Lancaster County adventures.

Drive south on PA 222 (South Prince Street). Make a left on South Andrew Street and continue until you come to a five-way intersection (Andrew Street, East Strawberry, North Street and Cemetery Avenue). Look for **Bethel African Methodist Episcopal Church** (450 to 512 East Strawberry). This church was originally founded in 1817 and the present building dates from 1879. This church served as an important station on the Underground Railroad for many years. For the first 50 years of its existence, members assisted slaves escaping to the north. Several African Methodist Episcopal preachers and Bethel pastors including the Reverend Joshua P. B. Eddy, the Reverend Thomas Henry and the Reverend Robert Boston, among others, were connected to the Underground Railroad and the abolitionist movement. The church was a critical center of spiritualism and social activity for the many free African-Americans who lived in and around the city of Lancaster. Each year the church conducts the Living the Experience re-enactment—"an interactive spiritual journey to the times of the Underground Railroad."

Return to PA 222 and head south. Make a left turn on Seymour Street, drive for a short distance and then make a left on PA 222 north. After a short distance, make a right onto Chesapeake Street, follow it for about one mile and then make a right onto East Strawberry Street. Look for the sign indicating the **Rock Ford Plantation**.

Standing on the wooded banks of the Conestoga River, this Georgian-style

FAST FACT: Edward Hand also served as a presidential elector, the chief burgess of Lancaster, a delegate to the convention for the 1790 Pennsylvania Constitution and a member of the Pennsylvania Assembly.

brick mansion is a remarkably preserved remnant of 18th-century living. It was the colonial estate of Edward Hand, who rose to become Adjutant General to George Washington in 1781.

Hand was originally an Irishman and, following medical training at Trinity College in Dublin, was sent to garrison at Fort Pitt (site of present-day Pittsburgh). He resigned from British service in 1774 and eventually arrived in Lancaster to practice medicine. However, history had other plans for him.

In July 1775 Hand joined the Continental Army as Lieutenant Colonel of the First Battalion of Pennsylvania Riflemen. He led troops at Boston, Long Island, White Plains, and Trenton before being selected by General Washington as his Adjutant General. After the war, Hand returned to Lancaster County and built Rock Ford in 1794. He began a life in politics, eventually serving in the U.S. House of Representatives. He continued to live at Rock Ford until his death in 1802.

Rock Ford is an excellent example of refined country living, particularly during the 18th century. The four floors of this house remain exactly as they were when Hand and his family lived here more than two centuries ago. As you walk through the house (all tours are self-guided), you will notice the meticulously furnished rooms with period antiques and original artifacts belonging to the Hand family. Pay particular attention to the original rails, shutters, doors, cupboards, paneling and windowpanes.

Your visit will include a walk down the grand hallway or entryway with the wall display of General Hand's original military epaulets and his certificate of membership in the Order of Cincinnati, signed by George Washington. Walk into the blue parlor and notice the game table, the covered sweetmeats jar and the beautiful tall-case clock—all originals. Next tour the gold parlor and dining room, where a portrait of George Washington hangs over the fireplace. The study, adjacent to the blue parlor, was likely used as a plantation office.

Go up the staircase to the second floor and you'll be able to view the girl's bedchamber with its rope beds and mattress sacks, as well as the boy's bedchamber and its collection of toys and games. Stroll over to the master bed-

Rock Ford Plantation (circa 1794)

chamber and notice the size of the bed. Try to imagine how in the world six-foot, four-inch Edward Hand was able to sleep in this bed (you'll learn how when you visit). You may want to peek into the "necessary" to see what a late 18-century bathroom looked like.

Complete your tour in the basement where the kitchen was located. Note the original fireplace, mantel and crane, as well as the various utensils and implements used for food preparation.

This is a most delightful place and worth a visit on any tour of Lancaster County. You'll enjoy the rustic grounds as well as a lovingly restored home that breaths new life into the lives and times of those who lived here.

After departing Rock Ford direct your car over to US 222. Drive south until you come to the town of Willow Street. Just north of town, US 222 changes over to PA 272. Stay on US 222 (it diverges sharply to the left at a traffic signal) and continue south. You are headed through the towns of New Providence and Quarryville to the **Robert Fulton Birthplace**, which is located just before US 222 intersects again with PA 272 in southern Lancaster County. The driving distance from Rock Ford to Fulton's birthplace is about 20.1 miles and will take about 30 minutes.

Robert Fulton is probably best remembered for having built the steamboat *Clermont*, which in 1807 successfully navigated the Hudson River. He was born in this tiny stone house, not far from the Maryland border, on November 14, 1765. As Fulton grew up he displayed a natural artistic talent—drawing political caricatures and painting tavern signs. He also designed firearms and built a unique double crank paddle-wheel boat, which he used on the Conestoga Creek.

As his artistic talents grew, he moved to Philadelphia, where he was known for his mechanical drawings and miniature portraits. He later sailed for England where he continued his artistic studies. It was there that he met the scientist James Watt, who had developed the steam engine.

It was during this time that Fulton's interests shifted from matters artistic to matters mechanical. He experimented with torpedo and submarine-type boats, among other interests. After 20 years in Europe, he returned to the United States, created a torpedo that blew up a boat in New York Harbor, and built his famous vessel, *The North River*, later renamed *The Clermont*. This was the ship that eventually demonstrated the future of steam power in this country by successfully sailing up the Hudson River. Robert Fulton died on February 24, 1815, at the age of 49.

After the Fultons moved to Lancaster, the house in which Robert Fulton was born and lived in as a child was owned and occupied by several generations of the Swift family. The Swifts maintained the house and surrounding buildings, including a store, post office, and tobacco and grain warehouses. In 1965 the prop-

FAST FACT: Although Fulton is credited with several inventions during his lifetime, history has forgotten that he was also one of the most accomplished artists of his time. His miniature portraits are considered to be some of the finest ever produced in this country.

The Robert Fulton Birthplace, near Quarryville

erty was turned over to the state, and the Pennsylvania Historical and Museum Commission has faithfully returned the house and grounds to its appearance when Fulton lived there.

You'll be able to see what life was like in the mid-1700s as authentic reproduction furnishings have been returned to this rustic dwelling. The home looks much the way it did when Fulton was a child—the simplicity of the furnishings are testament to the simplicity of life in 18th-century Lancaster County. Among other things, you'll be able to view an exhibit that faithfully presents the life and accomplishments of Robert Fulton (including a scale model of *The Clermont*). Be aware, however, that this historical treasure has limited weekend viewing hours during the summer months only.

After departing the Robert Fulton Birthplace, turn right out of the driveway and continue heading south on US 222. You will quickly come to the intersection with PA 272. Make another right turn and head north on PA 272. Continue up PA 272 until you get back to the city of Lancaster. Drive through Penn Square and make a left turn onto Orange Street. Travel on Orange Street until you come to its intersection with PA 23 (also known as Marietta Avenue). Turn right and proceed for about .7 mile until you arrive at **James Buchanan's Wheatland** on the left side of the road. The driving distance from the Robert Fulton Birthplace to Wheatland is about 23.1 miles and will take approximately 35 minutes of driving time.

The home of our country's 15th president is spectacular and gracious. History, however, has not been kind to James Buchanan. Whenever historians put together a list of U.S. presidents from greatest to worst, Mr. Buchanan almost always occupies the bottom of those lists. His inability to impose peace between two sharply divided sections of the country in the years before the Civil War has cast him as one of our country's most ineffectual leaders. The fact that he was often referred to as a "doughface"—a Northerner with Southern sympathies—did not endear him to many people. His vain attempts to maintain peace between North and South alienated both sides. It was during his presidency that several southern states, in a prologue to the Civil War, declared their independence and succeeded from the Union. That he was eventually overshadowed by the towering figure of Abraham Lincoln did little to add any luster to his presidency and he quickly passed into the shadows of historical obscurity.

> **F**AST FACT: James Buchanan was our country's only bachelor president.

But let's not dwell on incompetent presidents, or the only president from Pennsylvania. Let's look at his house.

In the early 1800s a house was constructed on a parcel of land just outside the city of Lancaster. Known as the Wheatlands (perhaps because of its proximity to a wheatfield), it was eventually purchased by one William Meredith in 1845. Meredith sold the house and property to James Buchanan in December 1848 and Buchanan moved into the mansion several months later. After the 1852 election, Buchanan was appointed by President Franklin Pierce as Minister to Great Britain. Buchanan did not return to Wheatland until 1856.

Shortly after his return, Buchanan was nominated by the Democratic Party to be its candidate for president. Unlike presidential candidates of today, Buchanan decided not to campaign across the country; instead he conducted a "front porch campaign"—doing much of his campaigning from Wheatland. One of the most unusual campaign tactics Buchanan used was to print and circulate lithographs of Wheatland, principally in southern states, "as a polite way of informing southerners that the Democratic candidate, though from the North, had a 'plantation estate' and held a course of life similar to their own."

Not surprisingly, Buchanan carried all the Southern states.

While he was president, Buchanan returned to Wheatland occasionally, but never for very long. When his term was over, he retired to his beloved mansion in 1861. He died in a room on the second floor on June 1, 1868. After a succession of owners, Wheatland, along with five acres of land was purchased by the James Buchanan Foundation for the Preservation of Wheatland in 1935. It was designated a National Historic Landmark in 1961 and listed on the National Register of Historic Places in 1966.

President James Buchanan's Wheatland

Tours of this Federal-style house are available throughout the year. The interior of the house boasts furniture original to the time Buchanan lived here. Mid-19th century decorations bring an additional sense of authenticity. The only modern additions to the house are the heating and lighting systems; everything else is just as it was in the 1800s.

Your tour of the house will include the parlor, the library, two dining rooms, and kitchen. The dining room in the western wing was used for informal meals like breakfast and afternoon tea. The other dining room was reserved for more formal occasions such as state dinners.

Off the hallway in the east wing is the library where Buchanan wrote his inaugural address and presidential memoirs. The second floor is accessed via an elliptical stairway. Embedded in the newel post at the base of the stairs is a glass "peace stone" placed there after the mortgage was finally paid off. All of the living quarters are also on the second floor.

The house is complimented by exquisite gardens, a carriage house, ice house, frog pond, and privy. During my visit, leaves were dropping from the trees surrounding the house, adding a golden luster to this architectural gem.

Return to your car and turn left back onto PA 23 west. Head northwest for approximately 12 miles. As you cross over PA 441, the road changes its name to East Market Street. You are now in the old-time river town of **Marietta**, where more than half of the town has been designated as a National Historic District. This former industrial town, hanging on the edge of Lancaster County and clinging to the banks of the Susquehanna River, once entertained a president (Ulysses S. Grant) and numerous statesmen. Drawn directly from the late 19th century, it was once the center of the lumber and iron industries with a healthy dose of saloons and boarding houses to prove it.

Marietta began in the early 1700s as a trading outpost on the American frontier. James Anderson, who operated a river-crossing site here originally named it Anderson's Ferry. However, it was Scotch-Irish immigrants who saw the strategic location of this settlement and brought together four separate settlements in the area to create Marietta, which was officially chartered in 1812. As you wander through the town you will immediately be struck by its elongated configuration—testament to the significance of the river in its overall economic development. Business and commercial enterprises sprang up, often overnight, along this stretch of river—accelerating its growth and development.

The Railroad House B&B and Restaurant in Marietta

During the early 1800s Marietta was a processing center for timber floated down the Susquehanna River from the center of the state. Look at the homes lining Market, Biddle, Front, and Waterford Streets and you'll see an abundance of wood-framed and wood-sided houses in contrast to the many brick and stone houses throughout much of Lancaster County. With the advent of the Pennsylvania Canal between 1825 and 1830 more businesses and entrepreneurs established themselves in the area to take advantage of the increased water traffic as well as people traffic.

In the late 1800s, iron was king in Marietta. At one time there were at least eight separate iron furnaces east of Marietta. With all the wealth generated from

FAST FACT: The Marietta Historic District—a collection of 373 buildings in the business district and residential areas of town—is listed on the National Register of Historic Places.

both the lumber and iron industries, it wasn't long before opulent mansions began to spring up throughout the town. Several of those grand homes are still standing as a paean to the business people who saw this town as a viable commercial center beside the Susquehanna. As the lumber and iron industries began to wane around the turn of the century, however, the economic energy that drove this town began to dissipate. It is now a river dowager—but one that still retains its classic lines, its 19th-century charm and a unique personality that continues to draw visitors.

Drive around this classic town and if you don't get discombobulated by its strange configuration, you will discover an array of classic buildings and homes—all without the flash of neon lights or endless lines of strip malls. This is a piece of the past well-preserved and waiting for your discovery. As you roam around town you might want to look out for the following distinctive buildings:

The Railroad House B&B and Restaurant (280 West Front Street)—the building was once a former ticket office for the Pennsylvania Standard and was constructed between 1820 and 1823. It also served as a restaurant for travelers on the river or canal.

Old Town Hall Museum (corner of Waterford Avenue and Walnut Street)—This building, since its construction in 1847, has served many uses including town hall, public school, jail, and lodge headquarters.

Shank's Tavern (36 South Waterford Avenue)—Built in 1814, this is Lancaster County's oldest continuously operated tavern. It was originally operated by retired riverboat captain James Stackhouse.

B. F. Hiestand House B&B (722 East Market Street)—This home was originally owned by one of the town's 19th-century lumber barons.

For a good glimpse of the town, you may wish to park your car near the river and stroll along Front Street (which is actually East Front Street, West Front Street, and South Perry Street—all depending on where you are along the road). Glance at the buildings and the eclectic styles and architecture they represent. Look at the river and imagine this place as a once-bustling river town filled with music and laughter and lots of commercial energy in a now bygone era.

Wright's Ferry Mansion, in Columbia

When you are ready to leave, drive through the middle of town until you get to East Market Street. Head south until you arrive at the intersection with PA 441. Make a slight right hand turn and proceed south to the town of Columbia. You'll be following a portion of the Susquehanna River as you head toward another river town.

Continue into Columbia (PA 441 becomes North Third Street). Make a right turn on Locust Street and then a left turn on South Second Street. Just after I Av-

> **F**AST FACT: Benjamin Franklin was a guest of Susanna Wright in this house in April 1755, while on a mission for the British Crown.

enue and before Cherry Street will be **Wright's Ferry Mansion** (38 South Second Street) on your right.

Columbia was originally settled in 1726 and known as Wright's Ferry, since the Wright family owned a ferry that crossed the Susquehanna River here (the site of that original ferry is on the eastern shore of the Susquehanna River directly beneath the bridge that connects Lancaster County with York County). Most of the early settlers were Quakers, and the mansion is a stately remnant of a privileged life in colonial Lancaster County in the early 18th century. Originally constructed in 1738 by Susanna Wright, the house reflects English Quaker elegance and simplicity. Known as "the bluestocking of the Susquehanna," Susanna Wright was versed in both law and medicine along with an extensive literary background. Her library contained the works of Milton, Swift, Pope, Racine, and other literary giants and she was fluent in Latin, Italian, and French. She was a confidant to Benjamin Franklin with whom she would share food products grown in the area, while Franklin would seek her advice on matters of the impending revolution.

Susanna was well-known as one of the earliest silk entrepreneurs in the country. She maintained 1,500 silkworms and was able to transform raw silk into some of the finest gowns and trappings of the day. The Queen of England wore one of Susanna's silk dresses at a birthday party for King George III. Susanna continued to maintain ties with her native country throughout her residence here.

The mansion has been faithfully restored and furnished with authentic trappings of the early 18th century. The furnishings are Queen Anne and Philadelphia William and Mary—a delightful blending of American and English styles. Windows without hangings and bare scrubbed floors, common in the time, help accentuate the decorations. A stroll through this home is like a stroll back through the early 1700s—as though you were a guest and had just been admitted into the house awaiting Susanna's arrival from upstairs.

This two-and-a-half story early Georgian-style limestone house is distinguished by a rich combination of artistic, academic, and cultural motifs that underscore Susanna's diverse interests. There is a superlative collection of Philadelphia furniture, English ceramics, needlework, metals, and glass, all produced prior to 1750. In 1979, the house was listed on the National Register of Historic Places.

CONTACTS:

Pennsylvania Dutch Convention & Visitors Bureau, 501 Greenfield Rd., Lancaster, PA 17601; (800) PA-DUTCH; www.padutchcountry.com/index.asp.

Lancaster Central Market, 23 North Market St., Lancaster, PA 17603; (717) 735-6890; www.centralmarketlancaster.com.

Bethel African Methodist Episcopal Church, 450-512 East Strawberry, Lancaster, PA 17602; (717) 393-8379; www.bethelamelancaster.org.

Rock Ford Plantation, 881 Rockford Rd., Lancaster, PA 17602; (717) 392-7223; www.rockfordplantation.org.

Robert Fulton Birthplace, 1932 Robert Fulton Highway, Quarryville, PA 17566; (717) 548-2679; www.padutchcountry.com/members/robert_fulton_birthplace.asp.

James Buchanan's Wheatland, 230 North President Ave., Lancaster, PA 17603; (717) 392-4633; www.lancasterhistory.org/index.

Wright's Ferry Mansion, 38 South Second St., Columbia, PA 17512; (717) 684-4325; www.padutchcountry.com/members/wright_s_ferry_mansion.asp.

The Amish way of life is simple and distinctive

12 An Amish Journey

Estimated Length: 50 miles

Estimated Time: 1 day

Combine this tour with: Chapter 11

Getting There: Beginning in downtown Lancaster, you'll drive toward the town of Willow Street. After Willow Street you'll head east toward Strasburg and then north to Bird-in-Hand, Paradise, and Intercourse. You'll follow portions of PA 340 and then take back roads past several Amish homesteads in a picture-postcard landscape.

Highlights: This drive will take you through bucolic farmland and country towns, as well as some of the commercialism that has crept into this part of the country. Look past all the glitz and you will see a lifestyle quite dissimilar from your own, but one that has endured in spite of neon signs, cell phones, and high-speed automobiles. This is a landscape that invites you to spend some time enjoying its vistas, rural independence, and unique way of life. Be respectful of the folks you meet along the way, and you will be rewarded with a most memorable tour.

Travel the roads of south-central and southeastern Pennsylvania and you will most likely come upon one of the most iconic symbols of the Pennsylvania landscape—the Amish horse and buggy with the state-required orange triangle on the back. You might peek inside that buggy and discover one or more individuals dressed in a very plain garb—the men with beards and straw hats, the women with black shoes and scarves. You may wonder how these "plain and simple" people can live in a world that shuns modern conveniences and embraces simple living.

F AST FACT: Lancaster County is home to the oldest Amish community in the United States.

The Amish are frequently admired and observed, but rarely understood. Their way of life and beliefs are in opposition to much of what we take for granted. The fact that they have been able to survive and prosper in modern times is testament to their beliefs as well as their longevity.

Sixteenth-century Europe was in a state of religious upheaval. New Christian orders were being advocated by men such as Martin Luther and Ulrich Zwingli. In the midst of these changes a group known as the Brethren formed a new fellowship known as the Anabaptists (or "rebaptizers"). They believed the church should be a group of voluntary adults, baptized upon confession of faith, and separated from the state and world. As a result of their beliefs, they suffered enormous persecution throughout Europe. Leaders and worshipers were put to death and worship was held in clandestine locations. This persecution led many Anabaptists to develop an attitude of withdrawal from the larger society.

In 1536, a Catholic priest from the Netherlands—Menno Simons—joined the movement. He was a prolific writer and it was through his extensive writings and moderate leadership that widely scattered Anabaptists were brought together. Although there were others leaders who rose during this time, the believers soon became known as "Mennonites."

What we now know is the Amish began back in 1693 with a schism in Switzerland that occurred among a group of Swiss and Alsatian Anabaptists. The divide was led by one Jacob Amman, and those who followed him soon became known as Amish. It was their basic belief that the church consist of adults who had voluntarily committed themselves to the fellowship, or other like believers. As a result, the purity of the church was maintained.

Both Mennonites and Amish are considered Anabaptists, but they differ somewhat on their interpretations regarding the purity and faithfulness of the fellowship. As a result, they have split several times over the centuries. Nevertheless, most Amish groups consider themselves conservative cousins of the Mennonites.

The deadly persecution suffered by both the Mennonites and Amish in the 16th and 17th centuries forced them to go "underground." It soon became apparent that a new place—a place of tolerance—was needed in order for their beliefs to survive. As you may remember, William Penn was a strong advocate of religious freedom, and he "advertised" Pennsylvania as a territory where anyone could emigrate. The Amish saw this new land as an area ripe for immigration and the practice of their simple

> **F**AST FACT: Most Amish are trilingual, speaking English, Pennsylvania Dutch (a dialect of German), and High German.

ways. Thus, the early 1700s saw a migration of Amish to Pennsylvania. The fact that this new territory was also rich agricultural possibilities was further inducement.

The Amish settled in various regions throughout Pennsylvania—principally in the southern and eastern regions of the state. Along with their traditions and religion, they also brought their language. Known to most people as Pennsylvania Dutch or, more appropriately, Pennsylvania German, their language is a dialect that retains some of its Germanic precepts but is distinctive in both meter and cadence.

The Amish are family-oriented close-knit communities. Large families are the norm—with an average of seven children in each family. The Amish rely almost exclusively on the biological reproduction of their members, rather than on acquiring new members through conversion. Youngsters are typically not considered part of the Amish faith until somewhere between the ages of 16 and 25. It is during this time that the young are baptized and with baptism comes official membership in the faith and permission to marry.

There are several fundamental beliefs embraced by both Mennonites and Amish. First, there is a complete separation between church and state—neither has any jurisdiction over the other. Second, Anabaptists emphasize a simple obedience to the Word of God. As such, they tend to reject ritual and tradition. Third, they are true pacifists—refusing to participate in any war and embracing peace in all their actions with others. Fourth, they are strict Christians—believing that

> **F**AST FACT: Most Amish weddings take place between late October and December—after the autumn harvest. Weddings are typically held on Tuesdays and Thursdays.

> **F**AST FACT: Old Order Amish are opposed to the social security system. They are not opposed to paying the tax; rather, they are opposed to receiving the benefits of the system.

Christianity should be an expression of faith as well as of actions. Fifth, membership in the faith is voluntary, limited to adults only, full time, and extremely disciplined.

Anabaptists, both Amish and Mennonites, reject the notion of individualism—the good of the group is much more important. As you travel through Old Order communities you will quickly notice the lack of any labor-saving devices or electric lines coming into their homes. Part of their belief is that anything that might make one less dependent on the community is immediately frowned upon or rejected.

The lack of telephones, automobiles, electric appliances, and any modern convenience by Old Order Amish is both a choice and a requirement of the faith. In addition, the Amish neither purchase any form of insurance, nor tap into any form of government assistance.

The Amish are often referred to as "plain and simple" people and nowhere is this more apparent than in their dress. They wear clothes that are simple in design and coloration. Men and boys wear black suit coats that have no lapels and fasten with hooks and eyes. Their pants are usually held up with suspenders. Shirts are solid colors and they wear brown shoes for work and black shoes for dress-up. You'll often see them in straw hats when they are outdoors. Young men are clean-shaven; however, as soon as they marry they grow beards, but no mustaches.

Women and girls wear dresses with full skirts of solid colors. Quite often an apron is worn and a cape frequently covers the bodice of the dress. Black shoes are always worn—whether at home or when traveling. Amish women and girls do not cut their hair. They wear it parted in the middle and combed back from the face. They may twist it into a bun at the back of the head or nape of the neck. A head covering, most often white, is always worn indoors and out. No jewelry is ever worn.

As you wend your way through the Amish countryside, you will most likely come upon the ubiquitous buggies of Amish life. Since the Amish reject modern conveniences such as cars and trucks, their preferred method of transportation—

the horse and buggy—is most often seen on highways and rural routes, particularly if you travel on a Sunday. That's when you'll be able to see the buggies lined up in the yard of an Amish farm or forming lines along the road as they return from their weekly

FAST FACT: William Penn, because of his religious beliefs (he was a convert to Quakerism), was jailed several times.

worship services. Each buggy will have an orange safety triangle on the back and be led by a single horse pulling a covered vehicle. The Amish observe all traffic laws, but be aware that their slower pace will require additional attention as you approach them on the road.

South of Lancaster and just east of the small town of Willow Street is the **1719 Hans Herr House**—which is where we'll begin this road trip. When William Penn was granted the land we now know as Pennsylvania, he wanted to protect people who had been persecuted for their religious beliefs. As we learned above, the Anabaptists were some of those people. In Europe, the early Anabaptists had received baptism as infants, but then, as adults, they came to the view that the only true baptism was of adult believers—thus they practiced adult baptism. Unfortunately, the state church saw this "second baptism" as a violation of both canon and civil law. Throughout Europe, Anabaptism was viewed as a crime punishable by either imprisonment or death.

In the spring of 1711 seven Mennonite men and their families traveled along the Great Conestoga Road to begin their lives anew on what was then the western edge of Pennsylvania. They had been granted a parcel of land ten thousand acres in size in what is now Lancaster County. Eight years later, in 1719, they would construct the first permanent building in the area—the Hans Herr House.

Hans Herr, a bishop of the Mennonite faith, and his wife Elizabeth are be-

When approaching and passing a horse-drawn vehicle, remember that horses are unpredictable and even the most road-safe horse can get upset by a fast-moving motor vehicle. Be sure to slow down and give buggies and horse-drawn equipment plenty of room when passing.

The 1719 Hans Herr House—the oldest home in Lancaster County

lieved to have been the first residents of this house. Over the years the house was home to several generations of Hans Herr's family until the 1860s. It fell into disuse and disrepair until it was eventually restored to its pre-colonial appearance in the 1970s. The house is now part of a museum complex that includes three Pennsylvania German farmhouses, two barns, a blacksmith shop, a smokehouse, an outdoor bake oven, and an extensive collection of farm equipment spanning three centuries. As you walk through this historic house you will get a sense of the simplicity of those early settlers—not only in terms of their everyday lifestyles, but also of the simplicity of their religious beliefs—beliefs they sought to practice in this new land of freedom and opportunity.

After your visit, follow PA 741 east to the tourist town of Strasburg (see Chapter 10). Slip through Strasburg and head up PA 896 to **The Amish Village** (199 Hartman Bridge Road) in Ronks. Please keep in mind that this is a commercial venture and, as such, it has pulled together many "authentic artifacts and buildings"—all of which you might not normally find at one time on a true Amish farm. Nevertheless, this is good introduction to everyday Amish life.

You can begin you visit with a tour of the site's "authentic" 1840 Amish farmhouse. Your guide will introduce you to "today's Amish lifestyle, their centuries-old heritage and their religious beliefs and traditions." After the house tour you can walk around the grounds and view other Amish outbuildings such as a springhouse, bank barn, horse paddock, one-room schoolhouse, and blacksmith's shop. There's also a variety of farm animals, equipment, and shops with food items and handmade goods for sale.

After departing the Amish Farm, head up PA 896 north, make a right onto PA 340 east and drive into the town of **Bird-in-Hand**. This small community (pop-

The Amish Village offers varied Amish experiences.

A hardware store in the town of Bird-in-Hand

ulation: 402) was founded in 1734. The name of the town comes from a sign that was at the former McNabb's Hotel. The sign is said to have "portrayed a man with a bird in his hand and a bush nearby, in which two birds were perched." Thus, the inn was more popularly known as the Bird-in-Hand Inn. The name of the inn then became the official name of the town in 1873. Prior to that, the town was known as Enterprise.

Many visitors quickly note that this county may be home to more towns with singularly distinctive names than anywhere else in the country. These would include the towns of Bird-in-Hand, Intercourse, Blue Ball, Bareville, Mount Joy, and Paradise. I will spare you any discussion about other Pennsylvania towns such as Pigs Ear, Number Thirty-Seven, and Elephant—none of which you'll find in Lancaster County.

As you drive through Bird-in-Hand you'll notice a profusion of markets, quilt shops, candle shops, country knives, buffets, craft shops, and Amish restaurants and eateries. Most of the wares and collectables are probably unobtainable in your own local stores.

After departing Bird-in-Hand continue east on PA 340 for approximately .8 mile and make a right on South Weavertown Road. Just after the turn, there will be a white Amish home on the right. You'll immediately notice several features about this farm (as you will with all Old Order Amish farms). There are no electric wires going to the house and there are no automobiles. If you happen to see any farm machinery on the property (and look very closely) you might notice that there are, for example, no rubber tires on the tractors. You are certain to see one or more gardens on the property and, depending on the time of the year you visit, the gardens will have a profusion of vegetables. Whether it's a small plot of land for table food or a large sprawling expanse of tobacco or corn, farming takes up most of the life of the Amish.

Continue down South Weavertown Road and after .4 mile make a right at the T in the road. The road curves around to the left and you will come to another T in the road. Make a right turn at this T (onto Irishtown Road). Just before you turn, you will notice an Amish farm on the left and just after that another Amish farm on the right (just before you make a curve to the left).

You may be surprised to see that many Amish farms grow immense fields of

> **F**AST FACT: Pennsylvania is home to more than 58,105 farms. There are 7.7 million acres of farmland under cultivation in the state. Ninety-two percent of the farms are family-owned and the average farm is 133 acres.

One of the staple food items throughout the Amish countryside is shoo-fly pie. Although there is no consensus on this matter, it is believed that this calorie-rich desert got its name from the fact that it was made with very sweet ingredients that tended to attract lots of flies. When you have lots of flies in your kitchen, you want to "shoo" them away—thus the name.

> **F**AST FACT: Fifty percent of Amish are under the age of 18 and not technically part of the Amish church.

tobacco—a very profitable crop. The Amish regularly rotate their crops of corns, alfalfa, and tobacco.

At the next stop sign, make a left turn onto North Ronks Road. You will then drive under an overpass and find yourself in the tiny town of Ronks. Just on the other side of Ronks you will pass by another Amish farm on the left (white house, red barn).

You'll come to the intersection of North Ronks Road and US 30 (Lincoln Highway East). Travel through the intersection and continue on Ronks Road. The first farm you see on the right is an Amish farm (red and white house). Again, you'll notice there is no electricity—no telephone or electric wires going into the house.

Continue on Ronks Road for 1.1 miles and turn right (you will have passed Herr Road on the right) off Ronks Road at the stop sign. After .2 mi there will be a Y in the road. Take the left-hand part of the Y (Paradise Road). You'll notice a brick home on the left (there may be a horse and buggy in the garage) and a tobacco field on the right. As you continue down the road, you'll see the **Red Caboose Motel** on the left (definitely not Amish).

You'll come up to an intersection (with traffic signal) with PA 741 (Gap Road). Turn left onto PA 741. You'll soon see several Amish farms on the right side of the road. Notice the multiple buildings—many of which are painted white. You'll also notice a sprinkling of "English" homes here and there along the road.

After 2.5 miles you'll pass by an Amish schoolhouse on the left—a white building with a picket fence all around. One of the most iconic symbols of Amish life, the one-room schoolhouse, can be found throughout the Lancaster County countryside. Formal education for the Amish goes up to grade eight and classes are taught by young girls (typically 17 to 20 years old) who were good students while they were in school. After grade eight, the young are expected to work in the fields (boys) or tend to household chores (girls).

> **F**AST FACT: If someone broke into an Amish home to steal something, the Amish would not report them to police. They don't want any affiliation with government agencies.

Stop by Fisher's Produce for great Amish treats.

At this point the road has a new name—Strasburg Road. Depending on the time of year, you may see lots of greenery—gently rolling hills and farmland as far as the eye can see. Most of the land will be farmed with vehicles with steel wheels and drawn by horses or mules—no mechanization whatsoever. Houses, too, are all plain and simple. The fences may be white or may be unpainted and the landscaping is simple.

About 1.2 miles from the school house will be **Fisher's Produce**—an expansive roadside stand on the left-hand side of the road. Stop here for some great Amish food. There is an incredible variety of canned goods—everything from honey to green tomato relish to elderberry jelly to vegetable soup to garlic chips to chow-chow to apple butter. You'll also get a great selection of produce (depending on the season). Be sure to get some homemade root beer and an ever-classic "whoopie pie."

FAST FACT: Old Order Mennonites and Amish pay public school taxes. However, in 1972, the U.S. Supreme Court ruled that these and other related groups were exempt from state compulsory attendance laws beyond the eighth grade.

Turn your vehicle around and head back on PA 741 (Strasburg Road); 2.5 miles from Fisher's Produce you'll make a right turn onto Black Horse Road. After .6 mile on Black Horse Road, you'll come to another Amish schoolhouse on the left side. This one, too, is a one-room tan-colored schoolhouse with a simple fence all around.

You'll soon arrive at the intersection of Black Horse Road and US 30 (Lincoln Highway East). You are now in Paradise, a classic Lancaster County small town (population: 1,028), with an abundance of brick homes and a plenty of traffic zipping along the main route. This is a town that has charm to spare, so you may want to stop and roam through some of the shops for authentic Pennsylvania Dutch gifts.

From Black Horse Road make a left turn onto US 30, then after .2 mile make a quick right turn on Leacock Road (there's a Wells Fargo Bank on the corner). After .5 mile you'll see an Amish bookstore (Gordonville Book Store) on the right side of the road. The Amish print shop is about a mile away; it's where the Amish print the materials sold in the bookstore.

About 1 mile from the Gordonville Book Store is another one-room school house (on the left). This one has a white fence around it and a small ballfield in the rear. Drive for another .4 mi. and you'll come upon the **Leacock Shoe Store** on the left. This store is frequented by the Amish, who shop here for shoes and clothing.

Drive for another .4 mile and you'll come to the intersection of Old Leacock Road and PA 340. As you are waiting at the intersection, you might want to consider a brief detour to the **Plain and Fancy Restaurant** a mere .4 mile to your left. If the thought of an old-fashioned Amish farm feast sounds like epicurean heaven, then make that left turn onto PA-340 and pull into the restaurant's spacious parking lot on the right side of the road.

For 53 years, this restaurant has continued the tradition of pass-the-platter, all-you-can-eat, family-style dining that will remind you of a Thanksgiving feast on steroids. You'll sit down at a long table with lots of other folks you've just met for the first time and pass heaping platters of food to each other. Included on those heaping platters will be fried chicken, roast beef, chicken pot pie, baked sausage, mashed potatoes, buttered noodles, veggie medley, dried sweet corn, chow-chow, cole slaw, raisin bread, rolls, apple butter, assorted beverages and a panoply of desserts. Loosen your belt and dig in. The feast will set you back a few pennies (adults—$19.95; children—$9.95), but what a meal!

Continue your journey by making a left turn back onto PA 340. After about 1.2 miles, you'll arrive in the town of **Intercourse**. For decades, tens of thousands of postcards have been sent from the Intercourse post office by tourists with "cute" snippets of humor referencing two of the villages in the immediate area ("After Intercourse we'll soon be in Paradise!"). Everyone chuckles at these double-entendres, but the naming of the town has less to do with sexual in-nuendo than it does with physical ge-ography.

As the story goes, the village, which was originally founded in 1754, was at the intersection of two important roads—the Old King's Highway from Philadelphia to Pittsburgh (now the Old Philadelphia Pike) and the road from Wilmington, Delaware, to Erie. The intersection of these two roads is claimed by some to be the basis for the town "Cross Keys." The name was officially changed to its synonym, Intercourse, in 1814.

The town's current claim to fame is that select portions of the Harrison Ford movie *Witness* (1985) were filmed here. These included the filming of the phone booth scene on the porch of Zimmerman's grocery store, the fight scene on Queen Road, and the local police office (the former township building that is now Peace-ful Valley Amish Furniture).

Intercourse offers an interesting congregation of restaurants, services, car-riage rides, tours, attractions, museums, lodging, and other businesses perfect for a peaceful stroll around town or a quiet interlude in a busy travel schedule.

After your visit, turn onto PA 772 north (also known as West Newport Road). After .7 mi you'll see an Amish farm on the left. This is one of the larger farms in

> **F**AST FACT: The typical Lancaster County Amish farm has about 40 acres. Crops include alfalfa, corn, tobacco, and grains.

the area and you'll note several outbuildings and a sophisticated farming operation in place. In .4 mile, another large Amish farm will be on the left. Look for a large assembly of horses, mules, and other field animals.

Continue your drive on PA 772 (West Newport Road). After a while PA 772 will bend around to the left, but you'll want to continue your drive straight ahead on Hess Road (careful—the sign may be difficult to see). Notice the farmlands all around as you travel north on Hess Road. You'll see a profusion of Amish farms on both sides of the road. When you come to a stop sign make a left turn onto Eby Road (there will be an Amish farm directly ahead of you.).

After .2 mile you'll pass by Hess Road on the right—be sure to stay on East Eby Road. In a very short distance, you'll see an Amish schoolhouse on the left (a tan building with a chain link fence). After another .2 mi. you'll come to the Myer Homestead with its graveyard on the right. Park your car off the road and walk over to the iron fence surrounding this 1759 homestead. Just outside the perimeter of the fence is this historical marker:

> Herein lies Abraham C. Myer (deceased 1792) and his heirs. Of German descent, he arrived 1758 and purchased 100 acres of land to the north and east of this point. Eight generations of farmers followed and were a stable influence as community and church leaders, pump and furniture makers, blacksmiths, inventors and educators. Abram Hess married Caroline Myer in 1894 and continued farming followed by their son Titus M. Hess (deceased 1991) and wife, Anna Haldeman, their six children and grandchildren.

In 1976 the farm was identified by the U.S. Department of the Interior as a Bicentennial Family farm. After 237 years of farming in 1994 the heirs donated an easement to the Lancaster Farmland Trust as a farmland forever.

Immediately after the graveyard (on the right) is **Riehl's Quilts and Crafts**. This is where you want to be if you're in the market for an Amish quilt. The selection here is unparalleled and the quality exceptional.

From here, make a left turn onto Stumptown Road. Notice the expanse of Amish farms off to your left and all the way to the horizon. If the light is right, you'll see an incredible sight of Pennsylvania agriculture as it once was…and is currently maintained by the Amish. This is a calendar view—one that just can't be duplicated anywhere else.

You'll shortly arrive at the intersection of Stumptown Road and PA 772 (Newport Road). On the southeast corner of this intersection is a unique Lancaster County landmark offering visitors a magical glimpse into the past. The **Mascot Roller Mills**, built in the mid-1730s, was an economic and social center where Amish and Mennonite farmers had their corn ground into cornmeal, exchanged their wheat for flour, bought and sold wheat at the end of the season, and had their grain ground into animal feed. What you will see here is a documentation of the rural milling industry in the United States—from its earliest beginnings as a business enterprise to its current place as a living museum. While many U.S. mills have fallen into disuse and disrepair, this structure has been lovingly preserved by the Ressler Mill Foundation in order to educate the public about grain milling and a way of life quite distant from our own.

Also located at the site is the **Ressler Family Home**—the house where the owners of the mill lived for more than two centuries. Visit the home and you will step back into the pages of history. The house, home to three generations of the Ressler family, and its contents has been faithfully preserved (there are no replicas and re-creations here) as a window into 19th and 20th century rural living. Here you'll see a coal-fired stove, Mother Ressler's rocking chair, a bride's box and period antiques that were part of the home's furnishings in a bygone era. Step through the home and you will quickly get a sense of what the "good old days" were really like.

AMISH PROVERBS

1. The kind of ancestors you have is not as important as the ones your children have.
2. Very few burdens are heavy if everyone lifts.
3. Pray for a good harvest, but continue to hoe.
4. Keep your words soft and sweet in case you have to eat them.
5. If at first you succeed, try not to look astonished.
6. A word to the wise is unnecessary.
7. To grow old gracefully, you must start when you are young.

The Ressler Family Home, more than two centuries old

After departing the Ressler Family Home and Mascot Roller Mills, you can turn right on PA 772 and return to the town of Intercourse. Or you can make a left turn on PA 772 and head towards Leola where you can pick up PA 23 and wend your way back into Lancaster. Whatever direction you head, you're sure to remember this trip as one that combines both past and present into an unforgettable journey through "Amish country."

CONTACTS

Hans Herr House, 1849 Hans Herr Dr., Willow Street, PA 17584; (717) 464-4438; www.hansherr.org.

The Amish Village, 199 Hartman Bridge Rd., Ronks, PA 17572; (717) 687-8511; theamishvillage.net.

Riehl's Quilts and Crafts, 247 East Eby Rd., Leola, PA 17540; (717) 656-0697; www.riehlsamishquilts.com.

Mascot Roller Mills and Ressler Family Home, 443 West Newport Rd., Ronks, PA; 17572; (717) 656-7616; www.resslermill.com

DINING

Plain and Fancy Farm, 3121 Old Philadelphia Pike, Bird-in-Hand, PA 17505; (717) 768-4400; www.plainandfancyfarm.com.

York has its roots in Revolutionary War times.

13 In Old York Town

Estimated length: 2–3 miles (walking); 1 mile (driving)

Estimated time: ½–1 day

Combine this tour with: Chapters 10 and 14

Getting there: Leave your car behind in a parking garage and hoof it along some of York's historic streets to see some delightful architecture and monuments. After the first part of the walking tour, you'll take a short drive up North George Street to the Prospect Hill Cemetery to see more York history.

Highlights: This journey combines two walking tours into an all-encompassing visit back into Revolutionary and Civil War times. You will glimpse some historic buildings, sample incredible food, and visit some incredible individuals. You will see parts of York many visitors miss—segments of the city's history that will inform and delight.

York may well be a city with a split personality—or several personalities split among assorted commercial enterprises. Depending on whom you talk to, York is the Snack Food Capital of the World (many of America's favorite potato chips, candy, pretzels, ice cream, and cookies are baked, popped, fried and seasoned here), the home of the country's longest-running county fair (the York County Fair, held every September, has been going on every year since 1765), or perhaps it's proudest moniker, the First Capital of the United States. This last title is one subject to great debates and constant arguments—with a firm resolution probably never forthcoming.

Nevertheless, here is one indisputable fact: the city (and county) of York has a fascinating history—a history that will lure you with all manner of interesting sites and informative artifacts.

FAST FACT: York briefly served as the capital of the new nation in 1777 and 1778 when the British captured Philadelphia and drove the Continental Congress west. However, most historians designate York as the fourth capital of the United States. The first three national capitals would be Philadelphia, Baltimore, and Lancaster.

The area in and around the town of York was originally purchased by William Penn in a 1736 financial transaction with the Iroquois Indians. The county of York was officially created on August 19, 1749 from part of Lancaster County. Its name may have come from one of two sources—it may have been named for the Duke of York, who was an early patron of the Penn family. There is also speculation that the name came from the city and shire of York in England. The town of York, just like the county, also has a long ancestry—having been originally founded in 1741 by folks who had moved away from Philadelphia in order to start a settlement on the other side of the Susquehanna River. The settlement was eventually named "York" in honor of the English city by the same name. Most of those early settlers were not English, however, but rather Germans and Scotch-Irish. Eventually the town grew sufficiently large to become an official borough (September 24, 1787) and eventually an incorporated city (January 11, 1887). Interestingly, the city of York was known as "Yorktown" during the colonial period.

One of York's claims to fame lies in the fact that the aforementioned Articles of Confederation were developed and written here. The Articles, also known as "The First Constitution," came to fruition at a time when most Americans did not care much for the concept of a centralized government. Most of their loyalty and allegiance was to their home state, with which they felt a closer kinship. Nevertheless, the Articles of Confederation were in force from March 1, 1781, until March 4, 1789, and were eventually replaced by our present-day Constitution. In spite of the fact that the Articles of Confederation proved to be inadequate in addressing the many problems of the new nation, they were a critical first step in the transition to a fully democratic form of government.

York achieved additional historical significance during the American Civil War. It achieved the dubious distinction of being the largest northern town to be occupied by the Confederate Army. Under orders from Robert E. Lee, Major General Jubal Early and his 6,000 Confederate troops rode into town (they were on their way east) on June 28, 1863. Early and his men camped in and around York and being possessed of both weaponry and a large number of hungry and ill-clothed men demanded that the good citizens of York hand over substantial amounts of provisions and good old American currency. The list included the following:

165 barrels of flour or 28,000 pounds of baked bread

3,500 pounds of sugar

1,650 pounds of coffee

300 gallons of molasses

1,200 pounds of salt

32,000 pounds of fresh beef, or 21,000 pounds of bacon or pork

2,000 pairs of shoes or boots

1,000 pairs of socks

1,000 felt hats

$100,000

Knowing their city would be "put to the torch" if they didn't comply, the citizenry of York scrambled to fulfill the order. By four o'clock that afternoon they were able to satisfy all of Confederate's demands, except for the shoes and, not unexpectedly, the cash. They were, however, able to raise about $28,600 in ransom money. As fate would have it, two days after their arrival, Early's troops were recalled west by General Lee. (It seems he needed some troops for the conflict that was soon to take place in nearby Gettysburg.)

It's also worth noting that another Confederate brigade under the command of General John B. Gordon also arrived in York at the same time as General Early's troops. Although Gordon did not stop in York, he did relieve the city of the 35-foot flag flying in Centre Square (today's Continental Square). Gordon marched on to the small town of Wrightsville on the Susquehanna River (eventually turning around and returning west after General Lee also ordered him back towards Gettysburg). Wrightsville had its own significant Civil War event—a story we'll visit in the next chapter.

FAST FACT: In June 1776, the Continental Congress began to work on the Articles of Confederation. It took five years for it to be approved, first by members of Congress and then by the states.

York played an additional significant role during the Civil War when the U.S. Army Hospital was established on Penn Commons. The Hospital served the medical needs of thousands of Union soldiers wounded at both the battles of Antietam and Gettysburg. Many of the troops who died there were eventually interred at Prospect Hill Cemetery—a delightful chunk of history also on this tour.

As York began its march into the 20th century, it slowly established itself as a significant industrial center. Several large-scale industries were based in the city including companies manufacturing railroad equipment, steam engines, automobiles, and pottery. Papermaking was also a significant industry. Since then, the city has branched out and diversified in a number of areas. But its historical roots continue to hold the greatest fascination for both visitors and residents alike.

For this journey back into the past, we're going to take two walking tours, separated by a very short drive. When you first arrive in York, drive over to the Philadelphia Street Parking Garage (near the intersection of Philadelphia and North George Streets and directly across from the Strand Theater). This garage is in the downtown area and a good starting point for our first tour. After you park your car, exit the garage and begin walking east on Philadelphia Street. You'll immediately cross over North George Street. Continue eastward on Philadelphia Street until you come to the the **William C. Goodridge Freedom House and Underground Railroad Museum** (123 East Philadelphia Street). This house was owned by ex-slave William Goodridge who was one of York's most well-known citizens in the early 1800s. As a young boy he apprenticed as a tanner and was eventually hired as a barber in what is now downtown York. In the years that followed he purchased the barber shop and expanded it considerably—selling a wide variety of merchandise includ-

The William C. Goodridge Freedom House

ing a universal tonic for baldness ("Oil of Celsus and Balm of Minerva"). He continued to purchase several properties in York—at one time owning nearly 20 of them.

FAST FACT: William Goodridge was the first person to introduce the sale of daily newspapers in York.

But Goodridge's greatest contribution to York was in his role as a conductor on the Underground Railroad. His house had a secret room in the back of his basement, which was a safe place for many slaves escaping the south. In 1842 he established a rail line (the Goodridge Reliance Line) between York, Philadelphia, and more than 20 other cities. Unknown to all but a few select individuals, he ingeniously created secret compartments in several of his railroad cars so that he could ferry scores of runaway slaves northward and away from marauding bands of slave catchers. He also hosted many anti-slavery meetings with several noted abolitionists. (You can view an oversize mural of William C. Goodridge on West Market Street in York by the Market & Penn Street Farmers' Market).

Continue east on Philadelphia Street until you come to Queen Street. Turn right and walk to East Market Street. Before beginning your travels westward, turn left and look for the **First Presbyterian Church of York**. The grounds for this building were donated by John Penn and John Penn Jr., the grandsons of Pennsylvania founder William Penn. James Smith, a signer of the Declaration of Independence, lies buried in this churchyard.

Keep walking a short distance east on Market Street and check out the **Charles Billmeyer House** (225 East Market Street). This urban Italianate structure was originally built in the early 1860s for noted businessman Charles Billmeyer. He co-owned the Billmeyer & Small Co.—a manufacturer of railcars for several railroad companies including the Rio Grande and the Mexican Central Railroad.

Note the distinctive architectural features of this house—including the cupola on the roof. The interior of the house is adorned with frescos done by artists involved with paintings in the U.S. Capitol. Shocking as it may seem, this building was literally inches from being demolished in the mid-1970s. The reason—somebody needed a parking lot.

Turn around and walk west on East Market Street. You'll soon arrive at the **Horace Bonham House** (#152). This structure dates from about 1840, although

The Billmeyer House, a high-style Italianate mansion

when it was first built it was somewhat smaller than it is today. When Horace Bonham purchased the house in 1875 he added to it considerably. Bonham was a prominent York resident who was trained as a lawyer and had also been appointed as a revenue collector by President Abraham Lincoln. He was also a painter—focusing on landscapes and portraits and displaying his extensive collection throughout his home.

The three-story home has been occupied by generations of the Bonham family—at least up until 1965. It was then donated to the Historical Society of York County and is now a popular house museum. You might want to tour this upper-middle class home and view rooms decorated in a variety of styles—everything from the late 1800s to the early 1900s. The tour begins at 250 East Market Street.

Continue on East Market Street and just before Duke Street will be the **Zachariah Spangler House** (114 East Market Street). It's now a law office. The Federal style of building was extremely popular in York—particularly during the late 1700s and early 1800s. This building, one of the classics of early York architecture, is a noteworthy example of a distinctive design. It was occupied by Zachariah Spangler, a sheriff and a justice of the peace in the early 19th century.

You will immediately note the keystones (remember that Pennsylvania is "the Keystone State") above the windows on both the first and second levels. Also note the distinctive dormers on the third floor. To put this building in proper, or at least surrealist, perspective, note the 20th-century parking meter immediately in front of the house.

Continue your stroll west on Market Street and at Duke and Market is the **Lafayette Club** (59 East Market). This building was constructed in 1839. Immediately across the street is the **Yorktown Hotel** and old courthouse. Just after you pass the parking garage on your right is a historical market entitled "The First National Thanksgiving." The sign refers to nothing the Pilgrims had done, but rather something that was the result of a singular victory during the Revolutionary War.

You see, in the fall of 1777 the Continental Congress was convening in York (since the British had taken over Philadelphia). On October 31, a messenger arrived with news of an Ameri-

The Zachariah Spangler House (note the keystones over the windows and door)

THE FIRST NATIONAL THANKSGIVING
WAS PROCLAIMED FROM YORK BY THE CONTINENTAL
CONGRESS ON NOVEMBER 1, 1777 TO BE CELEBRATED
ON THURSDAY, DECEMBER 18. IT WAS WRITTEN BY
SAM ADAMS OF MASSACHUSETTS, "THE FATHER OF
THE REVOLUTION," WHO ADVOCATED FOR THE FIRST
TIME "ONE DAY OF PUBLIC THANKSGIVING" FOR
ALL OF THE STATES AFTER THE BATTLE OF
SARATOGA, "THAT WITH ONE HEART AND ONE VOICE
THE GOOD PEOPLE MAY EXPRESS THE GRATEFUL
FEELINGS OF THEIR HEARTS."

BY VARIOUS HISTORICAL AND PATRIOTIC SOCIETIES
AND
THE NATIONAL THANKSGIVING FOUNDATION

can victory at the Battle of Saratoga in New York. It seems as though the British general, John Burgoyne, had unconditionally surrendered to the American general, Horatio Gates (whose house we'll visit shortly), after a long, casualty-laden battle. This was extremely good news since it helped persuade the French to jump into the war on the American side. The result was a much-needed influx of both men and supplies.

Congress' reaction was to appoint a committee of three individuals, including Samuel Adams of Massachusetts, Richard Henry Lee of Virginia, and Daniel Roberdeau of Pennsylvania. These men were charged with drafting a report and resolution on the victory. The report, adopted November 1, officially declared Thursday, December 18, as "a day of Thanksgiving," so that "with one heart and one voice the good people may express the grateful feelings of their hearts, and consecrate themselves to the service of their divine benefactor." While there are those who argue that the first Thanksgiving took place between the Pilgrims and the Indians at a place much further north, others argue this one was the first Thanksgiving since it was an official proclamation by Congress. Nevertheless, there is an official historical marker certifying York as the location of "The First National Thanksgiving."

Continue your walk westward and you will eventually cross over North George Street. At this point East Market Street becomes West Market Street.

> **F**AST FACT: The official date of Thanksgiving (the fourth Thursday in November) wasn't established by Congress until 1941.

After one block you will come to the corner of East Market Street and Beaver Street. Here you will find the **National House** (53 West Market Street). This structure is quite easy to find because of the wraparound balconies that give it a somewhat southern feel.

This building was originally built in 1828 and has gone through a succession of names changes. It has been variously known as the White Hall Hotel, National House, National Hotel, and Jack's Department Store. Its historic claim to fame is that this is where President Martin Van Buren stayed on his visit to York; it was also temporary lodging for author Charles Dickens, who wrote about his York experience in "American Notes."

Just after the National House is a historical marker for the **General Wayne Headquarters** (the building no longer exists).

Stroll westward along Market Street, past Beaver Street, and look for the large wall murals. The two on the right are entitled *York County 250th Anniversary* and *The Four Chaplains.* However, it is the one on your left-hand side (on the Pershing Street side of the Junior League of York building) that you want to pay particular attention to. It is titled *The Articles of Confederation* and it will provide this section of your tour with a unique punctuation mark that underscores the incredible architecture of this city and its place in the pantheon of significant American historical sites.

We'll now visit a set of four historic buildings. This complex of colonial structures is known as "the Colonial Complex" and includes **the Colonial Court-**

> **F**AST FACT: One of the major weaknesses of the Articles of Confederation was that there was no executive branch to enforce any acts passed by Congress.

house, **the Golden Plough Tavern**, **the Horacio Gates House**, and **the Bobb Log House**. Collectively, they offer a unique look into the past and offer visitors to York a "one-stop" history lesson that underscores the importance of this city in early American history.

The first building in the complex is the **Colonial Courthouse** on Market Street. Actually this building is a reconstruction of the original county courthouse, which was built in 1754 and stood in Centre Square. That building endured until 1841 when it was replaced by a Greek Revival building over on East Market Street. The Colonial Courthouse was where the Continental Congress met for nine months in 1777-1778.

After approving the Declaration of Independence in 1776 the Second Continental Congress continued to meet in Philadelphia. However, as British troops began to occupy the city, by the end of 1777 it quickly became apparent that the Congress would have to depart Philadelphia for a safer location. They decided to meet in York to continue their work. It was here that the Articles of Confederation were officially adopted. The Articles of Confederation was an agreement among the original 13 colonies that officially established the United States of America as a confederation of sovereign states and served as its first constitution. This is why York often refers to itself as the "First Capital."

The current Colonial Courthouse is actually a replica of the original—it was built in 1976 in honor of the country's bicentennial. Step inside and you'll be able to see back to 1777 when delegates such as John Hancock, Henry Laurens, and Sam Adams hammered out the design of the new country.

After visiting the courthouse, you'll want to walk across North Pershing Avenue to the **Golden Plough Tavern**. This building was originally constructed as a tavern in 1741 by Michael Eichelberger and its architecture is a classic German Colonial style. Many of York's early settlers were from Germany and this building is a reminder of German Palatinate structures.

FAST FACT: During the deliberations in the Colonial Courthouse, the delegates were seated at tables representing each of the colonies. The tables were arranged from north to south.

The tavern also operated as an inn for weary travelers. There were simple quarters on the second floor where visitors could spend the night. The tav-

Rear of the Golden Plough Tavern in York

ern's chimney is located in the center of the structure—a common German design. As you walk through the interior, just imagine folks like George Washington, Sam Adams, General Horatio Gates, and French General Marquis de Lafayette also strolling through these rooms with a pint of ale in their hands and thoughts of independence in their heads. A statue of General Lafayette stands outside the tavern.

Right next door to the tavern is the **Horatio Gates House**. Gates had a most unusual military career. He began it as an officer in the British army. As a British officer he discovered that advancement in rank was often dependent on either money or influence—of which he had little. Frustrated by military hierarchy, he sold his major's commission in 1769 and brought his family to America. He originally settled in Virginia; however, when he heard about the outbreak of war in May 1775 he contacted George Washington and offered his services to the American Army. On Washington's recommendation, Gates was commissioned as a Brigadier General in the Continental Army. His most significant military encounter was the American victory at the Battle of Saratoga.

The Horatio Gates House was constructed in 1751 by Joseph Chambers and was connected to the Golden Plough Tavern by means of a shared kitchen. Built in the Georgian-style it is a two-and-a-half story brick and limestone dwelling. This house was General Gates' home while the Second Continental Congress was meeting in York from September 30, 1777, to June 27, 1778.

Take your time to walk around both the Golden Plough Tavern and the Horatio Gates House and marvel at these two 18th-century buildings (both in their original appearance and both in their original locations) in terms of both their architecture and their historical significance.

Walk north on Pershing Avenue to the **Bobb Log House** (corner of Pershing and Philadelphia Streets). When viewed in the context of the previous three structures, this building seems somewhat out of place. That's simply because it is the only structure within the Colonial Complex that is actually not colonial. This house was originally constructed in 1812 and was originally located at the corner of Pershing and College Avenues, a few blocks south of its present location.

The house was moved to its present-day location in 1968 so that it could become part of the Complex. Although definitely not American colonial (it is, however, built in the English Colonial style), there is a museum inside that will give you a glimpse into what life was like in the early 19th century.

> **FAST FACT:** A *log house* (like the Bobb Log House) is constructed using hewn (cut and shaped) logs. By contrast, a *log cabin* is constructed using rounded (un-shaped) logs.

Exit the Bobb Log House and walk east on Philadelphia Street to the **1776 Friends Meeting House** (135 West Philadelphia). Constructed by William Willis (who also built the first courthouse) in 1766, this building is one of the oldest Quaker meetinghouses in

The Bobb Log House

the area. It was originally a religious center for Quaker men; it was expanded in 1783 so that women could meet there as well.

Quakerism (the Religious Society of Friends) has been around for more than 350 years and is based on four core beliefs: 1. Simplicity—A commitment to living simply; 2. Equality—there is that of God in each person; 3. Integrity—Being in harmony with oneself; and 4. Peace—A belief in nonviolence.

The city of York was originally settled by Germans and Scots; however, English Quakers also made up a significant portion of that early population. As a result, there were several English Quaker meetinghouses constructed in the region, of which this is the oldest. If you are visiting on a Sunday, please know that all are

The 1776 Friends Meeting House

welcome to participate in a Quaker meeting. Note that the worship begins when you sit down. There is no announcement.

As you stroll along Philadelphia Street and back to the parking garage, you will come upon one of the historical stalwarts of downtown York—the **Central Market** (34 West Philadelphia Street). This venerable institution has been engaged in farm-to-market sales ever since 1754. It was then that a Royal decree was issued granting permission for the operation of York's first center square market:

> The inhabitants of the town of York are become so numerous that they find it necessary to have a public market...or the better supplying and

accommodating them with goods and wholesome provisions under proper regulations. The proprietor upon the humble request of the inhabitants of York grants and ordains that they and their successors shall and may forever thereafter hold and keep within the town, in every week of the year, two market days, the one on Wednesday and the other on Saturday.

The current 35,000-square foot building—consuming almost an entire city block—was constructed in 1888 at a cost of $45,000. It was designed by noted local architect J. A. Dempwolf and was named to Pennsylvania's Inventory of Historic Places in 1977 and was listed on the National Register of Historic Places in 1988.

Walk into the York Central Market and you can just smell the aromas of hundreds of different foods and flavors. Culinary offerings include freshly made burritos at Roburritos, made-to-order sandwiches at the Busy Bee, homemade fried chicken at Bairs Fried Chicken, fresh-squeezed lemonade at Brunners Exotic Fruits, Mediterranean salads at Tina's Greek Salads, and sushi at Nama Sushi

There's always something good at York's Central Market.

264 ❖ HISTORIC TRAILS OF EASTERN PENNSYLVANIA

> **F**AST FACT: York's Central Market was one of the first structures in the city to have indoor plumbing.

Bar. My favorite place for lunch is J. R.'s French Fries, where I get the hot sausage sandwich and their sinfully delicious french fries. Try their fries and you'll never go back to anything else. They are *that* good.

After you finish your meal you can walk around and take a look at all of the different stands, including the Fish Market, Martin's Potato Chips, Charles Family Market, Henry's Ham, Dietz Fruits and Vegetables, Hartman's Fruit Farm, the J. L. Miller Sons Meat Market, or dozens of other stands waiting to satisfy your culinary desires.

The Central Market is York in miniature. For many residents, this is more than a market—it is a place where stories are shared, informal meetings are held, friendships are solidified, coffee is consumed, and the business of the city is conducted. It is also a place of fond memories and long-established traditions. In York, this is the place to be seen and the place where the pulse of the community can be felt. You'll hear and taste and smell and feel the heartbeat of authentic commerce as you walk around sampling the wares and enjoying the fresh farm food. If you've never been to a farm market, this is certainly the place—it's history, culture and food all bound together in a delightfully historic venue.

After exiting the market, walk across the street and pick up your car at the parking garage. Exit the garage and make a right turn onto Philadelphia Street. Drive to the intersection at Beaver Street and make a right turn. Drive north until you go over the railroad tracks. Make an immediate right turn at the next street (it's North Street, but there's no sign). Drive one block to North George Street. Make a left turn at the signal and cross over Codorus Creek. Move into the right-hand lane and you'll soon come to a traffic light at North George Street and Parkway Boulevard. Just after that signal (and just after you start going uphill) on the left side of North George Street will be **Prospect Hill Cemetery**. Make a left turn into the cemetery's Main Gate (between the two stone arches), drive up the short brick road just inside the wall on your right and park in front of the main office.

On June 7, 1864, Hiram Young, a reporter for the *True Democrat*, wrote, "We know no spot more charming, nor one to which a visit is more amply repaid, than Prospect Hill Cemetery.... Our citizens find much pleasure in visiting this burial

FAST FACT: Phillip Livingston, one of the signers of the Declaration of Independence, died in York (June 1778) while attending the Continental Congress. His grave is in the cemetery.

ground for the dead, and we would urge all strangers visiting our town to pay Prospect Hill a visit." That admonition is just as appropriate today as it was when it was originally written 150 years ago. This is a historical and cultural stroll through the lives of people from four different centuries—all of whom who have left an indelible mark on the York community.

During the War Between the States an estimated 6,000 soldiers from York County served in the conflict. Of that number about 4,100 Civil War soldiers have been buried in York County, with more than 1,000 buried in Prospect Hill Cemetery alone. All told, there are approximately 100,000 burials on the 327 acres of this historic cemetery. This is a history book waiting to be discovered.

After exiting your car, check in with the folks in the main office and let them know you would like to take a short stroll around the grounds (visitors are welcome, but the staff appreciates knowing who is on the grounds). Exit the office and turn left. Begin walking up the incline. As you do, notice the unusually shaped bricks on which you are walking. They look quite different from normal bricks and there's a good reason why. Prospect Hill Cemetery has its roots deep in the York community and was initially chartered on March 9, 1849, well in advance of the Civil War. Cars were non-existent in the early days of the Cemetery and hearses were typically horse-drawn carriages. Because Prospect Hill is on a hill, it would have been very difficult for the horses to get a foothold (called a "purchase") on flat, often slippery, bricks. As a result, special bricks were made with one edge beveled so that horses' hooves would have something to catch onto as they were trying to pull a heavy wagon or hearse up the hill. Those same odd-shaped bricks are still used today on this historic property.

FAST FACT: The number of war-related deaths from 1861 to 1865 is greater than the total number of American deaths in all other American wars.

As you walk up the incline you will come to a Y in the road. Bear to the right and straight ahead of you will be Soldier's Circle and its imposing and iconic statue of a Civil War soldier holding his rifle. Here is what the Historical Society of York County said about this monument in the 1930s:

> Surrounded by a broad avenue, Soldier's Circle has a row of trees around the edge. The graves are arranged in two circles, with the heads towards the outer edge. The same head boards mark the graves that were on the lots where the bodies were first interred but will be replaced before long by head stones furnished by the government. These stones when erected in their places will form a fence or enclosure for the lot. The number of bodies removed to this lot is one hundred and sixty-two, arranged so far as possible in states. Erected by the Ladies Aid Society and Citizens of York, PA in memory of the defenders of the Union 1861-65. US Hospital established at York, PA 1862. The dead here interred were soldiers of the Union from 16 states who died at the Hospital, at their homes or on the battlefield.

Prospect Hill Cemetery was initially chartered in March 1849.

Before you come to the monument, look to the right side of the road and you will begin to see a series of signs erected by the York County Heritage Trust. They are all part of a walking tour of the cemetery and identify significant grave sites in addition to some

biographical data about the people interred. The first signs are directly across from the cemetery office.

#8—To the right of the main drive and directly across from the cemetery office is a marker with the following: "Remembering 5 unknown dead 3 here, 2 near. The Twenty First Century Confederate League."

#3—This identifies the monument for Civil War soldier Murray Cross (1835–1897) who served for a total of three months in the Union Army. He participated in a number of significant battles, primarily in Virginia, and was recognized as "a brave soldier and an able and honorable man."

Continue your ascent until you get to Soldier's Circle. Begin walking in a counterclockwise direction, taking time to read the inscriptions on the headstones around the circle. When you get to the first road on your right, make a very short detour about ten yards up the road and look for the next sign.

#1—Here are the graves of Henry and Sarah Ann Bayler. The Baylers provided food, lodging and nursing care for wounded soldiers during the Civil War. Their house was located near the present-day intersection of Pershing and King Streets in York.

Return to Soldiers Circle and continue your counterclockwise journey. You'll soon arrive at markers #5 and #6.

#5—Here you'll note the grave of Daniel Kraber (1808–1882), who operated a lumber business on West Market Street in York. Kraber was affiliated with a number of benevolent societies after the Civil War, including the Committee of Safety and the Benevolent Association.

#6—There are two markers here—one for Cassandra Small Morris, who was a volunteer during the war—providing aid and comfort to wounded soldiers. The marker adjacent to hers is that of Charles Morris—the owner of the Morris Drug Company, which provided medicine for injured Union soldiers at Gettysburg.

Continue around the Circle and return to the road you came up on. Walk

FAST FACT: During the Civil War there were more Northern-born Confederate generals than Southern-born Union generals.

down about 20 yards and make a sharp right turn on the first side road. Walk about 30 yards until you come to another road on your left. At the intersection of those two roads will be a series of four signs clustered together.

#7—Here is the marker for David Small (1812–1885) who was the owner of *The York Gazette* and was also the chief burgess of York during the Civil War. He was one of the individuals who met with Confederate troops prior to their occupation of York.

#9—This is the gravestone for Margaret Duncan Fish (1846–1911) who worked for the Children's Home of York in the early part of the 20th century.

#10—Henry L. Fisher (1822–1909) was an attorney in York during the Civil War. As a regiment of soldiers returned home in September 1864, Fisher proclaimed, "You have nobly performed your duty, and your services will be recorded on the bright pages of history."

#13—Henrietta Yocum (1811–1875) was the sister of Confederate General Johnson Kelly Duncan and lived in York.

Walk down the road on your left (the road begins to slope downward) and in about 20 yards you will come to a small triangle of land on your left (just beyond you will note that the road on the other side of the triangle changes from asphalt to concrete). In the triangle are three signs.

#12—Nearby is the gravestone for Michael P. Small (1831–1892), who was instrumental in helping to quell the riot at Harper's Ferry in 1859 (known famously as John Brown's Raid). He was also at Appomattox for the official cessation of the Civil War.

#36—Hugh Whiteford McCall (1839–1931) helped to raise and organize a troop of soldiers in York County in June 1862. He later went on to become a lawyer, helping Civil War veterans with their pension applications.

#37—James A. Stable (1830–1912) worked a variety of jobs during the Civil War eventually rising to the rank of lieutenant colonel. He was also a representative for the 19th Congressional District of Pennsylvania.

Continue your walk down the slope until you get to the concrete road. Bear right along the road. When you come to a grassy road on your right you'll discover three more signs:

#11—Peter McIntyre (1806–1869) was a member of the York Committee of Safety during the Civil War. He was originally from Scotland and his occupation was: whip manufacturer.

#14—Thomas Andrew Ziegle (1824–1862) shares the tombstone with Peter McIntyre. He was a lawyer in York and also served in the Union Army.

#15—Thomas Evans Cochran (1813–1882) was the editor for *The York Republican* for several years in addition to providing counsel to the Committee of Safety during the time of the Confederate occupation.

Continue your walk along the concrete road until you come to the next intersection on your right (the road on your right will be asphalt). Just before the juncture of these two roads will be three signs:

#17—George Hay (1809–1879) was one of the men who met with General Gordon when Confederates arrived to take over the town of York. He was a cabinetmaker and undertaker.

#34—John A. Denig (1845–1876) was awarded the Medal of Honor for fighting with "skill and courage" at a pivotal battle on August 5, 1864. However, when he returned to York his life took a series of dramatic turns. Read the sign to discover the "interesting events" he got into.

#35—Abraham Rudisill (1811–1899) was one of the Civil War's oldest soldiers, having entered the service at the ripe old age of 50.

Make a right turn and head up the asphalt road toward Chapel Circle. On the right side you'll see the next sign.

#21—Charles A. Shetter (1839–1862) died at the tender age of 21 after being wounded at the Battle of Antietam.

Continue your walk and just as you begin to bear right around Chapel Circle will be cluster of four signs:

#16—John F. Fisher (1808–1862) was injured during the raising of a 110-foot flagpole in the center of York.

#18—Charles Henry Hgenfritz (1837–1920) was awarded the Medal of Honor "for most distinguished gallantry in action at Fort Sedgwick, VA."

#19—T. Kirk White (1826–1901) made sure the U.S. flag did not touch

FAST FACT: Surgeons in the 1800s never washed their hands after an operation, because all blood was assumed to be the same. They never washed their instruments either.

FAST FACT: Prospect Hill Cemetery is the final resting place for patriots from *every* war in which the United States has fought.

the ground during its lowering by Confederate troops.

#21—Charles A. Shetter (1839–1862) was another young soldier (23 years old) who died as the result of wounds at the Battle of Antietam.

Walk around Chapel Circle a quarter-circle and turn down the first road on your right. You'll pass by another asphalt road. Continue on for a few more yards and you'll arrive at two more signs:

#2—Margaret Duncan Beitzel (1815–1872) was the sister of Confederate General Johnson Kelly Duncan—one of the Confederate occupiers of York.

#4—Jacob Horlebein (1836–1865) was a Union soldier who was captured and imprisoned at the infamous Andersonville Prison. He died shortly after his release and return to York.

Continue your walk toward Stewart Circle (identified by the large mausoleum). Make a quarter turn to the right around the circle and head down the first road on your right. As you walk down this road you will begin to see Soldier's Circle directly in front of you. Bear left around Soldier's Circle, down the incline, and return to your vehicle.

During your walk throughout this cemetery you will see, not only the graves and tombs of Civil War veterans, but also the markers for folks from many different eras in York's history. You might want to take note of the various decorations on the grave markers, the architecture of the various monuments, and the decorative styles prevalent during various ages in the history of the city. Gothic, Corinthian, Greek Revival, and other styles considerably more simple in their design and execution are scattered throughout the grounds. Take time to read some of the inscriptions or gaze at some of the design features and you will be amazed at the incredible diversity of remembrances and the equally incredible diversity of individuals who walked this city throughout its history.

I have had the good fortune to visit Prospect Hill Cemetery on several occasions—each time coming away with new information and a deeper appreciation for the chronicles within these acres. Prospect Hill should be on every visitor's list of things to see in York. While a cemetery might not be the first thing you think of when considering sites and attractions in a new town, you will discover that this extraordinary place is a treasured step through the history pages of York.

CONTACTS

Downtown York Visitors Information Center, 149 West Market St., York, PA; (717) 852-9675; www.yorkpa.org.

York County Heritage Trust, 250 East Market St., York, PA; (717) 848-1587; www.yorkheritage.org.

Central Market York, 34 West Philadelphia St., York, PA 17401; (717) 848-2243; www.centralmarketyork.com.

Prospect Hill Cemetery, 700 North George St., York, PA 17404; (717) 843-8006; www.prospecthill.org.

The National Civil War Museum in Harrisburg

14 Civil War Trails

Estimated length: 186 miles

Estimated time: 2 days

Combine this tour with: Chapters 13, 15, and 16

Getting there: This journey begins in Harrisburg at the National Civil War Museum—a must-see for anyone with even a passing interest in this time period. Then we're off to a succession of small towns—Mechanicsburg, Carlisle, Chambersburg, Mercersburg, Greencastle, Cashtown, Hanover Junction, and Wrights - ville—all of which witnessed various episodes and events of the Civil War with varying degrees of victory and defeat.

Highlights: Any Civil War buff will love this tour. It starts off at an excellent museum and takes you around to various towns and burgs that felt the onslaught of this grand conflict first-hand. You'll encounter interesting people and sites and witness some of the events closer than you ever thought possible.

Tourists from around the world have long recognized southeastern Pennsylvania as a mecca for Civil War buffs. A proliferation of historical sites, acres of battlegrounds, untold numbers of museums, annual re-enactments, and all manner of artillery and artifacts lure visitors in droves each year to this area rich in history and ripe for exploration.

The American Civil War was a conflict that defined this country in ways both political and geographical. It was a war of rights—the rights of individuals as well as the rights of states—and though it resulted in the greatest number of casualties of any American conflict, it also cemented the viability and strength of our constitutional government.

A Union officer's uniform at the National Civil War Museum

The underlying construct for the hostilities between North and the South was the complicated issue of slavery—or rather whether slavery was an out-of-date evil or a practice protected by the Constitution. Anti-slavery forces (primarily in the North) wanted to prevent the expansion of slavery and eventually eliminate it from the American landscape. Southerners, on the other hand, believed that slavery and its practice was one of their Constitutional rights.

During the early 1800s, slavery was a constant source of political tension between the Republican party and many legislators in the South. Republicans were determined to eradicate slavery and many Southern legislators threatened to secede from the Union if Abraham Lincoln, the 1860 Republican candidate for president, was elected.

By the late 1850s the issue of slavery was ripping the country apart. The polarization—politically, socially and economically—was clearly evident in almost every aspect of American life. It was a time of intense turmoil and national upheaval.

The election of Lincoln as our country's 16th president was the spark that ignited the Civil War and plunged the United States into a bloody four-year conflict that resonates even today. Here are some of those early events:

November 6, 1860	Abraham Lincoln is elected President.
December 20, 1860	The South Carolina legislature votes to leave the Union.

January 9 to February 1, 1861	Mississippi, Florida, Alabama, Georgia, Louisiana, and Texas join South Carolina to form the Confederate States of America.
February 18, 1861	Jefferson Davis becomes president of the Confederacy.
March 4, 1861	Lincoln is sworn in as president of the United States.
April 12, 1861	The Confederates attack Fort Sumter, South Carolina.
April 17 to May 20, 1861	Virginia, Arkansas, Tennessee, and North Carolina join the Confederacy.

As a northern state, Pennsylvania was immediately thrust into the conflict. The state provided both men and the industrial complex that helped support and fuel the Union cause from the first days of the war until the very end. Four days in advance of the Confederate attack on Fort Sumter, Pennsylvania, Governor Andrew Gregg Curtain met with President Lincoln. He quickly returned home and petitioned the Pennsylvania legislature to increase the number of available soldiers. When war erupted on April 12, 1861, Curtain dispatched five companies of men to Washington, DC. Although they arrived without weapons and a lack of military training, they were quickly placed around the Capitol building to guard it against any potential invaders. By the end of the war Pennsylvania had contributed in excess of 427,000 men—the most of any state—to the Union effort.

Most of the Civil War took place in southern locations and for the first few years of the conflict northern states were spared the destruction and pillaging of their landscape. Pennsylvania was no different. Although there were battles across its southern neighbor Maryland (the Battle of Antietam), for the most part Pennsylvania was spared the gore and destruction. However, that was all to change in October 1862 when Confederate troops under the command of Major General J. E. B. "Jeb" Stuart raided the small Pennsylvania town of Chambersburg. By spring of 1863, there were rumblings and rumors of additional Confederate troops poised to invade the gentle Pennsylvania landscape and ravage every hamlet and burg north of the Mason-Dixon Line.

FAST FACT: According to one estimate, 2 percent of the American population died in the Civil War.

> **F**AST FACT: At one time in our country's history, one out of every seven Americans belonged to another American.

After a decisive victory at the Battle of Chancellorsville in late spring 1863, General Lee made the bold decision to move his troops north into Pennsylvania. The decision was a calculated one—one that would reveal the strength of the Confederate forces and their ability to tackle the Union army on northern soil and one that might persuade European countries to come to the aid of the Confederacy. Lee had also hoped that that a significant conflict in Pennsylvania would divert Union forces from western operations and eventually spare several southern cities (most notably Vicksburg) from vicious and substantial attacks.

Lee commanded his troops to invade Pennsylvania in late spring 1863 and to obtain goods and supplies from every farm and town they could. Horses, cattle, machinery, crops, and anything else that might supply the troops was plundered from farms and homes throughout the southern tier of Pennsylvania. Lee's mapmaker, Jedediah Hotchkiss noted:"We shall get nearly a million dollars worth of horses and supplies of all kinds from Franklin County alone, and we have also invaded Fulton and Adams Counties, and shall levy on them in like manner. We are supporting the army entirely on the enemy."

In June 1863 Lee moved large numbers of his troops into the northern end of the Shenandoah Valley—a critical piece of geography that allowed easy access into Pennsylvania as well as a direct route to Washington, DC. After a rout of Union forces outside Winchester, Virginia on June 13, 1863, Lee saw an opportunity to move war-tested battalions north and into the politically and militarily fertile fields of the Keystone State.

Your journey along some of Pennsylvania's Civil War Trails is a historical trek into some of the lesser-known, but equally significant, regions where this great conflict was fought. While this tour won't visit the pivotal battlefield near Gettysburg (we'll devote all of Chapter 15 to that), you will have an opportunity to tra-

> **F**AST FACT: A number of women passed themselves off as men and served in military units during the Civil War. About 450 cases of female soldiers have been documented.

verse a region that was as much a part of the Civil War as was any naval bombardment, prisoner of war camp, or military engagement.

We'll begin this tour at the **National Civil War Museum** in downtown Harrisburg. This is unquestionably one of the finest museums you will ever visit (it's affiliated with the Smithsonian Institution so you know it's good). The curators have made a conscious effort to portray the Civil War without showing any favoritism to either the North or the South. The museum's goal is to tell the complete story of the conflict—focusing on the issues, people, and lives that were affected. The causes and ramifications of the conflict are investigated and both Northern and Southern viewpoints are authentically presented.

This is what a museum should be: there's something for everyone, from the youngest to oldest member of the family. As you walk from room to room you are

"Moment of Mercy" statue outside the National Civil War Museum

presented with lifelike displays, fascinating information, mesmerizing artifacts, illuminating characters, spellbinding events, and a unique attention to historical accuracy. The combination truly makes this museum a "class act." My first visit consumed the better part of the day: I was swept up by the grandeur and professionalism of the exhibits, along with the intriguing details that are so often missing from staid history textbooks.

As you approach the entrance, one of the first things you will notice is the three-dimensional bronze statue entitled "Moment of Mercy." It depicts a young Confederate sergeant, Richard Rowland Kirkland, engaged in an act of incredible compassion and courage during the horrific Battle of Fredericksburg on December 13, 1862. The story of this young man sets the stage for the journey you are about to take.

After purchasing your admission ticket, walk to the rotunda and ascend the staircase on your left. Your self-guided tour begins on the second floor in the first gallery—**A House Divided, 1850-1860**. Here you will learn about the incidents and issues that propelled the nation toward the Civil War. Both Northern and Southern views are presented, including John Brown's Raid and Lincoln's election. In the second gallery (**American Slavery: the Peculiar Institution, 1850-1860**) you are confronted with the cruelty of slavery including an authentically created slave auction.

The next three galleries (**First Shots, 1861**; **Making of Armies**; **Weapons and Equipment**) bring you face to face with the beginnings of the war. Here you'll see a three-dimensional and lifelike diorama of the bombardment of Fort Sumter, recruiting posters for both Union and Confederate troops, and an unbelievable assembly of firearms, swords, accoutrements, ammunition and very distinctive weapons from both the Northern and Southern armies.

Galleries 6, 7, and 8 focus on the **Campaigns and Battles of 1862**, a lighted **Battle Map, 1861-1862**, and a diorama of **Camp Curtin** in Harrisburg, the largest Union camp of rendezvous in the North. Throughout the museum are videos and simulated sounds of soldiers marching, singing, and working along with commanders giving battle orders. The following two galleries, **Why Men Fought, 1861–1863** and

FAST FACT: The melody of the popular Civil War ballad "Aura Lee" was later used for Elvis Presley's "Love Me Tender."

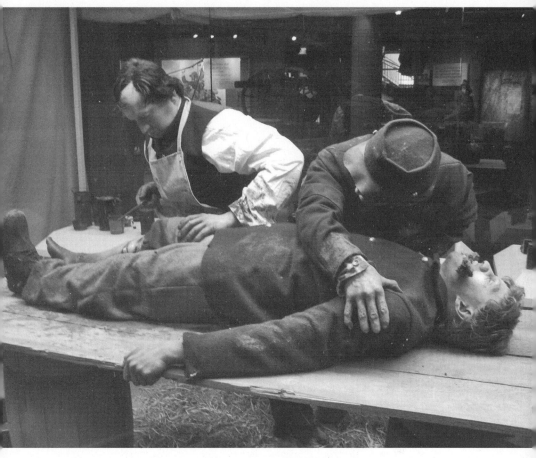

Amputations were a common procedure during the Civil War.

Civil War Music, offer up information on why soldiers enlisted and how they entertained themselves once they did. You can even play your favorite Civil War song.

At this point, you will descend to the first floor and get an up-close-and-personal introduction to the **Battle of Gettysburg** in Gallery 11. The next several galleries present aspects of the war that don't get much attention in history books or television documentaries. These include the **Cost of War**—the physical suffering experienced by so many soldiers (be prepared for the lifelike leg amputation); **Women in the War**; **Navy**—a reminder that not all the battles were fought on land; and **Campaigns and Battles of 1864-1865**. One of the most touching

> **F**AST FACT: The Civil War Museum has catalogued over 4,000 artifacts and 21,000 archival documents.

artifacts is the Bible carried by Robert E. Lee from 1847 until the end of the war. You'll also view the **Battle Map**, which depicts significant events that took place throughout the duration of the war.

Finally, you'll view **Lincoln: War and Remembrance**—a tribute to our 16th president, a retrospective of the war, and the role of veterans after the war. Here, via an interactive exhibit, you'll be able to ask questions about war strategy, the evils of slavery, and significant events in Lincoln's life. Afterward, you may want to saunter over to the gift shop and their expansive collection of Civil War books, maps, guidebooks, and memorabilia.

Please don't pass up the opportunity to visit one of the great museums of the country. You could spend an entire day here drinking in the beautifully mounted displays, the exquisite dioramas, the unbelievable statistics, and engaging stories that were so much a part of this conflict. This museum is just as much about the human experience as it is about the war itself.

Exit the museum and Reservoir Park and turn right onto Market Street. Make a left turn on South 17th Street and then turn right to merge onto I-83 south. After about two miles make a slight left onto PA 581 west (headed toward Camp Hill/Gettysburg). Travel for about 2.5 miles and continue onto US 11 south. Take exit 4 toward PA 641 west (Mechanicsburg). Stay on PA 641 west until you come into Mechanicsburg (the road changes over to East Main Street).

In 1863 the good citizens of Mechanicsburg came face to face with the realities of the war. On a certain Sunday morning they exited their respective churches to discover their town under siege by Confederate troops. Many folks had heard about the impending arrival of soldiers and had wisely shipped many personal belongings out of town to prevent their confiscation.

Nevertheless, Confederate General Albert Jenkins (whom we will meet again in another town) demanded provisions and supplies. It was through the courageous actions of then-mayor George Hummel that the town was not completely ransacked and burned to the ground.

If you have a desire at this point in your journey for some Civil War memorabilia, plan to stop in at **Civil War and More** at 10 South Market Street in Mechanicsburg. The staff will also be able to point you to several Civil War sites around town.

Depart Mechanicsburg and continue on PA 641 toward the quaint and historic town of Carlisle 10 miles west.

> **F**AST FACT: The *Alligator* was an experimental Union submarine, which was declared useless in battle.

With its tree-lined streets, historic architecture, romantic restaurants, and genuine small-town feel, Carlisle resembles Bedford Falls—the town in the classic Jimmy Stewart film, *It's a Wonderful Life*. More importantly, it was the site of the Battle of Carlisle.

During the early evening of July 1, 1863 (note the date), Confederate troops under the command of Major General J. E. B. Stuart entered Carlisle looking for supplies. The town was "protected" at that time by Union General William Smith who declined an offer to surrender. As a result, the Confederates commenced bombarding the town. After several hours of continuous shelling, Stuart received word of an engagement that was currently taking place in a little town south of Carlisle—Gettysburg. Stuart immediately ordered his troops to set fire to the Carlisle Barracks and at 1 AM on the morning of July 2, the Confederates left town and marched toward Gettysburg.

While you are here, be sure to stroll the picturesque campus of Dickenson College. At the time of the Civil War, the student body was evenly split between Northern and Southern sympathizers. Many of the students enlisted in the two armies, occasionally facing each other on the field of battle. In the archives of the college is an autograph book that chronicles the parting words of 118 students headed off to war. Here, students penned their final goodbyes to both friends and family.

> **F**AST FACT: The Medal of Honor, the nation's highest decoration for valor, was first authorized in a bill passed by Congress and approved by President Lincoln in December of 1861. Over 1,200 Medals of Honor were awarded for gallantry in action during the Civil War. Sixteen Army Medal of Honor and 8 Navy Medal of Honor recipients were African-Americans.

On your way out of town, drive past the Old Cumberland County Courthouse on North Hanover Street. Look up at the old pillars and you'll be able to see the scars from the bombardment of Confederate troops during the Battle of Carlisle.

The next portion of this tour will be less about the Civil War and more about the scenic beauty of rural Pennsylvania. Depart Carlisle on PA 34 south (South Hanover Street). Continue on PA 34 south for four miles and make a right turn onto PA 174 west. Travel on PA 174 west for about 7.5 miles past endless acres of farmland, red barns, and rolling hills. When you come to the intersection of PA-233 south, make a left turn. For the next 20 miles you'll be traveling through beautiful Pine Grove Furnace State Park. If you're traveling in late spring or summer be sure to open up your car windows and fill the interior with authentic pine scent.

When you come to Pine Grove Furnace Park, PA 233 makes a slight right turn. Immediately in front of you will be an old ironmaster's house (circa 1829). Continue along the road and pass through beautiful Caledonia State Park (the perfect place for a picnic lunch if you happen to have one in the back of the car). You may want to park your car in the park and do as my wife and I love to do on long summer days—stretch your legs out on one of the many trails that wind their way through the dense woods and bubbling streams of this state treasure

When you come to the traffic signal at the intersection of PA 233 south and US 30 west (Lincoln Highway), make a right onto US 30 and head west toward Chambersburg. Just after the turn you'll see the old blacksmith's shop of Thaddeus Stevens (on the right side)—an individual we met in Chapter 3 and will meet again in Chapter 16.

Continue along US 30 west. You'll come into the less-attractive end of Chambersburg—a slew of fast-food restaurants, shopping malls, and chain restaurants—before you get to the quaint and considerably more civilized section of town.

If we were to look at Chambersburg through the lens of the Civil War, I suppose we should rename it "Conflagration City" or "Flaming Acres" or "Burning Estates." Between 1861 and 1865, Chambersburg seemed to attract a bevy of Con-

---

FAST FACT: General Robert E. Lee's father fought in the Revolutionary war.

FAST FACT: By the beginning of 1862, the Civil War was costing the U.S. government over $1 million a day. To finance the war, Congress passed the first income tax in U.S. history in July 1862. The federal Civil War Income Tax formed the basis for the present income-tax system.

federate arsonists and a host of Southern pyro technicians. It was set aflame three separate times during the four years of the war.

The first "invasion" of Southern troops into this geographically strategic town was on October 10, 1862. Eighteen hundred Confederate forces under the command of Major General J. E. B. Stuart raided Chambersburg. In the process they gathered up hundreds of horses, confiscated about 500 guns, cut telegraph wires, and demolished approximately $250,000 worth of railroad property. One of their primary targets was the burning of the railroad bridge across the Conococheague Creek at Scotland, about five miles north of town. They didn't quite succeed in that venture...but they would be back.

In the weeks prior to the Gettysburg campaign, a brigade of Confederate soldiers under the command of Brigadier General Albert G. Jenkins came into town and proceeded to set several warehouses, railroad structures, and the aforementioned bridge on fire. From June 24 to 28, 1863, large segments of the Army of Northern Virginia tramped their way through Chambersburg on their way to Gettysburg. Robert E. Lee also set up some temporary headquarters at a nearby farm.

As luck or circumstance would have it, the citizens of Chambersburg saw Confederate troops (commanded by General John McCauslend) enter their town for a third, and most devastating, time. The weary town decided not to cooperate with the invaders and refused to pay a ransom of either $500,000 in U.S. currency or $100,000 in good old American gold. This irritated the invaders to no end, and on July 30, 1864, they commenced to set a large portion of the town on fire—leaving very few buildings standing and the city in complete and total ruins. The fire destroyed over 550 structures, including homes, businesses, and out-buildings. The devastation left 2,000 people homeless and caused property damage of $783,000.

Interestingly, in 1878 the city erected a seven-foot statue of a Union soldier in the center of town. The soldier is facing south—presumably to guard against the return of Southern raiders. Too little, too late, I guess.

Your first stop in town should be the **Heritage Center** on the southeast corner of the square (corner of US 30 and US 11). There is a small parking area behind this former bank building. The folks inside the Heritage Center will provide you with brochures, guides, and information about this historic town. If you plan to spend some time here, ask for a copy of the Historic Downtown Walking Tour—an easy-to-navigate guide to 21 historic sites in and around the downtown area. The town has been around since 1730, so it has lots of history to share with visitors.

Two buildings pertinent to our Civil War journey are located on East King Street. The first is the Old Jail and Library (175 East King Street). The jail was built in 1818 and it is one of the few buildings to survive the burning of Chambersburg in 1864. This building is one of the oldest in Chambersburg and was placed on the State and National Register of Historical Sites in 1970.

During more than 150 years of use as a prison, the Old Jail housed a number of notorious criminals including "Lewis the Robber" and Captain John Cook. The cellar contains five domed dungeons with rings in the wall and floors that were used to shackle prisoners. Tradition suggests that these cells were also used as a "station" on the Underground Railroad to shelter runaway slaves enroute to freedom in the north. The Old Jail Complex consists of the original 1818 building, a 1880 annex and a yard enclosed by a 20-foot high limestone wall. Today, the jail is home to the Franklin County Historical Society—an excellent source of Civil War history.

From here, take a short walk down East King Street to 225 East King Street. According to my guide, this unassuming house played a much more important role in the Civil War than its plain exterior might indicate.

In 1859, the house served as a boardinghouse owned by the widow Mary Ritner, whose late husband was an abolitionist and may have been a "conductor" on the Underground Railroad. In the summer of 1859, a knock on the door revealed an old gentleman with a white beard. He sought lodging for several months and indicated that his name was Dr. Isaac Smith. "Smith" was actually an alias for John Brown, one of the fiercest and most determined abolitionists of the time.

Brown had decided to make this house his base of operations for his eventual attack on the army arsenal at Harper's Ferry, West Virginia. There was a price on

Brown's head for murders he had committed in Kansas and he needed a safe place to stay and begin collecting weapons for his planned assault. In August of that year Brown met with Frederick Douglass in Chambersburg to discuss his planned attack and solicit Douglass's support. But Douglass refused and called Brown's plan "sheer madness."

Brown's plan was to use rifles and guns captured at Harper's Ferry to arm rebellious slaves in hopes that they might strike fear into Virginia's slaveholders. Ultimately, the raid on Harper's Ferry failed and Brown was tried for treason and sentenced to death. Hanged on December 2, 1859, John Brown was the first white man to use violence in an attempt to end slavery.

Brown's violent attempt to take over the armory at Harpers Ferry scared many in the South. As a result, Southern state militias began training for any further attempts by Northerners to take over their territories. The South became increasingly more militaristic toward the North—a stance that was to further fan the flames of discord and discontent that eventually led to the Civil War.

FAST FACT: One of the witnesses at John Brown's hanging was John Wilkes Booth—the future assassin of President Abraham Lincoln.

John Brown House historical marker

Depart Chambersburg via US 30 west and drive west for about 8.5 miles. Make a left turn on PA 416 south toward Mercersburg. Stay on PA 416 for about 7.5 miles until you come into the small town of Mercersburg.

Here you will discover one of those interesting anecdotes that personalizes

The John Brown House in Chambersburg

the Civil War and makes it much more than just an endless series of bloody battles. For it was in this tiny town that Confederate General J. E. B. Stuart paid a
visit to one Mrs. George Steiger. Stuart was intent on turning the Steiger house
into his headquarters while his men went about sacking and looting the town for
necessary supplies and food. However, the clever Mrs. Steiger rebuffed Stuart by
telling him that her husband was away on business and that all her children had
come down with German measles. She strongly suggested that it might not be in
Stuart's best interests to enter the home. He decided to have a quiet little lunch
outside instead.

In a most ironic twist of fate, the rebels, on their way out of town encountered a livestock dealer. They quickly took possession of his horses and wagon and took him prisoner as well. What they didn't know was that the gentleman was Mr. George Steiger. Apparently cleverness ran in the Steiger family, for later that night, while pretending to care for his horses, Mr. Steiger slipped away. Traveling via a roundabout route to avoid re-capture he arrived back at his house at around 1 AM. There to greet him were friends and neighbors who had arrived to console his wife. The celebration was joyous, to say the least.

At the onset of the Civil War, Mercersburg had a considerable African-American population. Unfortunately, African-Americans were forbidden to join the Union Army until President Lincoln signed the Emancipation Proclamation on January 1, 1863. Eighty-eight African-American men from Mercersburg immediately enlisted in the Army—serving with either the 54th or 55th Massachusetts Volunteer Infantry Regiments. Thirty-eight of those Civil War veterans are buried in Zion Union Cemetery. You can visit this historic cemetery and read the grave markers. To do so, travel along PA 416 south until it becomes a Y (PA 416 continues to the left and the right-hand portion of the "Y' becomes Linden Avenue.). Travel down Linden Avenue until you come to Fairview Avenue. Make a right turn on Fairview Avenue and then a left on Bennett Avenue. Zion Union Cemetery will be directly ahead.

Return to PA 416 and in very short order the road changes over to PA 16 east. Continue on PA 16 for 10.3 miles until you arrive in Greencastle. Greencastle is a quiet town with a pristine Main Street and well-kept side streets. Founded in 1782 it was named for a town in Northern Ireland and settled by both Irish and Scotch immigrants.

One of Greencastle's claims to fame occurred on July 2, 1863, during the Gettysburg Campaign. It was on that day that a small band of Union soldiers captured two Confederate couriers as they were passing through Greencastle's Center Square. The couriers had a message from Richmond to General Lee that Confederate troops would not be able to advance on Washington from Virginia while Lee was in Pennsylvania. This was a key piece of military information and pivotal in turning the tide to the Union's advantage during the second day of the Battle of Gettysburg.

Just before you enter the town of Greencastle, make a left turn onto US 11 north (also known as North Antrim Way). Just north of the intersection of PA 16 east and US 11 north is a tall granite obelisk that stands alongside the road in

FAST FACT: William Rihl has the dubious distinction of being the first Union soldier killed above the Mason-Dixon line during the Civil War.

front of a white farmhouse. This obelisk denotes the spot where Union Corporal William Rihl was gunned down.

Rihl was originally from Philadelphia when he joined the Union army in 1861. Two years later, on June 22, 1863, Rihl and his unit were ambushed by a group of Confederate cavalrymen right where the obelisk now stands. Struck in the head with a Confederate bullet, Rihl, only 20 years old, died instantly.

Rihl's remains lie in the same spot where he was killed. The obelisk was raised in 1886 by the state of Pennsylvania to honor "a humble but brave defender of the Union."

Return to PA 16 east and turn left. Travel a short distance to South Ridge Avenue and make a right turn. Drive down this street for a short distance until you arrive at the **Allison-Antrim Museum** on the right.

The Allison-Antrim Museum is a repository of select letters from several Civil War soldiers who enlisted from this area. Some of the letters written by two men, George Frederick Ziegler I from Greencastle and Samuel W. North from the Mercersburg area, were kept by several generations of each family and are now maintained by the museum. A third soldier from this area was Joseph A. Davison, and his Civil War letters are also here. For Civil War buffs, these letters provide a most interesting insight into the thoughts of these soldiers as they went about their daily business. But even more important, they reveal the changes these soldiers experienced as they became more practiced in the affairs of war and its consequences. The museum offers a unique insight into the thoughts of men in battle and the metamorphosis they underwent during the time of their enlistments.

After the museum, return along South Ridge Avenue to PA 16 east. Make a right and drive for 8.5 miles to the town of Waynesboro. Make a left turn onto PA 997 north and drive for 6.7 miles until you come to the very small town of Mont Alto. Make a right turn onto PA 233 north and drive for approximately 8.8 miles until you come to the traffic signal at US 30 east. You will quickly discover the journey along PA 233 reveals forested scenery that is as spectacular as it is beautiful.

When you arrive at US 30 east, make a right turn at the signal (you will be directly across from the entrance to Caledonia State Park, which you visited earlier

The Allison-Antrim Museum in Greencastle

in the day). Drive for 6.6 miles until you come to the blinking signal at the inter-section of US 30 east and Cashtown Road. Make a right turn onto Cashtown Road (also known as High Street) and travel .7 mile to the end of the road. Make a right turn and in about .1 mile will be the historic **Cashtown Inn** on your right. Pull into the spacious parking lot.

The Cashtown Inn was built around 1797 and initially served as a stagecoach stop along the newly constructed Chambersburg Turnpike. Its destiny was to change, however, during the Civil War and specifically during the Gettysburg Campaign of 1863. For a short time, the inn served as Confederate headquarters for General A. P. Hill while his 22,000 men bivouacked in the immediate area. At

The Cashtown Inn, where good food awaits

the conclusion of the Battle of Gettysburg, General John Imboden took over the inn as a staging area for the evacuation of wounded soldiers throughout the area. On July 4, the defeated and beleaguered Confederates began their long retreat south. Imboden wrote, "About 4 PM the head of the column was put in motion near Cashtown and began the ascent of the mountain in the direction of Chambersburg."

Today, the inn still stands in much the same manner as it did more than 150 years ago. But today it is a popular restaurant with a flair for culinary delicacies and expertly prepared repasts. These are meals that offer excitement for the taste buds and a lasting satisfaction absent from all those blazing neon chain restaurants down the road.

Some of my favorite dishes are the spinach salad, the herb-parmesan crusted New Zealand rack of lamb, the Mediterranean farfalle, and the pan-seared pork-loin. Bring your sense of culinary adventure to either the Victorian dining room or the historic tavern room and you will be most pleasantly

> **F**AST FACT: One historian calculated that 10 percent of all Northern white males and 30 percent of all Southern white males were killed during the Civil War.

satiated. You may also spend the night here in the equally charming B&B operated on the premises.

After your meal, return to the blinking light at US 30. Pause for a moment because you will need to make a critical decision. You can make a right turn onto US 30 and head east to Gettysburg, 7.9 miles down the road. If you haven't taken advantage of the tours described in Chapters 15 and 16, this would be an ideal time to put either one on your itinerary (adding another day or two to your journey). Whatever you decide, it will require you to pass through or by Gettysburg on your way across Adams County and into historic York County.

Continue traveling on US 30 east past Gettysburg (Just on the other side of Gettysburg US 30 makes a little jag to the left and picks up a new name—York

Hanover Junction: Abraham Lincoln was here!

Road.). Drive for approximately 24.1 miles (you will go through two traffic circles in the towns of New Oxford and Abbottstown) until you come to the intersection with PA 616 south (there will be a large gas station across the street). Turn right and drive for about 5.7 miles (you'll go through the town of York-New Salem). You'll eventually come to a tricky five-way intersection with only two stop signs. Slow down and make the second right (not the first, which is SR 3041 or Green Valley Road) onto PA 616 south (now called Seven Valleys Road). About 100 yards down this road on the left, will be a bar and pizza place ("open til 2 AM"). Travel for 1.3 miles to Hanover Junction on your left. Although it's a red building, it's easy to miss due in part to a small sign parallel, rather than perpendicular, to the road. Turn left into the parking area.

Hanover Junction was established in 1851 as a railroad junction of the Northern Central Railway and the Hanover Branch Railroad. A hotel and a handful of houses were built in order to serve railroad passengers transferring from one rail line to another. During the Civil War, the rail lines were essential to the Union efforts to quickly transport troops and supplies. Hanover Junction saw as many as 30 train stops daily, as the Northern Central carried troops and supplies heading to Washington for service in the Army of the Potomac.

The Confederates recognized the significance of Union railroads to their war effort and would do anything in their power to destroy or demolish rail lines and rail communities in their effort to isolate Washington, DC from the protection of Union forces. Thus, on June 29, 1863, Lieutenant Colonel Elijah White and the 35th Virginia Calvary raided the Hanover Junction railroad station and destroyed the building. Repairs were quickly made and the station served as a stopover for President Abraham Lincoln when, on November 19, 1963, he paused here for several hours waiting to change trains on his way to Gettysburg to deliver the Gettysburg Address. After Lincoln's assassination, the Northern Central carried his funeral train through New Freedom and Hanover Junction, stopping in the city of York to take on water for the train's boiler.

Added to the National Registrar of Historic Places in 1983, Hanover Junction has been faithfully restored to its Civil War appearance and reopened as a small museum. After visiting the museum and walking the grounds, you can board the **Steam into History Train (York #17)**—a faithful recreation of a Civil War train—and travel part of the Northern Central Railway, clickety-clacking over part of the same route President Lincoln did a century and a half ago.

The Columbia-Wrightsville Bridge still stands.

After your train ride, make a right turn out of the parking area to PA 616 north and return to US 30 east. Stay on US 30 east for about 16 miles. Take the exit toward PA 462/Wrightsville and merge onto Cool Springs Road/SR 1016. Drive for about .9 mile and turn left onto Hellam Street (PA 462). Continue driving for .7 mile and drive to the end of the road (on the left side of the bridge). Make a right turn and drive on South Front Street for about 400 yards. Park your car along the road or in the first small dirt parking lot on the left. Look over to your left and there will be the Wrightsville Bridge.

The town of Wrightsville itself began in 1730 with the establishment of a ferry service across the Susquehanna River by one John Wright. George Washington

FAST FACT: It is often erroneously believed that the South had more casualties than the North during the Civil War. Not so—in all, the North had 275,000 wounded and 140,414 killed in action, while the South had 137,000 wounded and 72,524 killed in action.

frequently used the services of the ferry to get across the Susquehanna. Unfortunately, the ferry became obsolete when a bridge was constructed across the river in 1814.

The bridge received considerable attention during the Civil War. The Confederates viewed it as a strategic way to move troops across the river into Lancaster County and eventually up to Harrisburg. As a result, southern forces under the command of General John B. Gordon sought to capture this valuable piece of real estate. However, Union forces were there first and dug entrenchments in a horseshoe shape around the bridge.

Unfortunately, the Confederates had superior numbers of troops—a fact that Union commander Andrew Frick quickly realized. He also knew his troops were weary and untested and would be an easy match for the much better-prepared Confederates. Thus, Frick decided to destroy the bridge. He initially assaulted it with explosives and gunpowder, but the bridge was well-built and defied significant destruction. Since it was constructed primarily of wood, the decision was made to set the entire thing on fire. As you might imagine this long span across the wide Susquehanna must have been a unique sight blazing in the night. A reporter for the York Gazette wrote: "The scene was magnificent.... The moon was bright, and the blue clouds afforded the best contrast possible to the red glare of the conflagration. The light in the heavens must have been seen for many miles."

FAST FACT: Little known to most people, the town of Wrightsville was once considered by George Washington as a strong possibility for the new nation's capital.

Although the Confederates tried in vain to save the bridge it was completely destroyed. As a result, Confederate troops were prevented from attacking Harrisburg. Today, you can travel across that same bridge as you drive from York to Lancaster County. As you do, imagine the townspeople of

Wrightsville dashing across the bridge—ahead of advancing Confederate troops—while Union soldiers were setting the entire structure on fire on a warm summer evening in 1863.

CONTACTS

The National Civil War Museum, One Lincoln Circle at Reservoir Park, Harrisburg, PA; (717) 260-1861 or (866) BLU-GRAY; www.nationalcivilwarmuseum.org.

Borough of Mechanicsburg, 36 West Allen St., Mechanicsburg, PA 17055; (717) 691-3310; www.mechanicsburgborough.org.

Carlisle Borough, 53 West South St., Carlisle PA 17013; (717) 249-4422; www.carlislepa.org.

Chambersburg Heritage Center, 100 Lincoln Way East, Chambersburg, PA 17201; (717) 264-7101; www.visitpa.com/chambersburg-heritage-center.

Old Jail Museum and Library; 175 East King St., Chambersburg, PA 17201; (717) 264-1667; www.pafch.tripod.com.

John Brown House (Franklin County Historical Society—Kittochtinny) 225 East King St., Chambersburg, PA 17201; (717) 264-1667; johnbrownhouse.tripod.com.

Allison-Atrium Museum, 365 South Ridge Ave., Greencastle, PA 17225; (717) 597-9010; www.greencastlemuseum.org.

Steam Into History, Inc., 221 West Philadelphia St., Suite E600, York, PA 17401; (717) 881-9966; www.steamintohistory.com.

DINING

The Cashtown Inn, 1325 Old Route 30, Cashtown-McKnightstown, PA 17310; (717) 334-9722; www.cashtowninn.com.

The Eternal Light Peace Memorial is a reconciliation between the Blue and the Gray.

15 The Battle of Gettysburg

Estimated length: 24 miles

Estimated time: 1–2 days

Combine this tour with: Chapters 14 and 16

Getting there: If you are staying in the town of Gettysburg, note that a few of the hotels have complimentary transportation to the park. If you are arriving from out of town or are staying at a hotel without complimentary shuttle service, you should drive your car to the National Park Service Visitors Center. From here, plan on using your vehicle to stop at all the selected locations on this tour.

Highlights: The first time you drive through the battlefield at Gettysburg you will, quite simply, be amazed. Nothing can prepare you for what you are about to experience—no history book, no brochure, no guidebook. This is an American venue that you truly need to see to believe.

The Battle of Gettysburg is often identified as the most crucial battle of the Civil War. It took place at a time when our country's history literally hung in the balance. It was the culmination of one of the most ambitious campaigns by the Confederates—an overwhelming and decisive invasion of the north. It was a battle of attrition as much as it was a battle of superiority. The "last man standing" would determine the fate of an army as much as it would determine the fate of a nation.

Almost by accident the Army of Northern Virginia and the Army of the Potomac met in a small crossroads town (population 2,400) in southern Pennsylvania. Generals Robert E. Lee and George Gordon Meade engaged in military battles of wit—pitting men and weaponry against each other and against the hilly

> **F**AST FACT: General George Meade was only in command for three days before the battle.

terrain. The stakes were high and the ferocity and desperation of the fighting forces was palatable. Although the Confederates scored some early successes, the advantage in men and firepower helped secure eventual victory for the Union forces.

After the battle, Lee limped back to Virginia. He knew, above all else, that the Civil War had now become long months of survival. He had been defeated mightily and his strength had been eviscerated. A corner had been turned and a fate had been sealed on the rolling countryside of Gettysburg. This was the beginning of the end—Confederate hopes for independence had been effectively quashed during three days in July 1863.

The Battle of Gettysburg is also one of the most studied battles in American history. It was the only major Civil War battle fought on Union soil. It was also the largest engagement of the Gettysburg Campaign—a campaign that began in early June 1863 and concluded in mid-July 1863. The campaign was the second attempt by Confederates forces to invade Union territory and bring the Civil War directly to the North. The first attempt occurred in 1862 at the Battle of Antietam Creek. Up to that point in the Civil War, all fighting had occurred in southern states.

The Union troops at Gettysburg numbered approximately 90,000, while southern forces numbered approximately 75,000. Neither Meade or Lee had specifically selected Gettysburg as a place to fight a battle; nevertheless, as the two armies campaigned above the Mason-Dixon Line, it became increasingly clear that Gettysburg would be the spot where they would collide—the ten roads that led into town were ideal conduits for advancing armies.

DAY 1 (JULY 1, 1863)

The fighting began in the early morning hours west of Gettysburg and continued for several hours. At that time, neither General Meade nor General Lee was on the field and only small portions of the two armies were in place. The fighting escalated throughout the day as additional Confederate and Union reinforcements arrived.

The fighting eventually expanded to positions north of town. During the afternoon, there was additional fighting both west and north of the town. Initially, Union forces were able to withstand the Confederate attack, but by the end of the day, the Confederates had succeeded in pushing Union troops from their original positions. The first day ended as a Confederate victory.

DAY 2 (JULY 2, 1863)

By the time fighting resumed on the afternoon of July 2, both armies had significantly more men on the field. The Union army outnumbered the Confederates, had more artillery on the field, and their cavalry was ready for battle. They had also gained valuable high ground south of town. As Union reinforcements arrived, they developed a "fish hook" position that covered Culp's Hill, Cemetery Hill, Cemetery Ridge, and the Round Tops. The Confederates took a position in a similar shape in front of the Union lines. The lines ran around Culps's and Cemetery Hill, through the town, south along the Seminary Ridge and onto the Warfield Ridge.

General Meade wanted to hold his positions in order to prevent the Confederates from moving toward Baltimore or Washington. General Lee's intent was to attack both ends of the Union line in an effort to break their position. The fighting began in the afternoon with engagements on the Union left in front of Little Round Top. Some of the heaviest fighting took place in areas known as the Peach Orchard, the Wheatfield, the Devil's Den, and the Valley of Death. Later in the day, Confederates also attacked positions on the Union right in the vicinity of Culp's Hill, Cemetery Hill, and Spangler's Spring. By the conclusion of fighting on July 2, no clear winner emerged. The intense battle, however, produced a significant number of casualties.

DAY 3 (JULY 3, 1863)

The third and final day of fighting began early in the morning on the Union right. Union forces were able to push the Confederates back from some minor positions they had gained during the previous day. More Confederate cavalry had arrived and they developed positions east of Gettysburg near Union cavalry positions.

The main fighting took place at the center of the Union line along Cemetery Ridge. General Lee's plan was an attack against the Union center. General Meade's plan was to assume the defense and hold positions he had established

Cemetery stones of fallen soldiers at Gettysburg

the previous day. The attack at the Union center, now known as Pickett's Charge, began with an artillery duel in the early afternoon. Although there was a tremendous display of cannon fire, the duel accomplished little. General Lee had planned to move his cavalry against the Union rear; instead, they were forced to engage Union cavalry and were unable to move against the rear center of the Union line on Cemetery Ridge.

Pickett's Charge was a mass infantry assault that involved some 12,000 Confederates. In less than an hour, thousands of those attacking soldiers were casualties. The Union defenders succeeded in holding their positions along Cemetery Ridge and as a result, the Confederates were forced to retreat back to their positions along Seminary Ridge. Pickett's Charge effectively marked the end of the heavy fighting in Gettysburg. Late the next day, General Lee and his troops began moving away from Gettysburg. By the middle of July they had crossed Maryland and were reentering Virginia. The Union army followed, but at a cautious pace.

Although the Battle of Gettysburg is considered a Union victory, losses on

> **F**AST FACT: Pickett's Charge, despite popular belief, was not the largest charge (in terms of number of soldiers) of the Civil War. The Confederate charge at Gaines' Mill (June 27, 1862) involved approximately 57,000 Confederate soldiers.

both sides totaled approximately 51,112 soldiers. The Union army casualties included 3,155 killed, 14,529 wounded, and 5,365 missing and captured for a total of 23,049. Confederate casualties totaled 28,063. This included 3,903 killed, 18,735 wounded, and 5,425 missing and captured. Gettysburg was the most costly engagement of the Civil War and it marked the only major thrust of the Confederates into the North.

To begin your visit to **Gettysburg National Military Park** you should stop at **The National Park Service Museum and Visitor Center** as soon as you arrive. You can obtain a map of the park (including the 16-stop self-guided auto tour), information on how to visit the park, and tips on what to see in and around Gettysburg. While at the Visitor Center, there are several things you will want to see and experience (the first three require a fee).

First, you'll want to see the film *A New Birth of Freedom,* narrated by actor Morgan Freeman. This compelling film will immerse you in the sights, sounds, and emotions of the Battle of Gettysburg and its aftermath. It will also provide you with an orientation to the battle and its place in the larger context of the Civil War.

Next, you'll want to head upstairs to the **Cyclorama**. Here you'll be able to experience an unforgettable multimedia presentation of Pickett's Charge, the climatic final event of the Battle of Gettysburg. This sound and light show of the spectacular 377-foot painting by Paul Philippoteaux (completed in 1884) will literally surround you in the fury and drama of this heroic turning point of the Civil War.

Third, take some time (at least an hour is recommended) to tour the expansive **Gettysburg Museum of the American Civil War**. In 22,000 square feet of exhibit space you'll view relics of the battle, witness stories of the battle, and meet personalities face to face. All the events will come to life in the 12 exhibit galleries featuring numerous artifacts, interactive displays, and films. For visitors interested in additional resources, the **Resource Room** offers a bank of computers to research individual Civil War soldiers or other details.

Take some time to wander through the **Museum Bookstore**—certainly one of the most complete and most expansive park bookstores you'll likely see. On my most recent visit I found five separate titles (by five separate authors) on Pickett's Charge alone. Every personality, every conflict, and every skirmish is represented by one or more books in this extensive and sprawling collection. There are plenty of offerings for the kids and educators as well.

If members of your party need some refreshment or a full-course lunch, be sure to visit the **Refreshment Saloon** within the Visitor Center before you set out on your tour of the Battlefield.

There are several different ways you can tour the Gettysburg Battlefield, depending on the time you have available and the intensity of the information you wish to receive.

- Most visitors select the self-guided auto tour. The park has a most informative brochure that expertly guides you to each of 16 stops. The signage along the roads is excellent, and the descriptions are sufficient. You should plan on approximately three hours to complete the self-guided auto tour. This is truly one of the finest auto tours I've been on and you can easily decide if you want to see all 16 stops, spend some additional time at selected stops (for photos or time reading the signage), or skip a few along the way. Whatever you do, please pick up one of the complimentary brochures as soon as you enter the visitor center.

- There are licensed battlefield guides who, for a fee, will travel with you in your car or van and point out all the significant locations throughout the Park. This two-hour tour offers a first-hand account of the three-day battle and an opportunity to pose questions (and get reliable responses) from a well-trained and certified guide.

> **F**AST FACT: There are approximately 1,328 monuments, markers, and memorials at Gettysburg National Military Park.

- The museum bookstore has at least two different self-guided commercial audio tours available for purchase. Slip one of the CDs into the player in your car and follow the directions as the professional narrator describes in detail each of the locations (using the Park's official 16-stop brochure) in exact detail and with appropriate historical background. I "field-tested" one of these audio tours on one of my visits and found it to be well-researched, thorough and engaging. These are definitely worth the purchase price.

- You may opt for one of the self-guided walks the park has laid out for visitors. These walks should not be used to substitute for the guided auto tour, but rather to enhance your visit by providing some "up close and personal" contacts with featured locations. You may choose the Cemetery Ridge Trail—a 1.5-mile walk from the Visitor Center up to the area of Pickett's Charge. The National Cemetery Trail provides a walk through the grounds of Soldiers' National Cemetery. For the more adventurous, there is the 3-mile Johnny Reb Trail and the 9.5-mile Billy Yank Trail—both of which are used by Boy Scout troops as part of their Heritage Trails Program.

- There are several bus tour companies who will drive you over the battlefield. The Park has its own bus tour and there are several commercial outfits throughout the Gettysburg area that will be glad to (for a fee) escort you around the park on a narrated journey through history. Some outfits have very large buses; others considerably smaller ones. If you are traveling with a sizeable group, these can be the ideal way to see the park. Fees vary; check ahead before booking so you can get the most competitive rates.

- You may want to consider something different in your journey through the park. There are at least two commercial ventures who will take you on a one- to six-hour tour of the battlefield via horseback (one with re-enactors in Civil War dress). Another novel way to see the park is by guided Segway tour. Pick up a copy of the latest Gettysburg Official Visitor Guide or log onto Gettysburg's website (www.gettysburg.travel) to check out all tour possibilities.

If you come during the summer months, be sure to check at the information desk in the visitor center. Here you will be able to get a schedule of various walks and talks offered by rangers at various locations throughout the park. These value-added programs can enhance your visit considerably.

The driving tour that follows has been designed as a chronological tour—starting with the events on the first day of the battle (July 1) and ending with the events that took place on the last day of the conflict (July 3). The journey begins

SUGGESTED SCHEDULE FOR GETTYSBURG

I have visited Gettysburg National Military Park several times and talked with park rangers, certified battlefield guides, and other seasoned visitors. The consensus is you need a minimum of *one full day* to see everything. Here is a suggested schedule.

Morning: Tour the visitor center. See the Morgan Freeman film, view the Cyclorama, and stroll through the various exhibits in the museum. Stop by the bookstore and browse the selections. Total time: about 3 hours.

Midday: Have lunch in the Refreshment Saloon. Time: about 1 hour.

Afternoon: Jump in your car and take the driving tour as described below. As appropriate, exit your car to view selected sites up close, shoot some photographs, or read the informative placards or signs Total time: 3–4 hours.

If you have two days available (the ideal), I would suggest you plan your first day around all the offerings in the Visitor Center and the second day out on the road driving to and viewing the selected stops. A two-day visit will ensure that nothing is missed and give you sufficient time to see all the museum exhibits and read as many signs and plaques as you wish.

at the Visitor Center and takes you north on Washington Street (Again, the tour is well-marked with signs—each with a blue star and clear directions.). You'll make a left onto West Middle Street and then a right onto Reynolds Avenue. In short order you will come to McPherson Ridge.

JULY 1, 1863

1. MCPHERSON RIDGE

On the morning of July 1 the Confederate infantry was advancing along Chambersburg Pike (now US 30) toward the town of Gettysburg. Union General John Buford ordered his troops to defend the ridgelines west of town until reinforcements arrived. More soldiers from both side arrived and the fighting spread up and down the ridgeline. The Battle of Gettysburg had officially begun.

2. ETERNAL LIGHT PEACE MEMORIAL *(must see)*

Fighting in the afternoon centered around this hill as superior numbers of Confederate forces began to sweep southward and toward the significantly smaller number of Union forces massed at McPherson Ridge.

The Eternal Light Peace Memorial was dedicated in 1938 as a reconciliation between the men in blue and the men in gray (The memorial had been proposed by former soldiers in the Union and Confederate armies.). President Franklin Roosevelt addressed more than 200,000 people on the 75th anniversary of the battle—invoking some of Lincoln's thoughts from the Gettysburg Address. The eternal flame on top of the Monument burns 24 hours a day.

3. OAK RIDGE

Union soldiers amassed here on the afternoon of the first day. In short order, however, the superior numbers of Confederates pummeled Union forces—attacking on all fronts west and north of Gettysburg. The constant onslaught was too much for the dwindling Union troops and they were forced to retreat all the way back to Cemetery Hill. Thousands were taken prisoner as they made their way back through Gettysburg. The first day of the battle ended as a decided victory for the Confederate forces.

JULY 2, 1863

4. NORTH CAROLINA MEMORIAL

On the morning of the second day, Confederate troops had massed in this area, along Seminary Ridge, through the town of Gettysburg and north of Culp's Hill. Their position was like an enormous semi-circle around the perimeter of the Union troops. The Union troops, on the other hand were formed in the shape of

---

NOTE: Several stops on the tour have been denoted as "must see." These are places you should definitely visit in order to get a full appreciation of the scope and impact of the conflict. Please take time to get out of your vehicle and stroll around each designated area, read any signs or plaques, and take appropriate photos. Your tour through the battlefield will be all the richer as a result.

> **N**OTE: There are three observation towers along the route (at stop #3, shortly after #6, and at Culp's Hill just before stop #14). By climbing to the top of each one (the second one is a doozy), you can get an eagle's-eye view of the battlefield and the expanse of land the soldiers fought on. You'll also get an appreciation for the ebb and flow of the battle over those three days in early July 1863.

a giant fish hook just south of town. This shape allowed General Meade to quickly and easily move his troops back and forth along interior lines, reinforcing areas that were being pummeled by the enemy.

5. VIRGINIA MEMORIAL *(must see)*

The Virginia Memorial honors General Robert E. Lee—who sits astride his horse Traveller—at the top of this monument. This monument was the first Confederate state monument on the Gettysburg battlefield. This is a good place to exit your car and walk to the grassy area just in front of the monument. The large open field you see to the east is where Pickett's Charge would take place one day later—the penultimate event of the war.

> **F**AST FACT: There is a popular belief that if all four hooves on a statue of a horse are on the ground, then the rider died outside battle. That is the case for this statue (but not all statues).

6. PITZER WOODS

Union General Daniel Sickles, without permission from his superiors, moved his 10,000-man force to the elevated ridge in the Peach Orchard, thereby exposing them to the Confederate forces amassed along Warfield Ridge. Confederate Lieutenant General James Longstreet anchored the left side of that line in these woods. The Confederates clearly had a geographical advantage and quickly took advantage of it—resulting in one of the most intense and bloodiest battles of Gettysburg.

7. WARFIELD RIDGE

Late in the afternoon, General Longstreet began his frontal attack against Union troops hunkered down in the Devil's Den, the Wheatfield, and the Peach Orchard.

They also began their assault on the Round Tops where Union General Meade had an undefended left flank.

8. LITTLE ROUND TOP *(must see)*

One of the pivotal conflicts of the day, or perhaps the entire battle, took place on this rocky hill. Commanded by Colonel Joshua Chamberlain, 350 men of the 20th Maine were positioned on the extreme left of the Union line. If this line became overrun by Confederate forces, the entire Union line would be compromised. The 20th Maine fought valiantly, as the battle lines ebbed and flowed for almost two hours. Finally, Chamberlain ordered his men to attack with full bayonets. The charge was successful and the Union line was saved. As you walk across this hill site, gazing at the various monuments, you can almost see the waves of Confederate soldiers surging up the hill, being repulsed, and then surging up again.

As you drive toward the next numbered stop you will pass through the Devil's Den (not a numbered stop). You may want to park your car and walk about—for it was here that Confederate troops headed (from Warfield Ridge) overtaking a small band of Union defenders. The numerous boulders in the area were prime locations for Confederate sharpshooters as they set their sights on the Union soldiers on Little Round Top.

FAST FACT: The paved roads throughout Gettysburg National Military Park were laid down on the exact battle lines used by both Union and Confederate troops.

9. THE WHEATFIELD

The Wheatfield witnessed some of the bloodiest fighting of the entire day. The flow of battle ebbed back and forth between small Confederate and Union victories. When the day was done, there was more than 4,000 men wounded or dead upon this expanse of earth.

10. THE PEACH ORCHARD

The Union army extended from Devil's Den to the Emmetsburg Road and then north toward Gettysburg. As Confederate troops advanced toward the Wheatfield, they were subjected to a punishing bombardment by Union forces. However, Confederate William Barksdale was able to divide the Union army in two and by late

> **F**AST FACT: As the story goes, Major General Daniel Sickles "visited" his leg on several occasions after the war.

in the afternoon he had secured this piece of real estate.

As you drive toward the next numbered stop (# 11) you will pass the Trostle Farm on your left. It was here that Major General Daniel Sickles, while sitting on his horse, was struck in the leg by enemy fire. Damaged beyond repair, his leg had to be amputated. Sickles recovered completely and his leg bones were eventually displayed in the National Museum of Health and Medicine in Washington, DC.

11. PLUM RUN

This area was an escape route for Union soldiers during the intense fighting at the Wheatfield and Little Round Top. As the fighting raged on, troops used this ground to move from the Peach Orchard to Cemetery Ridge.

12. PENNSYLVANIA MEMORIAL *(must see)*

During the late afternoon of the second day, Union artillery was able to hold the line here against advancing Confederate troops. Meade recognized the tenuous position of his forces here and called for reinforcements from Culp's Hill and other locations. The additional troops were able to strengthen this line.

This monument, intended to honor all Pennsylvanians who fought in the campaign, was dedicated in 1910. It was constructed at a cost of $182,000 and was the result of a national contest to design the monument. Architect W. Liance Cottrel's design was selected as the winning entry. Part of the monu-

> **F**AST FACT: Cottrell received a total of $500 for his winning design.

ment includes 90 bronze tablets that contain the names of the 34,500 Pennsylvania soldiers who served during the Battle of Gettysburg. This is truly an impressive monument—one that will take your breath away.

13. SPANGLER'S SPRING

Late in the second day, after a withering and deadly attack on Union forces in this area, the Confederates were able to secure the lower slopes of Culp's Hill. As you gaze at the spring, you might be able to imagine a small band of Union soldiers being mowed down by superior numbers of Confederate troops. It wasn't until the following day, after seven hours of brutal combat, that the Confederates were finally driven off.

Before you get to the next numbered stop (#14) make sure you take the quick turn to the right and drive up to Culp's Hill. Climb the observation tower and look over the surrounding geography. It was here also that a small band of Union soldiers (numbering about 1,300) were able to secure themselves behind the earthworks that ran along the hill from the base to the top and hold off about 6,000 Confederates and successfully defend this territory.

14. EAST CEMETERY HILL

This is a most impressive sight. From here you can see several critical locations of the battle including Cemetery Hill, Culp's Hill, and the broad rocky fields to the north and east. Late in the day a force of Confederates had reached the crest of this hill. However, a tenacious band of Union soldiers was eventually able to drive them back down the slope.

JULY 3, 1863

15. HIGH WATER MARK *(must see)*

This is the setting of the famous (or infamous) Pickett's Charge—General Lee's last-gasp effort at striking a punishing and final blow to the Union army. It is often referred to as the High Water Mark because it was the apex of southern military achievement. This was a "once and done" effort—never again would Lee have the manpower or the firepower to effectively destroy Union troops.

After a punishing two-hour cannonade, 12,000 Confederate troops—one mile in length—marched toward the Copse of Trees, the angle, and the Brian Barn. They were met by 7,000 Union troops who effectively held their ground. The fighting was intense, brutal, and deadly for both sides. The field was littered with scores of wounded and dead and the ground ran red with blood.

> **F**AST FACT: Confederate losses were staggering at Pickett's Charge. At least 1,123 soldiers were killed and 4,019 were wounded. In all, there were approximately 6,555 Confederate casualties.

Soldiers' National Cemetery, site of The Gettysburg Address

16. NATIONAL CEMETERY *(must see)*

My most recent visit here was a late summer evening. As I walked through the cemetery, sunlight filtered through the trees etching animated shadows on the pathway. I strolled over to the spot just a few yards from where Lincoln delivered his oft-memorized Gettysburg Address. I was struck not just by the solemnity of the environment, but also by the presence of 6,000 soldiers who lie buried here. Many rest beneath simple numbered headstones; others have their names and battalion numbers etched on rustic marble slabs. I have always felt this is a good place to end one's tour of the battlefield, a place to reflect on the tens of thousands of lives that had been lost during this three-day battle. It's also a place to ponder the significance of that battle and what it stood for—North and South— one defeated and one victorious. The cemetery is a poignant exclamation mark for anyone visiting Gettysburg—bringing a unique sense of closure to the events and to your tour.

NOTE: If your time is limited and you would prefer a slightly abbreviated tour, these are the numbered stops on the auto tour you should include:

1. McPherson Ridge
2. Eternal Light Peace Memorial
3. Oak Ridge
5. Virginia Memorial
6. Pitzer Woods
7. Warfield Ridge
8. Little Round Top
12. Pennsylvania Memorial
15. High Water Mark
16. National Cemetery

CONTACTS:

Gettysburg National Military Park, 1195 Baltimore Pike, Gettysburg, PA 17325; (717) 334-1124; www.nps.gov/gett.

TEACHER RESOURCE BOOK

Fredericks, Anthony D. & Michael R. McGough. 2012. *The Gettysburg Address: The Complete Teaching Guide*. Charleston, SC: Create Space Independent Publishing Platform.

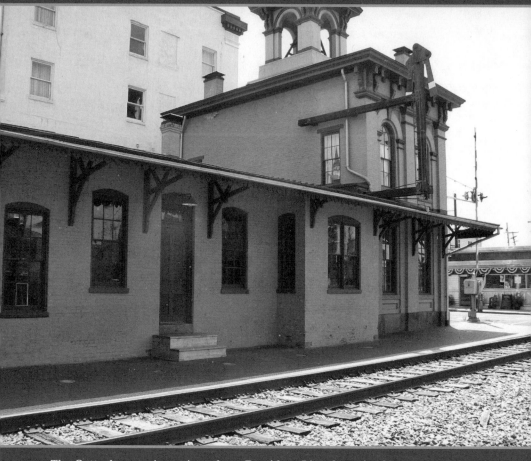

The Gettysburg train station where President Lincoln arrived on November 18, 1863

16 In Historic Gettysburg

Estimated length: 1–2 miles (walking)

Estimated time: ½–1 day

Combine this tour with: Chapters 14 and 15

Getting there: Just like in York, you'll begin this tour in a parking garage. Then, as soon as you step outside you will be transformed by visits to eclectic buildings, historic spots, and wondrous sites that will keep everyone in your party chattering away. Walk the streets, pop into the stores and chat with the locals…you won't regret a single step along the way.

Highlights: Consider this tour the "dessert" of your visit to eastern Pennsylvania. Gettysburg is, quite simply, a most delightful town. It will charm, entrance, and entertain you with both history and culture. The town gets tens of thousands of visitors every year for one reason—it has a lot to share. Come and be part of one of America's great small towns.

Say the word Gettysburg and most people will immediately associate it with the epic three-day battle that took place during the summer of 1863. Indeed, as you travel through this historic town you will be confronted with all manner of Civil War realia, artifacts, and history that transcends the earlier history of this pivotal south-central Pennsylvania town. Gettysburg continues its prominence today as both a hub of Adams County and a lure for millions of visitors who flock to witness battlefields, the living quarters of a former president, and the 19th-century buildings that crowd Lincoln Square and Baltimore Street.

But the roots of Gettysburg are buried deep in the early 18th century—long before it became a pivotal point for this country's greatest conflict. It was in 1736

FAST FACT: The athletic teams at Gettysburg College are nicknamed the "Bullets."

that the land in and around the present-day settlement of Gettysburg was purchased by the family of William Penn. Formally known as Marsh Creek, the Penn family secured it from the Iroquois Indians who inhabited the area at that time. The small settlement that was established was embroiled in the French and Indian War. There is a persistent (and documented) story of how one of the captives—a 16-year-old girl named Mary—was adopted by the Seneca Indians and later married two chiefs. Although offered several opportunities to return to the white world she adamantly refused and continued to live as a Native American until well into her nineties. Raids in and around this area were commonplace throughout the remainder of the French and Indian War.

Gettysburg got its start with the establishment of a tavern in 1761 by one Samuel Gettys. It was 25 years later (1786) when his son, James, finally laid out a town with 210 lots. The town consisted of a central square and was arranged radiating out from the now well-established tavern Samuel Gettys had built two-and-a-half decades earlier. Originally Gettysburg was part of York County, but a growing population in the area induced the citizens to establish a new county—Adams (named after President John Adams)—in 1790. Gettysburg was established as the county seat.

Gettysburg continued to swell—growing to 2,400 citizens by 1860. Ten separate roads led into the city and it fast became a center for business, industry, and trade. Now, the town was made up of approximately 450 buildings including banks, carriage makers, tanneries, taverns, shoemakers, and dry goods merchants. Two educational institutions—Gettysburg College (originally known as Pennsylvania College) and the Lutheran Theological Seminary (originally Gettysburg Theological Seminary)—also dotted the landscape.

History is often a record of circumstance, chance, and fortune. Frequently, events happen, not because they are arranged and deliberated, but because certain people were at the right place at the right time. Gettysburg was almost an asterisk to the Civil War—it was only through a series of unplanned events that the citizens of this town watched as 163,000 soldiers converged around their streets to wage one of the most significant battles in our nation's history. The 10 roads of Gettysburg brought vast armies, punishing artillery, and death and destruction to a town that little deserved or understood it. The citizens of Gettysburg were swept up in the conflict as their homes, churches, and businesses became makeshift hospitals, and their way of life was changed forever.

Gettysburg is one of America's best destinations—a town that will lure you in with its history and keep you captivated by its present. For three days in 1863 it was the epicenter of a great conflict that would turn our country and shape our inevitable and lasting philosophy.

The best way to see Gettysburg is via your two feet. The following walking tour will allow you to view some of the town's most historic buildings, savor the events surrounding its heritage, and see what this once-bucolic village was like back in the mid-1800s. You are welcome to deviate from this path. This is a tourist town, after all, and you will find all kinds of vendors—from the historic to the contemporary, from antiques to zebra-skin throw rugs. View the history, but enjoy the total experience.

The first thing you'll need to do is secure a parking space. If you happen to arrive in the summer you'll find parking at a premium and may find yourself circling the traffic circle (actually a square) hundreds of times in an attempt to secure a parking space. My suggestion: park in the East Race Horse Alley Parking Garage. It's easy to find, centrally located, and very cheap. You can leave your car there all day and easily access it from any direction. If you're coming into town via US 30 from York, make a right turn on Stratton Street just before the circle. Turn left onto East Race Horse Alley and there you are. If you're arriving into town via US 34 (Carlisle Street) from the north, make a left turn onto East Race Horse Alley just before you get to the circle. If you are coming into town via PA 30 (Chambersburg Street) from the west, travel three-quarters of the way around the circle and then up Carlisle Street for a few yards before turning right into East Race Horse Alley. If you are arriving from the south on US 15 (Baltimore Street), drive halfway around the circle, turn up Carlisle Street and turn right onto East Race Horse Alley.

After exiting your car, look for the small "Race Horse Alley Plaza" plaque that notes the site of the tavern of Samuel Gettys, whose son James laid out the town of Gettysburg in 1786.

Walk a short distance west until you come to Carlisle Street. Make a right turn and in half a block you will come to the first stop on our walking tour—the **Historic Gettysburg Train Station**. Railroad service in Gettysburg began in

FAST FACT: In September 2008, Haunted America Tours named the borough of Gettysburg the third most haunted city in America.

December 1858 with the opening of the western terminus of the Gettysburg Railroad Company, completing a 16.5-mile line to Hanover. The station is most noted, not for its beginnings, but rather by events that took place 4.5 months after the Battle of Gettysburg. For this is where President Abraham Lincoln arrived on November 18, 1863, for the dedication of the Soldiers' National Cemetery.

At noon on November 18, Lincoln and his party set out from Washington's B&O station for Gettysburg. After transferring to another train in nearby Hanover Junction (a stop we made in Chapter 14), Lincoln arrived in Gettysburg at about 6 PM. He exited the train and passed rows of empty coffins designated for soldiers yet to be interred at the cemetery. He was met by his host, David Wills, and escorted to Wills's House on the town square.

The next day Lincoln delivered his two-minute, now immortal, Gettysburg Address. After attending a few official receptions in the afternoon, Lincoln and his traveling party walked back to the Gettysburg Train Station and boarded their cars for the return trip to Washington, DC. The train pulled out of the station at about 6:30 PM—in its wake were 273 words that would immortalize this town and the three-day conflict between North and South.

After viewing the train station, turn around and walk back on Carlisle Street (south toward the circle). As you come to the circle you will note the historic **Gettysburg Hotel** on your left. The original hotel was built in 1797 when James Scott first opened his tavern on this spot. It also had a minor role just prior to the three-day engagement in July 1863. It seems that, four days prior to the Battle of Gettysburg, Confederate troops were marching through town. Fearing for their lives, the townspeople, hid wherever they could. Twenty-three people were able to secure themselves in a bank vault in the rear of the hotel and avoid detection. Today, you can walk through the hotel lobby to the rear of the hotel and see that same bank vault. Imagine what it would have been like to lock yourself inside a vault for an undetermined amount of time while your town is being pillaged and ransacked.

Just outside the entrance to the hotel is the "By the skin of our teeth" plaque.

The Gettysburg Hotel

On July 1, 1863, Union troops were trying to escape through town and up to the safety of Cemetery Hill. They were pursued by a relentless corps of Confederate soldiers. The Union soldiers tried to make a stand in the square but were clearly outnumbered. A hailstorm of bullets forced the Union troops to make a hasty exit. Colonel Gilbert Prey, the commander of the 104th New York whose regiment survived the bullets, recalled getting through the town "by the skin of our teeth." The plaque is a reminder of just how close the war had come to Gettysburg.

Directly across York Street from the hotel is the **David Wills House**, the third stop on our tour. David Wills was a prominent lawyer in town and purhased this large 1816 house in 1859. It also served as a shelter for wounded soldiers during and after the Battle of Gettysburg.

The David Wills House in Gettysburg

Approximately one week after the battle, Pennsylvania Governor Andrew Curtin visited the battlefield with Wills and was shocked by its condition. He immediately designated Wills as state agent, charged with seeing to the proper burial of Pennsylvania's dead. At a meeting of state agents in this house several days later, the idea of establishing a permanent national cemetery for all Union dead was advanced. Governor Curtin approved and gave Wills the authority to oversee its construction.

On November 19, 1863, thousands of citizens came to Gettysburg to honor the dead and dedicate the new cemetery (which was still unfinished at the time). President Lincoln stayed at the Wills House as a guest the night before the dedication. That evening there was a grand celebration with 38 dinner guests, including Governor Curtain, Edward Everett, Secretary of State William Seward, and other dignitaries. The house overflowed with people, and Mrs. Wills gladly gave up her own bedroom for the president.

It was in that bedroom that Lincoln completed his final revision of the Gettysburg Address (most of it had been written prior to his departure from Washington, DC). After a restful night, Lincoln and the other dignitaries left the Wills House and gathered near Baltimore Street. It was here that a parade had been organized for the procession to the Soldiers' National Cemetery. Lincoln climbed on a horse and rode down Baltimore Street to the cemetery where he would deliver one of the world's most memorable speeches.

The house has since been converted into a small museum. It is possible to take the self-guided tour and tour all the rooms in about 45 minutes. There are five galleries, two re-created rooms (including the same room where Lincoln stayed), two interactive stations, and two films. This house makes an incredible impression on one's image of the events prior to the delivery of the Gettysburg Address. It is a journey back to a time and place where real people participated in events and decisions that shaped history.

Just outside the Wills House (as you move toward Baltimore Street) is a statue titled "Return Visit" by sculptor J. Stewart Johnson Jr. Here you will see two figures—a life-size statue of Abraham Lincoln holding his hat in the air (toward the Wills house) and a statue of a contemporary man holding a copy of the Gettysburg Address in his hand. This sculpture was dedicated in 1991 and underscores the significance of Lincoln's speech—as much for modern-day visitors as for those who heard it back in 1863. It is so detailed that you can see the label on Lincoln's hat and the precision of his watch chain.

After viewing the statue, work your way clockwise around Lincoln Square until you come to Chambersburg Street. Walk west along the right-hand sidewalk to 27 Chambersburg Street, home of the **James Gettys Hotel**. It was here that James Gettys, the town's founder, sold his first plot of land in 1787 to John Troxell Sr. In 1804, Troxell opened the Sign of the Buck tavern and roadhouse to accommodate those traveling to the western frontier of Pennsylvania and beyond. As Gettysburg grew, the town eventually became the Adams County seat and the hotel expanded to house more travelers. By 1863, Gettysburg was booming with

"Return Visit" statue at Lincoln Square

2,400 residents and many businesses. The hotel, then known as the *Union Hotel,* served as a hospital for scores of wounded soldiers after the Battle of Gettysburg.

In the late 1880s the hotel was renamed The City Hotel. With an expansion to accommodate up to 250 guests, the hotel served as a major staging area for the 25th anniversary of the battle. In the intervening years, it has gone through several additional transformations—including an apartment building and a youth hostel. It is now a serene piece of Gettysburg history (listed on the National Register of Historic Places) providing B&B accommodations in twelve distinctive suites.

Two doors down from the James Gettys Hotel (on the same side of the street) are the **former law offices of Thaddeus Stevens**, who practiced law in the town from 1816 to 1842. Stevens was known as the "Great Commoner" and an ardent supporter of civil rights (we met him in Chapter 3 in his role as a defender of the accused in the "Christiana Resistance" as well as in our tour of Lancaster). He was also a strong advocate for universal public education in this country. Although Stevens eventually moved to Lancaster and had no direct role in the events surrounding Gettysburg in 1863, he achieved one of his greatest legislative contributions in drafting both the 13th and 14th amendments to the U.S. Constitution.

Walk to the intersection (Washington Street), cross over to the other side of Chambersburg Street and return along Chambersburg Street to **Christ Lutheran Church** (almost directly across the street from Stevens' old law offices). This is the oldest structure in Gettysburg continuously used as a church. It was founded in 1835 as the English-speaking Lutheran Church in Gettysburg (St. James Lutheran Church, in existence since 1789, conducted its services in German), and to be the primary assembly hall for both Lutheran Theological Seminary and Pennsylvania (now Gettysburg) College. The structure was one of the first hospitals established during the Battle of Gettysburg, and at its peak accommodated approximately 150 wounded soldiers.

Stand back from the church and gaze up at the cupola. If the light is right, you'll note the bell hanging there. This approximately 600-pound bronze bell was originally cast in 1788 for a Spanish or Portuguese convent. It has been in the Christ Lutheran Cupola since 1836. Also stop and read the Chaplain Horatio Howell marker in the middle of the front steps. Chaplain Howell, while tending to wounded soldiers on July 1, 1863, walked out the center door of the church and, after refusing to give up his sword, was gunned down by a Confederate soldier.

Continue walking down Chambersburg Street until you come to the circle. Travel one-quarter way around to your right and you will now be back at Baltimore Street. Make a right turn down Baltimore Street and immediately on your right will be the **Martin Stoever House and John Schick Store** (1 Baltimore Street). During the battle, this Federal-style building, erected in 1817, housed Professor Martin Stoever's family and J. L. Schick's general store. The ensuing battle

The Stoever-Schick Store was a hospital and hideout for Union soldiers.

turned this handsome building into a makeshift hospital for nearly two dozen seriously injured Union soldiers. As Mrs. Stoever recalled, "The Professor's recitation room became the amputation room." While the wounded were nursed upstairs, three fugitive Union soldiers were hidden in the cellar until discovered by a Confederate party on July 3. After the Confederates left town, the Christian Commission took over this building for their supply and distribution center. At the same time, the Stoevers provided an "open commissary" in their backyard, feeding a seemingly endless line of hungry soldiers.

Continue your journey down Baltimore Street until you come to 47 Baltimore Street and the **Fahnestock House** (now an apartment building). At the time of the battle, this building was a dry goods store. Because of its height, it also served as a critical observation post during the first day of the battle. At the conclusion of the battle, the U.S. Sanitary Commission established their local operations in the Fahnestock Brother's store. The Sanitary Commission was created by the federal government as a private relief agency in 1861. Their mission was to tend to sick and wounded Union soldiers throughout the Civil War. It was staffed with thousands of volunteers and operated primarily in northern states.

At the corner of Baltimore and Middle Streets is the **Adams County Courthouse**. Originally built in 1859, it was designed to replace the original 1804 courthouse located in Lincoln Square. This brick Italianate-style building was a focal point for the business of Gettysburg. The bell in the bell tower was cast in Philadelphia in 1804. Like many buildings in town, the courthouse was used as a hospital following the Battle of Gettysburg. It too is on the National Register of Historic Places.

The Fahnestock House was an observation point on the first day of the battle.

One of the unique stories associated with Gettysburg occurred in this structure. It seems that several local college and seminary students, part of the 26th Pennsylvania Emergency Militia, had been captured by Confederate troops during their initial foray into town. Apparently, Confederate General Jubal early took pity on the young and inexperienced soldiers and paroled them on June 26, 1863. He sent them on their way with the admonition "to go home to their mothers."

Continue down Baltimore Street. Shortly after you pass Breckenridge Avenue, you'll come to 309 Baltimore Street and the stately brick building now

Adams County Courthouse

The Schriver House Museum—formerly Shriver's Saloon and Ten-Pin Alley

known as the **Shriver House Museum**. During the Civil War this place was known as "Shriver's Saloon and Tin-Pan Alley." Constructed around 1860 it was the home of George and Hettie Shriver and their daughters, Mollie and Sadie. The family, concerned about their safety, vacated the house during the Battle of Gettysburg. Confederate soldiers, recognizing a good deal when they saw it, took over the house and set up a sharpshooter's position in the attic. Today you can take a guided tour of this house and see how common folks lived during the mid

1800s. You'll have an opportunity to explore all four floors of this structure—from the sharpshooter's nest to the saloon in the basement.

Continue your journey down Baltimore Street. As you cross over South Street, you'll note the **Farnsworth House** (401 Baltimore Street) immediately on your right. The building now serves as a B&B, restaurant, and tavern; it also bears mute testimony to the savagery of the battle that raged outside. The original part of the house was built in 1810, followed by the brick structure in 1833 (constructed by John McFarland). During the time of the battle, the house was occupied by the H. D. Sweeney family. Even today, the original walls, flooring, and rafters are intact— a testament to the carpentry skills of the original builders.

But the real story is on the outside. You see, during the Battle, the house was a haven for Confederate sharpshooters, who kept watch for troop movements in the immediate area (One unconfirmed story relates how Jenny Wade, the only civilian killed during the battle, was shot from this house.). Walk to the south side of the building and look back at the brick wall. There you will able to see more than 100 bullet holes still remaining from the battle.

Continue walking down the street, and at 451 Baltimore Street you'll come upon the site of the **John Rupp House Tannery**. This was near where John and Caroline Rupp and their six children lived. John operated a tannery, and all his property lay between the Union and Confederate armies. On the first day of the battle, Mrs. Rupp and the children fled across the street to their neighbors' cellar. John hid in his own cellar for the next three days.

On record is a letter from John Rupp to his sister-in-law. In the letter Rupp describes a cluster of Union soldiers on his front porch and Confederate soldiers on his rear porch—each firing at the other through the interior of the house. One Union soldier was killed in the exchange. Following the war, the Rupps chose to replace the original house with a larger dwelling that stands at this location.

Cross over Baltimore Street at the intersection of Baltimore Street and Steinwehr Avenue. At the top of the hill on the left is the **Jenny Wade House Museum** (548 Baltimore Street). Twenty-year-old Jenny Wade was visiting the home (this site) of her sister, Georgia McClellan, on the morning of July 3. Jenny was kneading bread when a musket ball traveled through the front

> **FAST FACT:** Jennie Wade was the only Gettysburg civilian to be killed during the Battle of Gettysburg.

door and the kitchen door and hit her. It pierced her left shoulder blade, went directly through her heart and killed her instantly. Unfortunately, her mother had just walked into the kitchen to witness her daughter's tragic death.

In a tragic irony, Jenny was engaged to Corporal "Jack" Skelly. Before news of her passing could be transmitted to Skelly, he was mortally wounded at the Battle of Carter's Woods near Winchester, Virginia. He died on July 12, 1863, without ever knowing the fate of his sweetheart. Today, you can tour this house and witness some of the damage it sustained during the battle, including more than 150 bullet holes and evidence of a cannon ball that entered a second-floor wall. You can also see the hole in the door through which the fateful bullet entered the small kitchen.

Cross back over Baltimore Street and stroll down Steinwehr Avenue to the **Springhouse Tavern at the Dobbin House** (89 Steinwehr Avenue). This building was constructed in 1776 by Irishman Alexander Dobbin and wife Isabella. Dobbin was a well-respected community leader and preacher who established the first classical school west of the Susquehanna River.

After bearing 10 children, Isabella passed away. Soon after, Alexander met and married Mary Agnew who arrived at Dobbin House with her nine children. After Alexander passed away, the Dobbin House was used as a "station" on the Underground Railroad. (You can still see the secret slave hideout close to the walk-in fireplace in the tavern.) The tavern also preserves the never-failing spring under the house that served the Dobbins as both a well and a "refrigerator." The spring is still working today much as it did more than 200 years ago.

The Springhouse Tavern on the lower level is one of my all-time favorite restaurants. It is also the perfect conclusion to a walk through Gettysburg. The atmosphere in the tavern is subdued, with light flickering from an array of table candles and silent stone walls that have been in place for more than two centuries. The authentic furniture, 200-year-old bar, and always-friendly servers dressed in period costume add both charm and gentility to the repast.

The menu is as expansive as it is authentic, and entrees are described in colonial terms. After dozens of meals here, my wife and I never tire of the expertly prepared and richly presented dishes, the warm and genuine greetings of the staff, or the romantic charm of this historic place.

We particularly enjoy visiting during lunchtime (although the evening offerings are equally delicious) on our frequent day trips through the surrounding

The Dobbin House & Springhouse Tavern

countryside. While you can eat at any of the tables scattered throughout this one-room restaurant, we particularly like hobnobbing with the locals at the bar. Here is my favorite lunchtime meal (as presented in the Springhouse Tavern menu):

BAKED KING'S ONION SOUP
Freshly made with beef and a variety of cheeses on top,
baked in a "quick" oven to succulent tenderness, and served
up hot and delicious in a tureen with snippets.

DOBBIN HOT BEEF SANDWICH
Tender roast beef piled high on a hearth baked roll. Served
up with its own juices for dipping. Choice of Potato
Sallade, Cole Sla, or Potato Chips.

RUM BELLIES VENGEANCE…the drink
of the Dobbin House! An absolutely incredible concoction of
light & dark rums, exotic liqueurs, & fruit juices, the
potency of which mandates a limit of two (2) per customer.
Truly, a genuine bargain.

Bon appetit!

CONTACTS

Gettysburg Convention and Visitors Bureau, 35 Carlisle St., Gettysburg, PA 17325; (717) 334-6275; www.gettysburg.travel.

LODGING

The Gettysburg Hotel, 1 Lincoln Square, Gettysburg, PA 17325; (717) 337-2000; www.hotelgettysburg.com.

DINING

Springhouse Tavern and Dobbin House, 89 Steinwehr Ave., Gettysburg, PA 17325; (717) 334-2100; www.dobbinhouse.com.

Acknowledgments

No book is truly the sole domain of the person whose name appears on the cover. This is particularly true of travel books—where the information gathered and presented is often dependent on the expertise, recollections, and insights of individuals with a plethora of local knowledge and a surfeit of regional experiences. I met many wonderful and informative people in my journeys through eastern Pennsylvania—far too many to list in this brief section. I am indebted to them all for helping make this book far more inclusive and much more engaging than a simple travel guide. Their suggestions on places to discover, visit, survey, search, seek, hunt, investigate, probe, and explore and their perceptions on history, archaeology, geography, ancestry, politics, culture, and sociology were instrumental in the book's scope and detail.

There were a few folks, however, who went "above and beyond" and deserve unmitigated cheers, standing ovations, and personal accolades. Many thanks go to Len Sherlinski, who alerted me to some of the outstanding covered bridges of Columbia and Perry counties; to Monica Trego and Christine Weaver of the Pennsylvania Dutch Convention & Visitors Bureau for their kind assistance in negotiating the byways and highways of Lancaster County; to Daniel Ness of the Mennonite Historical Museum for his help in locating Amish sites no visitor to Lancaster County should miss; to Tracy Cromeans and Jerry LaRussa of the Gettysburg Convention & Visitors Bureau, whose good cheer and knowledge of Gettysburg made my visits there so productive; to my good friend and colleague Mike McGough, whose knowledge of the Gettysburg Battlefield is beyond compare; and to Rachael Houser, a volunteer at the John Brown House in Chambersburg who expertly guided me through some complex history.

I would also like to salute Sharon, my guide at Mother Bethel African Methodist Episcopal Church, who graciously led me through two centuries of African American history; Scott, my tour guide at the Lackawanna Coal Mine Tour who opened my eyes (in a very dark place) to the trials and travails of anthracite coal mining; to Sarah, my guide on the *Josiah White II* and her expert narration about canal life; to the affable Mary Dugan, whose passion for the story of the Underground Railroad and the role Kennett Square played in that history were without equal; to Jan Reeps of the Brandywine Valley Tourist Information Center for her genuine personality; to Tom Maddock and Bill Traubel at Washington Crossing Historic Park whose good humor and friendly advice were both enjoyable and invaluable; to Glenn Wenrich of the Berks Heritage Center and his wonderful narration about another time and another place; and to Cornelia Swinson and Jim Crichton of the Johnson House, who offered me an abundance of stories, a wealth of anecdotes, and a passion for accuracy. Also, thanks to Jack Sommer of Prospect Hill Cemetery for his keen historical anecdotes and sincere commitment to the York community.

I am particularly indebted to the good folks at Countryman Press—truly a class act in the world of publishing. My heartfelt appreciation and infinite admiration go to Lisa Sacks, who is an absolute joy to work with. (She is particularly adept at working with authors who don't always pay attention). My sincere thanks also to Kermit Hummel for his continuing support of my literary sojourns.

True celebrations are in order for my wife, Phyllis, who (once again) patiently watched another summer go by without the attic cleared, the garage cleaned, or the deck stained. Her eagerness in supporting my travels to unknown destinations, far-flung locations, and long-ago sites was boundless…as is our more than four decades love affair.